MARGARET DAVIES *(Brown), 1923 –*

APOLLINAIRE

OLIVER & BOYD

EDINBURGH AND LONDON

1964

OLIVER & BOYD LTD
Tweeddale Court
14 High Street
Edinburgh 1

39A Welbeck Street
London W1

First published 1964

PRINTED IN GREAT BRITAIN
AT THE PRESS OF THE PUBLISHERS

Preface

MY grateful acknowledgments are due to Mme Apollinaire for her friendship and kindness in allowing me to see manuscripts of her husband's works, and for permission to reproduce pages from the manuscript of *Vitam impendere amori*; to the late M. André Rouveyre for his encouragement and support over the years, and for the valuable, unpublished material which he communicated to me; to Mlle Dormoy and M. Chapon for making available the rich resources of the Bibliothèque Doucet; to Mlle Pagès and Mme Delaunay, and to Messieurs Adéma, Billy, Kahnweiler, Férat, Léautaud, Raynal, Salmon, and Tzara for sharing their memories of Apollinaire with me, and showing me documents in their possession; to M. Décaudin for his interested help; to the late M. Jules Mouquet for his encouragement; and particularly to Dr Enid Starkie for her continual guidance and support.

I should also like to point out that the translations which appear in the footnotes pretend to be no more than strictly literal, and that the punctuation in all quotations—or rather, in the poetry, the lack of it—reproduces Apollinaire's own usage in definitive editions of his work.

London
December 1963

M. D.

Acknowledgments

For permission to quote from the works of Guillaume Apollinaire, acknowledgments are due to Editions Gallimard, Editions Stock, the Harvill Press Ltd., and New Directions.

Acknowledgments are also due to the following for permission to quote from the works indicated: Editions du Rocher (Toussaint-Luca: *Apollinaire: Souvenirs d'un ami*); Editions Seghers (André Billy: *Poètes d'aujourd'hui: Guillaume Apollinaire*); Editions du Seuil (André Rouveyre: *Amour et poésie d'Apollinaire*); Editions Stock (Fernande Olivier: *Picasso et ses amis*); *Les Lettres Françaises* (letters from Apollinaire to James Onimus, published in the issue of 13 Dec. 1951); and Librairie Plon (Marcel Adéma: *Apollinaire le mal-aimé*).

Contents

Illustrations

I

A Roman Childhood

IT is difficult not to strike some sort of defensive attitude about being illegitimate; and Guillaume Apollinaire, who was a deeply complex personality, could hardly be expected to be straightforward about the identity of his father. Once at the age of twenty he said casually to a friend that a photograph of an Italian officer which he had in his room was that of his father, and it is this person whom prolonged researches have finally proved to be at least the most likely candidate for paternity. To Annie, one of his earlier loves, he declared airily that he was the son of a Russian general. Here, naturally enough, he was using his mother's family to fill the gap. Later, in the more sophisticated atmosphere of Montmartre, he allowed more fantasy to play over his doubtful origins and enjoyed fostering the rumour that he was the secret offspring of some eminent dignitary of the Church. If one is different anyway, why not play up to it? Which he did with naïve unction.

His secretiveness certainly had the desired effect. During the whole of his lifetime, and for thirty years after his death, the mystery remained intact. Even now, when the key to the cipher appears to have been found, and it has been proved conclusively that for several years both before and after his birth his mother was at least living with the Italian officer, there are still dissenting voices from the people who cannot bear to have the titillating, priestly myth exploded, and even from a little coterie who have recently produced the delirious hypothesis that he was the grandson of l'Aiglon.[1] Even Apollinaire never thought of that, though he did boast that he looked like Nero. The supposition is that a maternal great aunt of Apollinaire's may have had an illegitimate son by the Duc de Reichstat—she did have both a picture of him and an

[1] Raymond Warnier, "Une Nouvelle Hypothese sur les origines d'Apollinaire," in *Studi Francesi*, No. 10, 1960.

illegitimate son and frequented the same Court circle in
Vienna—and that this son, who came to live at the Vatican,
may at the age of sixty have seduced his second cousin—
Apollinaire's mother—who was then a very attractive, lively
girl of twenty. At this rate almost any denizen of the Vatican,
or even of all Rome, in the year 1879 would do just as well.

In any case such fantasies still bear witness to the purposely
ambiguous nature of Apollinaire's background, and even now
many questions go unanswered. If his father was Francesco
Flugi d'Aspermont, the Italian officer who was openly his
mother's lover for many years, and if Apollinaire was sure of
this, why was he not equally open about admitting it? He
was always ready to boast of his mother's Polish ancestors
and his own Slav blood, but the d'Aspermonts were an even
more distinguished, aristocratic family, originating in the
Grisons district of Switzerland, and including over the genera-
tions a series of high-ranking priests and soldiers. Francesco's
elder brother, for instance, Don Romarino, became the *abbé
nullius* of the diocese of Monaco, and he himself had had an
honourable career both as soldier and courtier in the service of
François II, King of the Two Sicilies. Although after the
fall of the Bourbons he drifted into a vague playboy existence,
by all accounts he cut a most dashing figure as an accomplished
man of the world; and even if finally he came to be regarded
as the black sheep of the family because of his passion for
gambling and his debts and his liaison with Apollinaire's
mother—they were known as that "maladetto Francesco e sa
russa"—the family itself remained, and still remains, a respected pillar of Roman society, whom nobody, let alone a
stateless poet, need feel ashamed of. And yet Apollinaire,
who in the course of his unorthodox life had urgent need to
prove his identity, and who never ceased to proclaim his
allegiance to Italy as his second country, always welcoming
Italian writers and artists and speaking Italian with them,
preaching over many years a Pan-Latin spirit in the arts,
fêting in verse Italy's entry into the War, never once openly
admitted to Italian blood. Even when once taunted with being
a Levantine Jew, and this obviously irritated him, he replied
with dignity that he was "a Polish gentleman." But, if

Francesco was his father, he was in fact three-quarters Italian and only one-quarter Polish, for his maternal grandmother was also Italian. The ironical fact of the whole affair is that if Francesco and his possible offspring were for many years the skeleton in the Aspermonts' cupboard, they seem in turn to have been Guillaume Apollinaire's.

Does this turning of the tables point to any solution of the problem? Was Apollinaire so outraged because the Aspermonts had not thought his mother good enough to be a wife for Francesco and had never recognised her two bastards that he simply disdained to mention their name? Or did he genuinely not know about them? No doubt every illegitimate son has the right to ask, "Who was my father?" but obviously not every illegitimate mother feels obliged to tell the whole truth, or indeed any kind of truth; nor even if she does will the son feel obliged to believe her. He may well imagine that her natural reticences cover up much more shameful secrets.

Short of discovering new, more tangible evidence, which seems unlikely, one can only guess at possible answers, and finally turn to Apollinaire's works for clues; and then it is immediately obvious that these are very rare, and that more often than not they are designed to lead down the wrong track. It eventually becomes a sort of game in which one is trying to outwit the author, for Apollinaire had a very curious and ambivalent attitude to using autobiographical material. Like most writers, he felt the most urgent need to spill out his emotions and thoughts on to paper on the very instant, whether he was on the back of a bus, or in the trenches under fire; and his manuscripts are often written on bills, menus, old reviews, hotel writing-paper. "Each poem," he declared, "commemorates an event in my life,"[2] a natural enough cathartic process. He then, like an assassin returning to the scene of the crime to try to efface the evidence, not once but many times and in some cases over a period of ten or twelve years, would come back to his manuscript and cut out anything which seemed to give him away too much—quite literally

[2] Quoted by André Rouveyre in "La Poésie d'Apollinaire protégée par lui-même," *Le Divan*, No. 217, Mar. 1938.

with scissors and paste. The manuscript of *Le Poète assassiné*, his most autobiographical work, looks rather like a tailor's nightmare. This of course applied only to himself. He never minded leaving other people, such as Picasso or Marie Laurencin, fairly recognisable. But not everything disappeared under the scissors: the confessional for a writer is too sweet and insidious a temptation. Some secrets were too basic a part of the organism for him to bear the pain of amputation, so he would leave them, but twisted into strange shapes, or turned inside out, or bedded deep into fantasy. For publication, that is, because at the same time he took great care that the over-revealing manuscripts were jealously guarded; and it is from them, and from what has been deleted from them that one can piece together a part of the jigsaw of his early life.

There are, for instance, two references to the name of Aspermont. One is that of the hero of a group of stories in *L'Hérésiarque et Cie*, the Baron d'Ormesan, who was in manuscript called d'Ormespant, which, as people have pointed out, is an anagram of Aspermont. This character is generally known as having been based on the weird Belgian, Géry Piéret, who served Apollinaire as secretary, and got him into trouble over the Iberian statuettes stolen from the Louvre. Could Apollinaire, in using this name, have had any afterthought about Francesco himself? He too seemed to lead a rather fantastic life, and to be given to mysterious disappearances. Perhaps there were secrets which his son chose to keep. But this can only remain pure supposition, and there are no facts to confirm it.

The other reference also opens up another hypothetical possibility. In *Le Poète assassiné*, which critics are coming increasingly to regard as totally autobiographical under its sugar icing of lyrical fantasy, there is a character called François des Ygrées who marries the mother of the poet when she is already pregnant by a tramp. The resemblance of Christian name and particle may be only slight, but given Apollinaire's love of puns and plays on words, there is just a possibility of an echo of Grisons in Ygrées, as there is of "maquereau" in the mother's name, Macarée (feminine passive, the person used by a "maquereau"?). And so if one wanted to be both ingenious and literal one could deduce that Francesco may have been only a stand-in for somebody really disreputable.

And there one is falling headlong into Apollinaire's trap. The one thing that is certain at least is that he did his best to confuse the issue, and the most interesting question of all must be why. This seems to be the point where his mother, Angelica Kostrowitzky, must come into the picture, and she if anything was even more complex a character than her famous son.

About her father there are no doubts. She was born in 1858 in Helsinfors to Michel-Apollinaire Kostrowitzky and his Italian wife. The Kostrowitzkys were an old Polish family of the minor nobility. After the Polish insurrection against Russia in 1865 Michel's two brothers were sent to Siberia: but he managed to escape and, because his wife still had relatives in Italy, took refuge in Rome, where as a Roman and not Orthodox Catholic he was given the title of *cameriere d'onore di capa e spada* at the Vatican. On account of this honorary position, he managed to have his young daughter Angelica accepted at the very exclusive convent of Santa Trinità dei Monti, nursery of the fine flower of Roman nobility. There is a charming story of Apollinaire's which he originally dedicated to his mother and which could well be one of her own reminiscences about convent days, "L'Oeil bleu." The convent seemed like a prison, and when she eventually left she was dazzled by sunlight and air and liberty. Apollinaire once said that she was a poet, as he was, and certainly his story of a troop of little girls hearing a hunting horn in the distance and then imagining that one of the hunters is roaming about the convent in the shape of a solitary, disembodied eye which each of them does her best to attract, is a poetic enough fancy. As a more spectacular *envoi*, Angelica got herself expelled at the age of sixteen. She was too turbulent a girl for such still waters. Her father, realising that he might have trouble with her— she was very attractive too—did his best to launch her into Roman society in order to marry her off. He himself, although in a respected position, had not much money, and rightly thought that there might be some difficulty. There was indeed, but for a rather different reason. At a party Angelica had met the handsome, forty-three year old Francesco, and had immediately embarked on an affair with him. There was something of a scandal; Francesco, or his family, would not consider marriage, so the couple left Rome to lead a splendidly irresponsible life in the casinos of Europe, quarrelling and separating and then making it up, and trading on Francesco's name for their credit. From time to time the family would step in and pay the bills and try to persuade him to leave Angelica, whom they obviously regarded as his evil genius. But there was a very strong bond between the two and despite all opposition they managed to stay together for the best part of ten years.

In 1880, after about five years of this sort of life, Angelica came back to Rome, although she had by now lost both her parents, and in most elaborately secretive conditions gave birth to a male child on 26 August. About this child she seems to have had second thoughts. At first he is declared at the City Hall as Guillaume Albert Dulcigni, mother wishing to remain anonymous, father not named: a month later he is baptised as Guillelmus Apollinaris Albertus de Kostrowitzky, son of Angelica de Kostrowitzky, and finally the dual identity is reconciled in November by Angelica making a formal act of recognition of this her natural son, Guillaume Albert Wladimir Alexandre Apollinaire. Each step in her confession seems to be compensated by the addition of imposing names. No wonder that in later life one of the obsessive themes of his poetry should be the question "Who am I?", nor that the proud answer should be "Je suis Guillaume Apollinaire," that is, only the personage he had invented for himself.

It seems evident that Angelica's change of heart was caused by her religious belief: once the child was to be baptised she felt that she had to admit the truth. (In *Le Poète assassiné*, Macarée insists on going to Rome to have the Papal blessing on her unborn, illegitimate child, and, a minor detail which might have some connexion with Angelica who always looked very much the *grande dame*, equips herself with maternity clothes from the best *couturiers*.) What is less certain is the part that Francesco played at this time. Was he in Rome with her, or was this one of the times when he conveniently disappeared? Angelica, however, was equally determined that the baby should not interfere with her life, and very soon afterwards he was left with foster parents in Rome and the couple were together again on their round of the casinos, both now completely addicted to their passion for gambling. Two years later the same pattern was repeated. Angelica came back to Rome to give birth to another male child who was also declared under a fabricated Italian name: but him she did not bother to recognise until six years later. There has been a tendency in some biographers of Apollinaire to declare that he could hardly have failed to be the fantastic creature he turned out to be, with such romantic and fantastic beginnings. But his brother Albert, who shared the same beginnings, was the exact opposite, staid, stolid, and ordinary, content to remain a bank clerk all his life. And it was he, the docile dull one, who was his mother's favourite.

In 1884, the Aspermonts, in the person of Don Romarino, made a determined attempt to break up the liaison. He paid Francesco's debts, gave him money, and put him aboard a boat for America. He promptly got off at the first stop—Messina—and went back to Naples, where Angelica was waiting for him, an exploit not unworthy of the Baron d'Ormesan. But the next year Don Romarino did at last prevail and Francesco made his final exit from Angelica's life. She, however, seems to have carried on much as before, leaving her children in Italy while she wandered from casino to casino, until the moment came when she had to tackle the problem of their education. Despite her unconventional behaviour, she was always aware of what she considered due to her station in life, and was determined that her sons should be brought up as gentlemen. Her own resources being precarious, the obvious person to help shoulder responsibility for them, as he had driven Francesco away, was Don Romarino, who seems to have faced this task squarely. In 1887, Angelica arrived at a modest pension in Monaco with her two children, and Wilhelm, as she always called Guillaume, was sent as a boarder to the Collège Saint-Charles, which had recently been founded by the Bishop of Monaco, and which was as exclusive as her own Roman convent had been. Without Don Romarino's powerful influence, a child as fatherless as Guillaume would certainly not have been admitted. Angelica herself seemed to have more difficulty in being accepted by the authorities of Monaco as a resident, and in her official application used her son's school as if it were a reference for her respectability.[3] Albert was next settled at the same school and for a while Angelica's problems were over.

In a photograph which she had taken at that time, the two boys look like a couple of soulful Little Lord Fauntleroys in sailor-suits. (This was probably the source of the touching sailor-image which recurs in Apollinaire's poems: "Deux matelots qui ne s'étaient jamais quittés.") Like most mothers unrestrained by a husband, she dressed them over-preciously. This is one of the few characteristics which Apollinaire later saw fit to recall about his childhood—"ta mère ne t'habille que be bleu et de blanc." It certainly did not help when he made his first appearance at school. Nor did his foreign name. "Wilhelm—vilaine," the whole class began to chant, and the young nun in charge had the utmost difficulty in stopping the uproar.

This must have been an important, emotional experience in the small boy's life, and have underlined once and for all the fact that he was different, a foreigner, a mother's boy. But there is not a single reference to it anywhere in Apollinaire's writings: given his general attitude towards his early days this, however, is hardly surprising. It is as if he had sieved the ingredients of his life and, leaving out the raw lumps, kept only the surface dredging of flour. When he does talk of his childhood, it is to recall picturesque details which give nothing away. Only in one of the stories collected in the volume *Le Poète assassiné* does he appear to have abandoned himself to the temptation of reliving some of his earliest impressions. In fact this seems to be the sole *raison d'être* of "Giovanni Moroni," there being no plot or story, merely a string of incidents recalling a Roman childhood. They certainly leave us

[3] I have actually seen documents in the possession of André Rouveyre which appear to be photostat reproductions of an official list of some of the undesirable women of the Principality. Olga (another of Angelica's names) Kostrowitzky figures amongst them.

in no doubt about Apollinaire's remarkable powers of memory, and again confirm our suspicions that if he is silent about his childhood it is for some specific reason and not due to simple forgetfulness. All the details are as precise as those in an etching.

In particular Giovanni dwells on his memories of food: and this is clearly Apollinaire himself, the great eater, the catholic and *recherché* gourmand, enjoying his own reminiscences. For him the omnipotent, nostalgia-evoking sense was not that of smell, but of taste. The fir-cone kernels roasted over a wood fire at the age of three, the *dragées* made of orange-rind, the aniseed balls that symbolised the feasts of the Epiphany, the roast chestnuts that accompanied the evening walks in winter, and the ice-cold water-melon in summer, the tamarind paste to console him when he cried, the quince paste (*cotogniata*), the pancakes made of peach paste (*persicata*), macaroni with a sauce concocted from chicken liver, macaroni with sugar and cinnamon—how the little boy must have stuffed himself, and how the grown man must have enjoyed redigesting his past! And all these precise culinary analyses were registered before the age of seven!

There is another unmistakably Apollinairian trait in Giovanni: he is fascinated by words for their own sake and gives fanciful names to everything, not only to his toys, but to a dead fish his mother is about to cook, which he calls Bionoulor. This may not be particularly original in a budding writer, but Apollinaire was always especially fascinated by linguistic quirks and esoteric vocabulary.

More revealing, because it deals with an emotional experience, which could be the source of later obsessions in his writings, is an incident concerning Giovanni's mother, the handsome, dark-haired Attilia, who spent much of her time consulting priests and monks about such disparate matters as having her tooth out, or her fortune told. She takes the little boy with her and generally these encounters strike him as sinister and terrifying. One in particular stirred up a particularly strong response in the child. The monk fortune-teller is young and handsome, but filthy. During the long time that he tells the cards, he gradually lets his habit fall open and Giovanni, to his fascinated horror, sees that underneath it he is

B

naked. When he finally gets up he reveals himself as "bestiale-
ment impudique." There is a force behind the choice of those
two words, a vividness about the whole scene—the monk's
habit is full of "de petites saletés sèches et consistantes"—
which well convey the mixture of revulsion and fascination
of a small boy's first experience of sex, made more pungent
because it is his mother who is the object of a stranger's advances.

This could well be the starting point of Apollinaire's
obsessive interest in off-beat characters connected with the
Church, and of his harping on their curious mixture of sanctity
and obscenity. In fact they eventually form one of the favourite
themes of his stories and often excite some of his crudest irony,
a sure sign of personal, emotional involvement. Amongst
others, there is Benedetto Orfei, the lubricious, gourmandising,
self-flagellating heretic who gives his name to the volume of
stories *L'Hérésiarque et Cie*: there is in *Le Poète assassiné* "a big
monastic garden out of which rose laughter, sighs, cries of
pleasure as if a thousand couples were embracing";[4] there is a
last-minute baptism which turns out to be not valid because
the holy water was "du pissat de cheval" from out of the gutter;
there is a sick pilgrim girl who discovers her erstwhile lover
in a young monk and whose cries of "Kiss me, Amadeo" ring
through the church; there is the poem of the hermit in the desert
with his voluptuous dreams and the solitary witness of his
concupiscence; and the theme of blasphemy reaches its
apotheosis in the story of the fallen angel "Simon-Mage."
From a suspicion as a small boy that his mother's extracted
tooth—the only fee demanded by the Capuchin monk-cum-
dentist—later served as a holy relic, to an interest in demonology
is perhaps a natural progression.

There is also a precursory hint of this, combined with
another of his later and lasting interests—he once exclaimed
with delight when he discovered a treatise on the psychology
of the sewage-worker—in the continuation of Attilia's converse
with the monk. On another occasion he gave her a wooden
triangle bearing candles; and in the evening, when her husband
was out and she and Giovanni were alone she lit the candles
and went across the yard to the earth-closets chanting a

---

[4] *Le Poète assassiné*, 1959, p. 94.

rigmarole which terrified the child. He was even more terrified when she threw the strange, illuminated object into the hole and a great cloud of smoke issued forth. She must have been a simple soul, because she still went on going back to the monk, until at last he gave her a piece of mirror and told her that if it had belonged to a prostitute and she looked into it, she would become likewise "impudique." But his own glance was so "impudique" that finally she could be left in no doubt about his intentions.

Some biographers have chosen to identify Attilia with Angelica. Giovanni's attachment to her, the food-giver and comforter, seems authentic, and so do his sympathy and revulsion on her behalf, and little remarks like: "I loved her very much particularly because her ear-rings were big, heavy hoops of gold. And so I thought she was superior to my father, who had only little hoops as thin as wire." But the worldly Angelica could scarcely have behaved in such a simple-minded fashion. And then there is the father, Beppo the toy-maker, who occasionally drags his wife about by her hair and stamps on her breasts until they are stigmatised by the marks of his hob-nailed boots. Francesco might have been capable of stamping: he would not have been wearing hob-nailed boots.

A more plausible explanation would be that Attilia and Beppo represent Guillaume's foster parents with whom he spent the first seven years of his life in Rome. This would supply a concrete background to his childhood which has always been lacking—the toy-maker's house with the wooden toys made specially for the little boy clattering all over the floor, the child's mind full of the names and stories he had invented for them, the excitement of carnival time, the monthly holocaust when his foster mother caught cockroaches and then poured boiling water over them, the ever-present superstitious religion, the pretend Masses that he conducted in imitation, in short all the life and warmth and colour of a poor Roman family. And not only would this also make sense of the ending of "Giovanni Morani": it would explain why, with the minimum of effect, it is so moving. A stranger arrives and hands the couple a letter. Attilia cannot read and gives it to Beppo. When he has finished reading it aloud, the two simple souls burst into tears, and their despair is so infectious that the little boy joins in without knowing what it is all about. The next day Beppo takes him away by train to Turin. There he meets his uncle, who carries him off for good to Paris. "From that day to this," he says simply, "I have never seen my parents again." Angelica was away so much during those first seven years that it must have been the foster parents who were the mainspring of his existence; and the separation when she eventually took him away first to Paris for a brief visit and then to settle in Monaco, must have been an important and painful step in his growing-up.

However he was resilient enough even as a young boy. Giovanni Moroni completely forgets the sadness of the parting in the exitement of the long train journey and the puppet show to which Beppo takes him in Turin: and Wilhelm de Kostrowitzky very soon overcame the mockeries of the other little boys at the Collège Saint-Charles and became one of the popular ringleaders of his class. The picture that one manages to piece together from his own throw-away references and other people's accounts is of a bright, high-spirited boy generally at the top of the class, a born leader—it is he who was chosen to captain a paper cut-out army of Medes against his great friend René Dupuy who was in charge of the Persians—jolly, extroverted, and at the same time a great reader, already at the age of twelve writing poems and planning an ambitious adventure novel in the manner of Jules Verne with another of his friends, James Onimus. They got as far as choosing the title, *Orindiculo,* and the setting: it was to begin in Paris and end in the "savannas of America," but never in fact materialised at all. When he himself looks back at this untroubled period of his life from the lofty but clouded heights of his late teens, he exclaims with sentimental nostalgia about the limpid innocence of these days:

> Que mon âme était fraîche
> Et même j'ai connu la raison d'être des sphères[5]

---

[5] "Le Ciel se couvre un matin de mai," in *Le Guetteur Mélancolique, Oeuvres poétiques,* 1956, p. 525.

"How fresh was my soul
And I even knew the final cause of the spheres"

There is a photograph of him at the age of twelve dressed up for his first communion and looking very much as though he might be listening to the music of the spheres. Now that he has grown away from his mother's influence, he is altogether tougher, with his hair shorn and his pear-shaped face jutting out, his eyes solemn and fixed on the middle distance. This was the pious phase to which he refers as one of the landmarks of his childhood in the poem "Zone."

> Tu es très pieux et avec le plus ancien de tes camarades
> René Dalize
> Vous n'aimez rien tant que les pompes de l'Eglise
> Il est neuf heures le gaz est baissé tout bleu vous sortez
> du dortoir en cachette
> Vous priez toute la nuit dans la chapelle du collège
> Tandis qu'éternelle et adorable profondeur améthyste
> Tourne à jamais la flamboyante gloire du Christ[6]

Because religion seemed later to play no important part in his life, this is always dismissed as the normal religious crisis of early adolescence. There is surely more significance in it. To have a religious crisis may be normal, but actually to go to the lengths of stealing out of the school dormitory to spend the whole night in a Galahad vigil in the chapel would hardly be regarded by most schoolmasters as an everyday occurrence. The self-induced hallucination of the amethyst rose-window as Christ's glory spinning round in eternity, the power to sustain a visionary moment throughout a long night, the ability to act out his excess of imaginative fervour, even the longing for divine affection which shines through the indulgent evocation of the adult, seems to denote an out-of-the-ordinary sensibility and a particular capacity for whole-hearted devotion to an ideal.

[6] "You are very pious and along with your oldest friend René Dalize
You like nothing as much as the ceremonies of the Church
It is nine o'clock the gas is lowered and blue you steal out of the
dormitory
You pray all night in the School Chapel
Whilst the adored and eternal amethyst depths
Of Christ's blazing glory wheel round for evermore"

Although he loved everything about the "pomp of the Church," his particular allegiance was to the Virgin, and he proudly took up the post of secretary to the Congregation of the Immaculate Conception. Even later in life he would often refer to "la Vierge Marie" with a special note of grateful tenderness in his voice, as though she had for some while filled the role of a particularly charming tutelary spirit. It is tempting to see in this devotion to the ideal mother-figure a transference of the feelings he longed, vainly, to have for the un-Madonna-like Angelica—the crux, in fact, of all his early emotional life.

He had had to learn early how to live with a complex of contradictory emotions about his mother. He was both proud of her, her looks and bearing and aristocratic background, and yet profoundly ashamed of her conduct. She had wounded his pride, diminished his stature in the eyes of the world, yet he loved her so much that out of a child's highly developed sense of delicacy and loyalty he managed to suppress criticism, and then for the rest of his life to block out the memories and confidences which would give away her secrets—not his. There is one reference, and one only, that has escaped him in his works—and then it is so tortuous and obscure that it has taken years to be fully understood—to the difficulty that he had in reconciling the two warring poles of his feeling. It occurs in "Le Larron," a poem written when he was about nineteen, the thief being a ship-wrecked foreigner washed ashore on a Greek island and caught in the act of stealing fruit. At this particular stage in his life, Apollinaire had in fact good reason to identify himself with the foreigner in a civilised land caught on the wrong foot legally for a trifling offence.[7] The Chorus accuses the thief:

> Maraudeur étranger malhabile et malade
> Ton père fut un sphinx et ta mère une nuit
> Qui charma de lueurs Zacinthe et les Cyclades
> As-tu feint d'avoir faim quand tu volas les fruits

---

[7] Cp. the Stavelot episode, pp. 42-9 below.

and the thief replies:

> Possesseurs de fruits mûrs que dirai-je aux insultes
> Ouïr ta voix ligure en nénie ô maman
> Puisqu'ils n'eurent enfin la pubère et l'adulte
> De prétexte sinon de s'aimer nuitamment[8]

The picture that a careful analysis reveals is unequivocal. The father is an enigma ("un sphinx"), the mother a dark beauty radiating her charm over the Mediterranean scene; he himself, being taunted by more fortunate boys, possessors of proper homes and families, confronts his mother, and she in a voice that always reminds him of the Ligurian coast (though she had apparently no Italian accent in French) explains herself to him, keening ("nénie" is a funeral chant) over her wrongs with the familiar complaint, "I was very young, and we loved each other very much, and because we were not allowed to marry, our love had to remain secret [nuitamment]." Most revealing of all are the particularly emotional overtones of the two lines:

> que dirai-je aux insultes
> Ouïr ta voix ligure en nenie ô maman

Here the syntax is violated as his own sensibilities have been violated: it has taken the percipience of a scholar like Mme Marie-Jeanne Durry[9] to see that "que" stands for "pourquoi." "Why should I tell the people who insult me what my mother has explained to me alone in private?" And the keynote of that private colloquy is set by the sad lullaby sound of "en nénie," and the pathetic *cri du coeur* "ô maman" from the grown young man.

But the whole of Apollinaire's story with his mother is

---

[8] "O Foreign marauder clumsy and sick
Your father was a sphinx and your mother a night
Which charmed with its glow Zacinth and the Cyclades
Did you feign hunger when you stole the fruits

Possessors of ripe fruits why should I tell the people who insult me
What I have heard my mother tell me in the sad chant of her Ligurian
 voice
Since finally the adolescent girl and the grown man
Had no pretext but to make love at night"

[9] Marie-Jeanne Durry, *Guillaume Apollinaire, Alcools*, VOL. 1, 1956 (henceforth cited as Durry), p. 72.

touching. It is undoubtedly the reason for his defensiveness and secrecy, as well as the basis for the special brand of irony that gadflies over all his poetry, and for that strange criss-cross of tenderness and brutality that forms the warp and the weft of his love affairs. It is a perfect example of two people who were deeply attached to each other, but who could not be together for two minutes without quarrelling. "Immediately I see my mother she begins to curse me," he told André Salmon, and Salmon presents him as being terrorised by this redoubtable matriarch.[10] She disapproved of everything about Guillaume in later life. "Which of you has debauched the other?" she fired at him when he brought Salmon home. She, of all people! She had no interest at all in his writing and had read only *L'Hérésiarque et Cie*, which she found stupid. She was flabbergasted when people told her that they admired his work and said, "But my other son is a writer too." (Albert wrote articles for a financial paper.) She bitterly opposed his projected marriage to Marie Laurencin. She was possessive, dominating, apparently uncomprehending: but like a good mother she always did all she could to help him in her way, which was material but none the less useful. Marie-Jeanne Durry records[11] Marie Laurencin's statement that if Guillaume managed to escape from some of the more extreme excesses of poverty in his Bohemian days it was only because of his mother's help. She would pay his rent, the heating and laundry bills, give him money for suits, and then he would promptly spend it on a night out in Montmartre. She would also, more important still, send him jars of stew and jam and whatever she thought might quell his formidable appetite, of which she seemed to be rather proud. "With Wilhelm when there's enough for two, there certainly isn't for three," she said once, with maternal satisfaction. She also provided him with a whole set of ugly Breton furniture and a huge red eiderdown, which he religiously took with him in all his moves, despite the quips of his sophisticated friends. And that red eiderdown is given the honour, in one of his major poems, of bearing the full symbolic weight of the poor emigrants'

[10] André Salmon, *Souvenirs sans fin*, VOL. I, 1955, p. 86.
[11] Durry, p. 77.

yearning for home and family, affection and security. "Une famille transporte un édredon rouge comme vous transportez votre coeur," he writes in "Zone."

But even apart from this discreet, poetic revelation of all that the red eiderdown meant for him, it is evident in their whole converse that Guillaume never ceased to love her very much, that she was always the "maman" he cries out to as a young man, and he for her the "petit garçon." After his sudden death, these were the only words that her otherwise inarticulate grief could find. "Mon petit garçon," she kept repeating over his corpse.

He had never minded her treating him as if he were ten years old, and as he says to his *fiancée* at the age of thirty-five,[12] if she slapped him in the face even then he would think it quite in order. Yet although he took many things from her lying down, he was also capable of standing up all night to argue with her over a trivial question such as whether Valenciennes lace was made in colours or not. It was a part of his own pride to respect her and be proud of her, a *parti-pris* that he must have decided on from his earliest days: his loyalty to her was unbroken, in the face of many unpleasant scenes, and he in his turn helped her out financially when she was in difficulties. He always insisted on her good looks, and the distinction of her manners. "Elle est si racée," he said, and proudly took his friends home to meet the "grande dame." They were both fascinated and terrified by her, and made up a little ditty about "la mère d'Apollinaire" which went the rounds of Montmartre. It was a tempting pun, but they never dared to sing it in Guillaume's hearing. Any slight on her would have been a blow below the belt for him.

The heart of the matter was that, without having any interests in common, they were very alike. This explains Mme de Kostrowitzky's instinctive disapproval of failings in Guillaume which she recognised as basically her own, and her pride in Albert, who represented the respectability that seemed to elude her. Guillaume himself said that he resembled her very much, and that she too was a poet. She certainly invented an original way of life, and perhaps the fact of making

[12] *Tendre comme le souvenir*, 1952, p. 116.

your own conventions, or even of rigging up your sitting-room to look like an Arabian chief's tent, does show a creative turn of mind. As for the single-mindedness and enthusiastic devotion to one cause, which in Guillaume manifested itself in his attitude to poetry and the arts, well, she had her life-long passion for gambling.

There is no question that they both had the same ungovernable tempers, and at times the same violent behaviour. She would rage around her villa at Le Vésinet lashing out with a whip at her menagerie of animals, and the servants then were quick to get out of her way: one wonders whether certain of Apollinaire's erotic tastes derived from her. During a quarrel with her lover she did not hesitate to break all the windows in the bedroom, and André Salmon tells the story of seeing her in some miserable gambling den, locked in an all-in wrestling bout with another woman.[13] "Indomitable," said Guillaume of her proudly, "like all Slav women."[14]

She deserves a whole book to herself; but, again according to her son, Dostoevsky has already written it.

[13] André Salmon, *Souvenirs sans fin*, VOL. III, 1961, p. 248.
[14] *Tendre comme le souvenir*, 1952, p. 116.

II

Schooldays in Monaco

AT the end of the school year in 1896 the Collège Saint-Charles was closed by the order of the Prince of Monaco, and Wilhelm's settled school life was over. He did go for a term to the Collège Stanislas in Cannes and then in February 1897 for two terms to the *lycée* in Nice as a weekly boarder: but after shining as the star pupil in Monaco, he now became so ineffectual at his school work that he either left without taking his Baccalauréat, or actually took it and failed. This sudden falling-off has always presented itself as rather a mystery. There are, however, two simple explanations for his early diploma-less departure. First, that the Aspermont family had decided that they had done their bit and refused to pay any more school fees. In fact this happened to coincide with the beginning of a progressively impecunious stage in Angelica's own life; she was by now forty, and physical attractions, as everyone knows, do not last for ever. Secondly, Guillaume had already decided that he was going to be a writer and categorically nothing else. It is possible that the Aspermonts would have supported him further if he had been willing to take up some more orthodox career. There is a hint that this had been proposed and that he had actually refused it in one of the jottings found in a notebook dating from 1898-9. Talking of himself in the third person as A., he laments in a fit of depression and self-pity, his own poverty and lack of assured success:

> I would have done better to have swotted at my maths and tried for *Centrale*, become an engineer, got a secure job. No, instead of working, I wrote poems, I had dreams, I occupied myself with literature, *merde, merde*.[1]

---

[1] Quoted by James Lawler in "Le Séjour à Stavelot," *Mercure de France*, 1 Feb. 1955.

What poems, what dreams, what literature? It is always fascinating to watch somebody applying himself single-mindedly to a vocation from his earliest days; still more fascinating to discover how a boy of sixteen sets out consciously and entirely on his own to train himself for that most undefined of all activities, writing. For it was not merely a question of a story here, a poem there, although he was constantly dashing off poems and stories with characteristic facility, not merely the autobiographical confidences in the secret notebook, all the exhaust burst of the supercharged adolescent, but literature as a chosen way of life, and he as dedicated as a priest.

This stands out very clearly in the picture of the seventeen-year-old Wilhelm de Kostrowitzky as he appeared at the *lycée* in Nice to a boy of his own age, Toussaint-Luca, who soon became his closest friend and remained devoted to him all his life, as did three of his Monaco friends, James Onimus, René Dupuy (later known as René Dalize), and Louis Frick (Louis de Gonzague Frick). To retain four school-day friends must be an unusual feat, and it says much for his more than ordinary charm. From his first arrival at Saint-Charles he had known how to attract sympathy, and the pattern was repeated at the *lycée* in Nice. Now, more than forty years after his death, people[2] are still talking of his particular magnetic charm, how when he died, for them, high spirits and joy and fantasy died too. It must have had more than one ingredient: but basically it was an unusual degree of physical vitality and sheer energy which acted as the magnet. He was also always very anxious to please, craving the affection which blew hot and cold in his unstable family life; and if somebody actively needs to be liked and applies himself wholeheartedly and intelligently to it (and that means hiding all the chips that have settled on his shoulder), why should he fail? The adaptable Apollinaire succeeded brilliantly.

But although he joined in the other boy's activities and his was the loudest laugh of them all, he was more than just a good sort. At the same time he wore an air of precocious authority,

[2] André Billy, André Rouveyre, André Salmon, and Max Jacob before his death.

an indefinable gravity which impressed them most of all.
Even at this stage he succeeded in being taken at his own
valuation. Toussaint-Luca had noticed that his brief-case was
always stuffed with books and newspapers, therefore he
imagined that Guillaume must have on hand great anarchistic
plots, that he was a disciple of Kropotkin or Ravachol bent on
destruction. He soon discovered that Guillaume was indeed
imbued with a sense of his mission in life but that it was of a
totally different order. One day, bored by the stuffiness of his
schoolmaster, Toussaint-Luca wrote an essay into which he
dragged contemporary names like Régnier and Vielé-Griffin:
he also dug out what he thought were the most obscure lines
of Mallarmé and applied them to Racine. When it was read
out contemptuously by the master it acted on Guillaume
like a shot in the arm. His eyes began to pop out of his head
and he could hardly contain himself until the end of the lesson,
when he rushed up to Toussaint-Luca and machine-gunned
him with questions. Whom else had he read? Whom did he
like? What did he think of such-and-such? From then on
they enthused together.

Guillaume was in a state of cerebral effervescence, curious
about everything, passionate about the writers he liked,
falling on books and newspapers with a sensual avidity, as
greedy in this appetite as he always had been about food
and was to become about sex. Every morning he would
arrive with a sheaf of newspapers, which he would distribute
to his friends; and together they would comment on everything from politics to the gossip columns, particularly the
smart literary chats of Jean Lorrain, which gave them the feeling that they were in the know about the affairs of the capital.

This was one of the more impassioned moments of the
Dreyfus affair. The two boys were, as befitted young writers
of the time, pro-Dreyfus, and when Zola wrote his famous
letter *J'accuse*, he instantly became one of their heroes. It
was this ferment of enthusiasm which led them to found a
newspaper of their own written out by hand and given round
to be read at ten centimes a time. It was first called *Le Vengeur*
and then, mocking Rochefort, *Le Transigeant*. The contents
ranged from the two boys' own poems, and their versions of the

gossip columns, to political articles. all strongly anarchist in trend. This doctrine of destruction for destruction's sake with its unformulated, idealistic picture of a totally new world beyond, which was then in the air, matched well with Guillaume's own state of mind at the time, that of the rebel against a conventional society from which he is in any case excluded by an accident of birth, the young outsider, stateless and homeless, the clever boy obviously cleverer and more vital than his schoolmasters and knowing it, chafing all the time against the discipline of a formal education—and French education in uninspired hands can be particularly rigid—and the tyranny of accepted social order.

Toussaint-Luca reproduces two letters written during the year which Guillaume spent after he left school in Monaco devoting all his time and energies to becoming a writer. They are well-known, but they are repeated here because they reveal better than any description just how the cauldron of his mind was kindled to boiling point with the fuel of books and ideas and projects. Toussaint-Luca also adds that they give only a faint idea of his infectious verve and sparkle at this time.

Dear Toussaint,
This is only a short letter. I am in rather a hurry. Write to me sometime. I have lots of things to talk to you or write to you about.
What a difficult thing prose is! It's much easier to write good poetry. But you despise poetry. You are young and going through a crisis. Your case is fairly well described in *Les Déracinés* of Barrès. I am working. Could you find out for me what one has to do to have a brochure printed? The price, the place, and the means of distributing it. Thanks in advance.
Do you know that Max Régis (his enemies in Algiers call him Milano and the people who applaud him, Régisthériques) is in Monaco. Rochefort as well.
Last Thursday, I went and snooped around Rochefort's house, the villa Grimsil. It was pretty in the morning. He was on his doorstep—I wonder why—reading *La Libre Parole* [*sic*]. *La Libre Parole!* I had a sudden desire to speak to him. I unfolded my *Aurore* and went up to him and stupidly asked him where the rue Bel Respiro led to. After taking his eyes

away from his paper and looking at me for a second, the odd-
looking old man explained to me, what I knew anyway better
than he, that the road led out into the country, and didn't
go back into the Principality. (I don't think he noticed
L'Aurore.) I thanked him and then went away cursing my
confounded shyness that prevented me from speaking to him
when I had such a good opportunity. Any other person
would have enjoyed it very much, I think. Anyway . . . for
to-day that's enough, I shall leave you with a prayer for the
arrival of Souvarine, the man who must come, the fair-haired
man who will destroy towns and men. May 1899 hear once
again a voice like Zola's, and may the Revolution be its aim.
But Picquart-Athénée is behaving badly: he allowed himself
to be tormented. He has let them get hold of him, and they
won't let go. He is a martyr, and whilst I admire Picquart-
Athénée, I can't help thinking of Proudhon's saying: "There's
only one species more odious than executioners, and that is
martyrs." Whereupon I salute you.

GUILLAUME APOLLINAIRE.

P.S. Thanks for your offer of newspapers, but I read them all.
Books! books! books!

Dear Toussaint,

I am sending you some poems and the beginning of an
arduous translation which I hope will be successful. I am
trying to translate Boccacio and at the the same time keep its
original flavour. This *Fiametta* is a very charming little book.
They say that the lady who is supposed to recount her heart-
aches, was Boccacio's mistress and left him. This Fiametta,
who also plays a part in the Decameron, in which she is queen
during the day "delle novelle felici," came from the same family
as Saint Thomas Aquinas and Saint Louis. I don't think
that the *Fiametta* has been translated into French. In any
case, there can't be an æsthetic translation; and that's what
I'm trying to do. There are, in the prologue that I'm sending
to you, two sentences that I can't manage to translate at all
satisfactorily, and you'll be doing me a service if you get them
translated.

You haven't sent me any philosophy books.

I have read *La Volonté* from its first number until recently.
It was good. Luquet's *Urbs* is a charming novel. Now *La
Volonté* is no good at all and appears in the morning, and since

then I have been taking *Le Journal du Peuple,* anarchist and
directed by Sébastien Faure. So there's the situation.

I am reading Balzac very seriously with pleasure and profit.
He is an enormous, unformed predecessor of Zola, Bourget,
Tolstoy, Elimir Bourges; but he had no idea of the social
question.[3]

Once freed from the imposition of school and left on his
own to do exactly what he pleased, it is evident that Guillaume
was busy sublimating everything, his energy, his curiosity,
his appetites, his emotions, into a cerebral frenzy, feeding for
his staple diet on the constantly chewed cud of literature. Even
his diversions seemed to have a literary stimulus. When he
and Toussaint-Luca went to the fair in Nice it was not to try
the shooting-gallery, or pick up girls, but "to make a study
of people and of social habits"; and the highspot of the evening
was when they discovered an accompanist who said that he
was a poet called Charles, and had lived for a long time with
Verlaine (could this have been Charles Morice?). In their
excitement they willingly handed over all the money they had,
when he begged from them.[4]

There is another occasion when one of his pranks had a
literary flavour, and this is less to his credit than giving money
to a poor poet. There was an old man in Monaco, Adrien
Blandignères, who wrote ballads and acrostics and sold them
in the cafés. He eccentrically wore a badge of the Légion
d'Honneur to which he had no right, and dreamed of being
elected to the Académie française. For a joke Guillaume
wrote him a letter purporting to be from the Prince des Poètes
and announcing that he had been awarded the Légion
d'Honneur: to do the job thoroughly he also sent a copy of the
letter to a newspaper in Nice which actually published it.
Finally he walked the proud, drunken old man home with his
decorations on his chest. The incident ended with a police-
man asking Blandignères to produce his credentials. How
Guillaume extricated himself one is left to imagine.

Toussaint-Luca unfortunately makes no reference to any

[3] Toussaint-Luca, *Guillaume Apollinaire,* 1954 (henceforth cited as Toussaint-
Luca), pp. 26-8.
[4] *Op. cit.,* p. 21.

girl whom Guillaume knew at this time, and who might
correspond to the Mia who heads the chronological list of his
loves in the poem "La Colombe poignardée et le jet d'eau."
Again the maxim seems to hold good that when in doubt about
autobiographical material one should turn to *Le Poète assassiné*,
for here there is a delightful Monégasque Mia described, like
the monk in "Giovanni Moroni," in details which are odd and
precise enough to be genuine. "The colour of her skin and
her black hair bore witness to her Corsican blood. She was
always dressed in bright colours. She swayed as she walked,
her waist was sinuous, her bust was smaller than her hips, and a
slight strabism gave her eyes a vaguely lost look, which made
her all the more desirable."[5] This last detail certainly
sounds authentic. Why otherwise make a desirable girl
squint? But the trait in Mia which is unquestionably true to
life is her Monégasque way of speaking: and his interest in this
is the most revealing characteristic of Apollinaire at this time.
For even when his hero is watching Mia squint and desiring
her and pitying himself because she does not appear to desire
him, he is really most intrigued of all by her peculiar accent
and syntax which the author, Apollinaire, reproduces in
painstaking detail.

There is also a more intimate picture of Mia, which he
eventually deleted in the proofs. It is a little incident, common
enough to have been based on fact—the adolescent peering
through a keyhole to see a girl undressing—but which, instead
of being reproduced as a piquant slice of life, has been transformed into a precious literary conceit.

Mia's room was on the same floor as Nyctor's. Between them
there was only the bedroom of the Cecchi couple. One night
when he was going along the corridor and out into the garden
to dream, Nyctor saw a gleam of light coming from the keyhole
of Mia's room. With his heart beating at his own temerity
Nyctor bent down and put his eye to the keyhole. Then
immediately he knelt down so as to make himself more comfortable.

Nyctor saw a mirror and a pink, naked girl. Suddenly,
because of the mirror, there were two pink, naked girls.

[5] *Le Poète assassiné*, 1959, p. 27.

C

Each was looking lovingly at the taut breasts of the other. And ouf! the pretty girls turned round and there were two mobile behinds, firm and fleshy which profiled against each other as they were, seemed to be comparing each other incomparably. Then they went their separate ways with a funny rolling movement. Then again there was only one Mia. The other had vanished, disappeared out of modesty perhaps.[6]

Even the young man's desire is forged out of literature. This figure of Nyctor, cross between dreamer and *voyeur*, is interesting. He appears only in deleted passages in the manuscript of *Le Poète assassiné*. In the final version his role is split into those of François des Ygrées, and his poet-son Croniamental. He was evidently the first literary incarnation of Apollinaire himself, because many facts of their lives coincide. In another crossed-out passage Apollinaire lets Nyctor explain the reason for the choice of his name:

> At the *lycée* in Marseilles, in spite of the environment, in spite of the sea air, I became sad, dreamy, preoccupied. As I did not need much sleep, and often got up at night to go for a walk or to meditate at my window, my friends called me Nyctor, and I have chosen to keep my nocturnal name.[7]

(Although he abandoned it for the published version of *Le Poète assassiné*, it must have stayed in his mind because he uses it for another poet in one of his latest works of all, *Couleur du temps*.)

The Nyctor of these scattered, muddled autobiographical pieces is Apollinaire as he wanted to see himself in these days, the pale, sad dreamer. "I have had dreams." Dreaming or waking, or peeping through key-holes, he is acting out the role of the poet, more particularly as seen in the Symbolist vogue. His earliest surviving poem, which dates back to 1895, bears out this romantic, dreaming conception of himself. It amusingly foreshadows the calligram, being composed of a little drawing of a young man asleep above a huddled town and a nun at her prayers, with the title *Minuit* and the Verlainian incantation: "Dans la nuit sans bruit l'heure pleure

[6] *Le Poète assassiné*, 1959, p. 241.   [7] *Op. cit.*, Documents, no. 8.

trois fois," draped in trellis-work over it.[8] And this bundle of
energy, this boy who was so vital that he simply did not need
much sleep, who eventually chose to identify himself with the
sun-god latent in his pseudonym and to declare proudly, "I
am reborn with the dawn,"[9] in his *début* as a poet, saw himself
as the exact opposite and signed himself Guillaume Macabre.
It was a self-conscious, literary pose, and yet none the less
sincere. He was the melancholy dreamer as well as the
marvellously ebullient joker. It is hardly surprising if a young
man so self-aware, and so susceptible to the current tone,
with a personality so acutely developed that there is a constant
pendulum swing between two extremes, should be confused
by the diversity of his own potentialities and choose to empha-
sise one at the expense of the others. In fact these lightning
changes through different modulations of feeling and behaviour
are one of the lasting fascinations of Apollinaire as a man:
and as a poet it is perhaps his chief originality that he had the
sense and the ability to mirror these flashing moods and shifts
of key, here instanced by the dreamer mooning in the moonlit
garden and the Peeping Tom licking his lips over Mia's
duplicated nakedness.

He could easily, with his facile cleverness, the Nyctor
pose, his sense of mission and all his intense cerebration, have
become unpopular with the other boys. In his letters to
Toussaint-Luca there is a certain bossiness ("You are young
and going through a crisis," he wrote although he was the
younger), a sense of having read everything, an authoritarian
tone in his judgments ("Balzac had no idea of the social
question"), which might have irritated. But by some alchemy
he managed to turn even this dedicated passion for literature
into yet another ingredient of his spell-binding charm, a feat
less remarkable, certainly, in France than it might be else-
where, but still a rarity. "What a charming wit he had,
what an adorable *raconteur* he was!" writes Toussaint-Luca:

> His curiosity led him to hunt out anecdotes, eccentric stories,
> the oddest and least known of details. Already he knew all

[8] *Oeuvres poétiques*, 1956, p. 317.
[9] Louise Faure-Favier, *Souvenirs sur Apollinaire*, 1945 (henceforth cited as Faure-
Favier), p. 118.

the witty stories, all the little adventures which make up the
by-ways of history, and which are more than half the fun.
He could have told us whether a magician was dressed in blue
brocade and a pointed hat, if such and such a fairy wore a
sky-blue dress. He knew all the worries of the incubi and
succubi. He lived amongst legend, anecdotes, historiette.
He was passionately interested in teaching us all that we
were not aware of and that he knew already.[10]

He may well have been picking out the plums of his reading
as part of his conscious desire to please, like the diner-out with
his stories. Once, later in his life, he appeared at a dinner
party in the Ile Saint-Louis and held forth most com-
pellingly about the history of the island. After his hostess,
Louise Faure-Favier had exclaimed in delight at his erudition,
he confessed that he had read it all up just before he came.
"But that," he added, "is how you please the ladies,"[11] which
may seem very Gallic and dated, but at least his desire to
please was most potently effective.

But, as Toussaint-Luca says, it was not merely a question
of dredging up the tit-bits; he was actually living in a fantasy
world, which was so real and important and fascinating to
him that he had to share it with his friends. He was bubbling
over with imaginary gossip, beside which the life of the school-
room seemed two-dimensional. No wonder the other boys
loved to listen to him. What is more enchanting than to be
drawn out of one's own monotonous prison of self and to be
taken round an altogether airier and more curious domain?

His favourite hunting-ground for anecdote and adventure,
and even for the subject matter of his own poems, was in the
old Breton legends. The most important poem which survives
from the Nice *lycée* period, "Triptyque de l'Homme," describes
three little episodes of Gauvain and Myrdhinn (Merlin) and
Giglam son of Gauvain, which already show that he was well
acquainted with the world of King Arthur and the quest for
the Holy Grail, with Merlin the magician and the fairy Vivian
who enslaves him, and who later become the subject of his
first major work, *L'Enchanteur pourrissant*. Not that this was a
unique interest at the time when Symbolism was picking its

[10] Toussaint-Luca, p. 18.   [11] Faure-Favier, p. 34.

subject matter from the ruins of the past. What is typical of Apollinaire is that these legends are in no way misty, but very concrete, and even vague figures like fairies and gnomes and heroes have their individual peculiarities. His fairy with the white hands lets down her long red hair, in an attempt to seduce the knights, Merlin in his glass prison seems delighted to have been deceived, and Giglam the hero is frightened of ghosts in the moonlight. He also, and this gives some measure of the young Apollinaire's sense of his own place in the universal hierarchy, becomes proud only when he thinks of the pale men who will recount his heroic adventures invented by them. From the earliest days Apollinaire was sure that the poet is and must be more heroic than the hero.

From fairies and magicians to demons and alchemists and the esoteric world of the Cabbala was not a great step. He seemed to be interested in any subject which was bizarre enough to show men trying to escape from the limitations of convention and their own nature, and to be searching for figures in the past who would parallel his conception of his own extraordinary role. But even these researches, which were obsessive enough to occupy him for several years, were only a part of his catholic reading. He himself in a letter to André Breton in 1916 tends to minimise the extent of it:

> The only books I have read with care are specialised books on all sorts of subjects, linguistic studies, the Fairy Stories of Perrault, grammar-books, travel books, and poetry, whole stretches of Villon, Racine, La Fontaine. I read *La Chute d'un ange* a long time ago when I was eighteen. . . . As for Mallarmé it was *L'Hérodiade* which first struck me in what I read. Nevertheless Mallarmé must undoubtedly have influenced me although I found him above all Parnassian, pro-Parnassian. . . . Racine, La Fontaine, Perrault and also Madame Leprince de Beaumont were the great raves of my childhood.[12]

And yet even though he professed to dislike the Parnasse, there is a distinctly Parnassian flavour about one of his Nice poems, "Mort de Pan."

In fact, he gave the impression, as people with particularly

---

[12] Quoted by Marcel Adéma, *Guillaume Apollinaire le mal-aimé*, 1952 (henceforth cited as Adéma), p. 18.

good memories can often do, of having read everything. But he had a trick. He had early developed the reviewer's technique of snatching at the heart of a book through a fan of quickly turned pages, and with his quicksilver attention and swift powers of assimilation he would sort out the material which was to furnish his imaginary world, the recondite word, the bizarre trait, the freaks of history. Then, for this was all a part of his self-imposed training for becoming a writer, he would carefully note them down. The recent discovery of notebooks[13] belonging both to this and a slightly later period have shown the whole process at work. There are lists of words copied down from the dictionary, then strange words like "acousmate," "dendrophores," "Argyraspides," which crop up sometimes more than once and sometimes in poems of much later date; there is the medical term "pandiculation" which he uses afterwards in one of his pornographic novels; there are the famous "pi-mus," the Siamese twins amongst fishes, which he had apparently read about in a book of Chinese legends; there are anecdotes lifted from the newspapers of the time, such as that of the Zaporogue Cossacks who defied the Sultan of Constantinople, and who put in such an effectively obscene appearance in Apollinaire's lyrical *chef d'œuvre*, "La Chanson du Mal-Aimé"; there are lines of verse carefully scanned, in particular an oddity such as a nine-syllable line of Moréas, which he marks out, unusually for a poet writing in French, in anapaests; there are images taken from medieval chronicles—he wrote for instance "le topaze a le color d'or cuit," which later becomes in the poem "Palais":

> Nous aurions jusqu'au jour médité les topazes
> La veilleuse dans l'ombre est un bijou d'or cuit.

And in case this seems to justify the insult which was later cast at him, that he was nothing but a "junk-dealer," these notes are larded with his own inventions, amongst them some of the more luminous lines of later, completed poems, and all, for good measure, wreathed in fantastic doodling.

This self-teaching method may have been somewhat naïve and if he had had more mature guidance he would probably

[13] James Lawler, *op. cit.*

have learned to shed his early bookishness more quickly, although in fact his originality was so marked as to shine even through such a thick, derivative cloak. At least it shows him respectfully applying himself to preparing the raw material and sharpening the tools of his craft, which might well be a better apprenticeship in the long run than regurgitating undigested lumps of raw experience. In any case it is important to recognise that what André Gide later called "the ingenuous miracles of Apollinaire" had this background of intensive study and applied craftsmanship.

Another interesting facet of this period of solitary study, is that it was carried on against the most frivolous setting in Europe. Not that the pleasure domes of Monte Carlo ever seemed to hold any temptations for him. He was probably inoculated for ever by his mother's example against the mole-fevers of burrowing for money and social success, and ambitious though he always was for his status as a writer to be fully recognised, money as money and not merely barter for food and drink and freedom to write as he wanted, never had any valid lure. Nevertheless, that he was mordantly aware of the "social habits" and characters of the people who frequented the casino is evident in one short scene from *Le Poète assassiné*, and significantly it is not the picturesque setting which he saw fit to record, but the real tragedy behind it, and the inhuman condition to which an obsessive addiction can reduce a human being. His own defensive reaction to this, as to Mia's rebuffs, is an attitude of casual but conscious irony. A young man gets up and shoots himself in the "salle du jeu" because of his losses. "A few players turned their head a little, but nobody got up and the majority did not even notice." When François des Ygrées in his turn shoots himself, Mia cries out, "Now we'll have a room to let," and that night "sold her virginity to a millionaire who was a champion at pigeon shooting, and it was the thirty-fifth time that she performed this little commercial operation."[14]

Diluted as his enjoyment of the social setting may have been, there is no question but that he loved—as who could not—the physical *décor* of all that coast, although, because he was

[14] *Le Poète assassiné*, 1959, p. 34.

writing out of literature and not experience at that time,
definite Mediterranean images such as lemon trees and
cypresses do not appear until later in his poems. There are,
however, several stories in *L'Hérésiarque et Cie* and *Le Poète
assassiné* which have a very precise Piedmontese background.[15]
It is difficult to be certain when these were written. None was
published before 1902. André Billy in his Preface to the collected poetic works in the Pléiade edition states without further
reference that some were written during the year of liberty
in Monaco. Pascal Pia in his *Apollinaire par lui-même*[16] underlines in these *contes* the influence of Marcel Schwob whom he
did not meet until 1900. As neither of these is a particularly
clear indication, one is left face to face with the subject matter
and style which definitely appear to be of a different order
from those of the prose pieces that Apollinaire was turning out
before 1900.

Instead of the mythical fantasies of *L'Enchanteur pourrissant*
couched in a lyrical but opaque style which seems unable to
make up its mind whether to be prose or verse, these are
observations of real life transferred directly into an altogether
more mature, and authoritative language. "What a difficult
thing prose is!" he had written to Toussaint-Luca, and since
simplicity is often the result of extreme artifice, the fact that
he has had to chip and polish his words has given them such a
limpidity and precision that they reflect things seen as a
diamond reflects light. Such a clarity of impression is not
generally reached in the immediacy of the moment, but rather
from looking back nostalgically to a distillation of memories.
The way in which, in "La Fiancée posthume," "Les Pélérins
piémontais," "La Favorite," and the first part of *Le Poète
assassiné*, he savours his enjoyment of the sense impressions of
the Riviera and manages to analyse them precisely into unexpected components, is reminiscent of his loving evocations
of the roast chestnuts and orange *dragées* he ate as a child in
Rome, and would seem to indicate that they were written
after he left Monaco. The horrid smells of the old town of

[15] "Le Giton," "Les Pélérins piémontais," in *L'Hérésiarque et Cie*; "La Favorite,"
"La Fiancée posthume," in *Le Poète assassiné*.
[16] Pascal Pia, *Apollinaire par lui-même*, 1954, p. 139.

Nice coagulate into a delicious mixture, "old Nice with its scents of fruits and herbs mingling with the smell of raw meat, of sour pasta, of cod and latrines," just as the Manchester smell of coal and damp and cooked cabbage might have lingered in the memory of a prisoner-of-war in a Japanese camp.

But, whether or not he wrote these stories then or later, it is clear that even as a schoolboy he was keeping his eyes very wide open, probably even then noting down the incidents that he saw and his own reactions, as he would a line of verse or an odd word, already possessed by the characteristic need to formulate his continual converse with himself and the world into words. As in the books that he read, it is in other people the bizarre and the eccentric which excite his imagination. (And yet, paradoxically, as a poet dealing with his own emotions he becomes famous for his treatment of the simplest, most universal themes.) There is the couple who so worship their dead daughter's memory that they delegate their young lodger to be her posthumous *fiancé*; incidentally the young man has fallen in love with the mother and tells her that she is "as aromatic as the most scented of nutmegs, those which a pigeon has digested and rendered up whole";[17] there is the pretty boy who will sell himself to patrons of either sex and who is eventually impaled by his jealous contemporaries, dying "avec volupté peut-être,"[18] a macabre note of erotic violence which is repeated in "La Favorite" when a young man attacks his handsome, middle-aged mistress with his savage embraces on the bier of her dead husband. And, most dramatic of them all, there is the sick girl who discovers her former lover in one of the monks of the pilgrim church. "Les Pélérins piémontais" is a marvellous story, which makes one wish that Apollinaire had exploited his mastery in the *genre* more fully. It has everything one could wish for in a short story—a picturesque setting, extreme dramatic tension, an original twist for an ending, all told in the spare but fluid prose that he has managed to perfect.

The scene is painted with as much care and colour and sense of the infinite variety of human camouflages as is one of Breughel's village fairs.

[17] "La Fiancée posthume," in *Le Poète assassiné*, 1959, p. 175.
[18] "Le Giton," in *L'Hérésiarque et Cie*, 1936, p. 86.

The pilgrims were streaming out from every turning. Some of them were out of breath because they had climbed the steep slope of La Trinité-Victor. There were peasant women from Peille, carrying baskets full of eggs on little cushions on their heads. They walked erect, letting their heads sway impercept- ibly in order to keep their burdens balanced. As their hands were left free they were busy knitting at the same time. An old peasant with shaven head was carrying a basket of cakes sprinkled with little aniseed balls. He had sold some of his wares on the way, and walked painfully along smoking his pipe. Rich farmers' wives were sitting on their sure-footed mules. Girls walked hand in hand telling their rosaries. They wore the flat straw hats of the Nice local costume, which are like the Greek ones that can be seen in Tanagra statuettes. Some had gathered olive-branches which they used as fans, others walked along behind their mules holding them by the tail. They had loaded their beasts with presents for the monks, baskets of figs, casks of oil, clotted lambs' blood.

Troops of elegants pilgrims were arriving from Monaco, young ladies in silk dresses, groups of English people. There were the dandified croupiers as well and groups of Moné- gasque girls, simpering along in multi-coloured dresses.

All is movement, and it is no easy matter for a writer to convey the *perpetuum mobile* of streaming crowds, while still keeping the detail of sights and sounds concrete.

Their bare feet were shod in dust. Their eyes shone in their thin energetic faces. The women had put fig-leaves on their heads to protect them from the July sun. Some were chewing pieces of *polenta* on which swarms of flies had settled. Children with ringworm were nibbling away at the carob-beans they had picked up by the roadside. The Piedmontese were arriving in compact, interminable groups.

Once the multi-coloured crowd has filed in to the church, Apollinaire concentrates on building up the sound impressions, the convent bells a-clatter, the pilgrims with their ardent prayers, punctuated by the reiterated theme of "Santa Maria," a woman having an epileptic fit, a man vomiting up "waves of blood," a child howling, then shouting "Dolly" to the statue of the Virgin, and the continual counterbass of the monks' chant, their accents as broad in Latin as the pilgrims' in their

dialect. Then comes the first warning cry—not too loud yet—
from the paralysed girl who recognises the monk and sits bolt
upright on her stretcher. But the Host is about to be elevated
and all falls silent. Another contrasting voice breaks in, that
of a legless boy imploring a miracle, then roundly cursing the
Virgin; the bell rings and against the background of reverential
silence comes the crescendo shrieking of the girl. "Kiss me,
Amadeo. Since you left the days have been as dark as in the
wolf's maw." And it is here that Apollinaire's apparently
recherché interest in linguistics pays lavish dividends, for the
girl's mother repeats those last words in her dialect, "Schïr
cmé'n bucca a u luv," and the uncouth but poetic sounds ring
through the church like a discord on the organ. The assembled
pilgrims seem to hold their breath while the monk comes near
to her and the drama between the two is nothing but a tense,
whispered exchange of names. Suddenly the monk takes
action, strips off his habit and reveals himself, a peasant like
the rest. There is a relaxing of tension, a general muttering
and giggling of delight, and headed by Amadeo they stream
out of the church, happily homewards. Once they are all
outside there is an unexpected scream from the girl, and she
falls back dead. Terribly then the monk echoes her cry,
shaking his fist at the sky, "Brothers in Christ, the world is
badly made," and like the dying away of thunder, the pilgrims
take up his theme, "Fradei cristiang, ir mund l'é mal fâa!"

No other comment but the recording of calm after the
storm. The normal sounds of everyday life take over, other
pilgrims arrive, faith—or the cuckoo—is continuous, invariable.

> The mother brushed away the flies that had settled on the
> eyes and mouth of the dead girl. The mules pawed the ground
> in the stables. From the inns came the clatter of dishes. In
> the cloister, they were still singing the sad litany dominated by
> the name of the Virgin—Santa Maria.
>
> New pilgrims were arriving. Others were going away,
> happily sporting big rosaries with beads as large as nuts.
> In the woods, far away, a cuckoo let fall, at regular intervals,
> its peaceful, invariable, double note.

There is, however, in "Les Pélérins piémontais," as well
as the touch of the master hand in story-telling, an attitude

which might well indicate more maturity than we have yet seen in Apollinaire. The whole story is informed by a feeling of sympathy, even tenderness, towards these simple people with their naïve faith. "The wondering, detailed naïvety of the primitive art which is prevalent here can touch the hearts even of those who have no faith," he says of the pilgrim church. And it is not surprising that he should be susceptible to this gormless wonderment, for he too, under his patina of cerebration and irony, managed always to keep a sort of childlike capacity both for joy and for being hurt. In fact it reveals itself more as he grows older and more confident in being himself; not only does it become one of the most endearing characteristics in the sophisticated hurly-burly of his later life, but it shines through into his poetry and gives it its particular nimbus.

Here in these stories with the Mediterranean background, in his contemplation of a garden in Cannes, or a sunrise over Bordighera, it is his own "wondering and detailed naïvety" which makes him describe the narrow eucalyptus leaves lying amongst the dazzling mica of the sand as strands of sweet-smelling hair, or let fall an image as vivid as a child's of the rising sun like an armada on fire. Then, and the contrast is typical and a part of his complex charm, comes the un-child-like sensuality:

> Then he looked to the sea in the East, and it was as if a royal fleet were ablaze out there near Bordighera, that marine town with the white houses which supplies the palms for the Vatican feasts. He turned towards the still sentry of the garden: the big cypress wreathed in a flowering rose-bush that climbed right to its peak. François des Ygrées smelled the unparalleled fragrance of the sumptuous roses whose tightly compressed petals were naked as flesh.[19]

This is a delightful spicing. But it is important to remember that his whole kernel was meridional, that the Italian mixture in his blood predominates, that he was born and bred in sun-drenched places. It is a background which helps to explain the nature of "the ingenuous miracles" that are his poems,

[19] *Le Poète assassiné*, 1959, p. 28.

with their directness and music and freedom from rhetoric rare in French but not, for instance, in Provençal poetry; and which helps also to make clear the origins of the whole fabric of his imagery.

It would seem reasonable to suppose that a poet's most significant and obsessive images are those that have been registered in childhood. Apollinaire's favourite props for his poetic world may seem banal enough: the sun, light, shade, the sea, birds. Their use is not so. They all present the extreme contrasts of a world seen through a southern light. The light itself, linked often with fire and flames, is always blinding, the purifying but dangerous agent of the ideal; shadows are black and solid enough to be tangible and to chill the soul; his sea is the antique home of sirens, seductive but treacherous; birds, never the homely, hopping creatures of the hedgerows, are always on aspiring wing and clearly outlined against a pure expanse of sky; the sun is a flaming brazier often associated with cruelty—its rays are whip-lashes, it represents a decapitated, bleeding head.

But these were impressions only, being stored up on the plate of his memory for later use. At the time the precocious young man who had already chosen his definitive pseudonym, Guillaume Apollinaire, was not deeply concerned with the sun or the sea, however beautiful and full of meaning. A literary Rastignac, he was itching for the murk of Paris.

III

Adventure in the Ardennes

"I LEFT Monaco without a sou."[1] This is how Apollinaire later described to a friend his departure in January 1899, and from now on, poverty, and at times actual hungry want, is a constant in his life. He himself made light of it and could hardly do otherwise because it was the common lot of most writers and artists of the day. But as Mme de Kostrowitzky had known periods of great affluence in Monte Carlo, and was now being more or less forced to leave because of her gambling debts, this total eclipse of her fortunes must have come as a shock to the two boys who were still completely dependent on her and had not been trained for any jobs of their own. Again there is a complete and discreet silence from Guillaume about the change in their estate. One knows only that the incorrigible lady went straight to another casino, at Aix-les-Bains, flanked by her two full-grown sons. It would seem to be a tribute either to her optimistic faith in her own star, or to her maternal indulgence that she did not immediately turn them out to work. Guillaume's voracious appetite alone must have been a problem.

But although she fared no better at the gambling tables at Aix they all three still stuck together, and their next unexpected port of call was Lyons. Here again everything is conjecture and mystery. Apollinaire once said that he had read enormously in Lyons; on another occasion he showed that he was familiar with the Lyonnais dialect: and that is all. Mme Durry infers that this was the scene of another of Mme de Kostrowitzky's adventures, involving, since it was in Lyons, a rich silk manufacturer with a library well stocked and recondite enough to satisfy even Guillaume's greed for books. Although another woman might have found it embarrassing

---

[1] Article by James Onimus in *Les Lettres françaises*, 13 Dec. 1951.

to carry on an adventure in the boudoir, with her nineteen-year old son tucked up in the library below, for Angelica this was no doubt possible. It is also possible, but less piquant, that she stayed there independently or merely with good friends.

Le Poète assassiné, as is to be expected, makes use of the incident but complicates it still further. In the published version the hero Croniamental, after the respective deaths of his mother Macarée and his adoptive father, is taken from Monaco by a Dutchman, M. Janssen, to a *château* near Aix. There this accomplished scholar completes Croniamental's education, teaching him many languages and directing his reading from Virgil and Theocritus through Petrarch to Villon, Ronsard, Racine, and La Fontaine, with a sideways glance at the "romans de chevalerie," Shakespeare, Cervantes, Goethe.

The manuscript as usual is more specific. The *château* at Aix (now particularised as Aix-en-Provence), had belonged to the father of Nyctor who lived there during the first months of an unhappy marriage. M. Janssen is a man who had met Nyctor's father in Boston and who had promised that he would look after Nyctor in his absence. This is all heavily scored out. Assuming that in this work the truth had an irresistible fascination for Apollinaire and that his practice is to secrete his pearls of fantasy round the grains of it, as an oyster so deals with its grains of sand, one is tempted to ask a question which has not been posed before. Could the stay in Lyons have had anything to do with the Aspermont family? Francesco had once embarked for America. If he was still alive it would not have been surprising that he should have shown at least some interest in Angelica and his son, to the extent of asking a friend to look them up. But whatever the motive for the stay in Aix and Lyons, the figure of M. Janssen remains and needs to be explained. He is fully characterised—the celibate, learned, hypochondriac scholar—and that is an exception in Apollinaire's fiction, for normally his characters are merely the blown-up, fantastic embodiments of one particular foible. Did he have any prototype, or was he just a product of the wishful imagination of the fatherless, bookish boy, who never seemed to have found a real mentor amongst his school teachers?

One is all the more tempted to believe that M. Janssen did not spring, armed with his Latin verse, gratuitously out of the young poet's head, because Mariette, the young peasant girl whom Croniamental discovers doing her washing, and in his characteristically literary way compares with Nausicaa, could well be identified as the Yette, whom Apollinaire lists fifteen years later as one of his past loves in "La Colombe poignardée et le jet d'eau." Again characteristically, as with Mia, and it was to become one of his favourite erotic obsessions, he concentrates on her back view:

> He saw her from behind. Her petticoats were tucked up to reveal shapely calves in very white stockings. Her body was moving in the most agreeably titillating way because of the action of washing.

There is also a revealing detail about the pattern of his behaviour in love, obviously too revealing to be left in the final version. In the manuscript the young man, inflamed, tries to take hold of Mariette, and she rushes away from him, refusing his offer of money for his lodging. Suddenly his feelings change: "The sheer lust that had thrown me on to her changed into a passionate reverence. I was really in love with her."[2] In the course of Apollinaire's life there was much brave talk and writing about "sheer lust": "passionate reverence" is, however, never far behind, polar extremes of a richly endowed nature which, often fusing, enabled him to produce some of the most magnificent erotic poetry in the French language. The final result of these conflicting emotions with Mariette, and in this too the pattern of the future begins to reveal itself, is that his advances are not reciprocated and that once again he is, or thinks he is "unhappy in love."

It was in April that the family at last reached Paris, which had been Guillaume's goal all along. Mme de Kostrowitzky must still have had some money at her disposal because she took a flat in the elegant avenue Mac Mahon and there was still no question of the boys working. There she was joined by the young man who from now on figured as her constant companion and the boys' uncle, Jules Weil, who described

---

[2] *Le Poète assassiné*, 1959, p. 264.

himself as "a business man." He had come originally from
Strasbourg, but Mme de Kostrowitzky had already met him
in Monaco, part of his business consisting in gambling and
speculating on the Stock Exchange. He too was entering a
phase of bad luck: he had had money in some mines in South
Africa which were now worked out. Despite his playboy
reputation and his elegance, he seems to have been a rather
colourless character, or maybe any much younger man would
have appeared so in Mme de Kostrowitzky's shadow. From
later reports, he was at least capable of coming to blows with her.

Whatever the material preoccupations of his mother and
"uncle" at this time, Guillaume's thoughts at least could not
have been further removed from money matters. He had at
last arrived in the capital of his dreams, and it was in a state of
euphoria that he wandered around the streets. Paris was a
sort of living library to him, what with the ever-open stalls
of the *bouquinistes*, and all the passers-by looking like the famous
writers of the day, Barrès, Tarde, Moréas, Régnier. Like
Giovanni Moroni with the wooden toys, he was always capable
of creating his own fantasy characters out of the men in the
street: it was a lifelong diversion and the subject of some of his
more amusing short stories as well as one or two notable
poems. One man in particular took his attention at this stage.
He seemed to delight in everything he saw, patting stray dogs
and waving at a star. At first Apollinaire called him Le
Fabuliste; later he became Remy de Gourmont, who, Apollinaire had already decided, was a kindred spirit. "All things
interested him: beasts and the stars, books and the streets,
humanity and the love which inspires all nature."[3] Whether
it really was Gourmont seemed to have no importance, although
later the real Gourmont became an important influence in
Apollinaire's life and was responsible for introducing him to
the *Mercure de France*. Apollinaire's youthful admiration
never changed, despite, according to André Salmon,[4] his
fastidious avoidance of Gourmont's flat with its overall filth
and offending chamber-pot.

But apart from wandering about the streets, he was also

[3] Preface to *Pensées inédites de Remy de Gourmont*, Paris (Ed. de la Sirène) 1920.
[4] André Salmon, *Souvenirs sans fin*, VOL. I, 1955, p. 302.

D

deeply absorbed in his work. Poems and fragments of poems he was busy writing all the time: he was probably also planning his first major work *L'Enchanteur pourrissant* and for this he needed to work up a background of medieval legend. The Bibliothèque Mazarine was the obvious reference library and there he made the acquaintance of the Director, Léon Cahun, distinguished Jewish scholar and medievalist, and uncle of Marcel Schwob. Cahun was immediately attracted to the boy, took him under his wing and predicted a brilliant future for him. He was in short the first of Apollinaire's many influential contacts in the literary world. Could it have been he who was the original of M. Janssen? One detail seems to point to a possible *rapprochement*. In the manuscript of *Le Poète assassiné* M. Janssen has as friends "rabbis of Aix" who give way in the final version to "humanists of Aix," and, even there, he holds forth to Croniamental about the Hebrew origin of the name Adam. The most that one can say is that Cahun seems to be the most likely candidate for the role of the young man's master.

Meanwhile the two more practical members of the family had been planning a move to appropriate summer quarters, in the event the casino of Spa in the Ardennes. In June, Jules Weil was sent to reconnoitre the nearby district for a suitable billet for the Kostrowitzky rearguard.

The little town of Stavelot higher up in the hills near the German frontier was the obvious choice. Not only is it an excellent centre for bathing and fishing (the river Amblève is famous for its trout), and walks on the moors, but it is also an extremely picturesque place, with a store of local tradition and its own folk-lore, set on a steep hill overlooking the river, with narrow cobbled streets and cottage gardens and a dignified square which is reminiscent in miniature of the Grand Place of Brussels. As a relic of its former grandeur when it was the capital of a small state of thirty thousand inhabitants and twenty leagues, there still stands the impressive abbey of St Remâcle, once the home of a train of abbots who were princes of the Holy Roman Empire, and the church houses a marvellously wrought fourteenth-century shrine of St Remâcle and a silver statue of St Poppo.

Much has been written about Apollinaire's stay in Stavelot and with reason, for not only does it make a good adventure story with a fine melodramatic ending (in fact this furnished the ready-made plot of a play for Apollinaire himself), but it really does seem to celebrate his coming of age, an emergence out of the fantasy world of his adolescence into a more willing contact with reality. This would of course have happened anyway: but a sudden and complete change in surroundings, an awareness of himself in a totally new perspective helped to precipitate it.

Jules Weil, in a fawn bowler and a pastel silk shirt, presented himself at the Pension Constant in the main street as an officer on leave, took a room for himself and arranged for his two nephews to join him. He whiled away the time before their arrival reading financial papers, an occupation of which the villagers, rightly in this case, were highly suspicious. However, when Mme de Kostrowitzky arrived in July with the two boys, Guillaume now sporting a fine blond moustache and a floppy Rubens hat, Albert still the mother's boy in a sailor-suit, the impression of shabby distinction made by the two "young Russian counts" was very favourable, and the villagers began to feel proud of having such notable visitors. Mme de Kostrowitzky was off immediately to the gaming tables; Weil thought it expedient to stay a little longer, and then joined her at Spa, where the boys visited them occasionally. But Mme de Kostrowitzky's financial embarrassments must have been common knowledge in the gambling world for despite repeated attempts she was refused admission to the Cercle des Etrangers. There being then no reason to stay on in Spa, she and Weil made their way back to Paris, desperately but unsuccessfully trying to repair their fortunes at the odd casinos *en route*.

Their activities then begin to take on a very strange air, as though they, or perhaps Weil alone, were really on the run. At the end of August, Weil appeared in Paris at the Hotel Bellevue under the name of Kostrowitzky, soon to be joined by a tall, slim, blonde woman who appeared to be about twenty-eight and who said that she was his wife. Soon after this Weil must have left Paris altogether, for at the beginning of September, Angelica on her own took a furnished room at 9 rue de Constantinople, in the name of Olga Karpoff, age, audaciously, twenty-six. Weil, she later told the boys, had gone to the Transvaal to enlist in the British Army: one wonders if this was his only means of escape from a formidable piling-up of debts.

The boys, however, safely ensconced at the Pension Constant, did not seem to be affected by these suspect activities. Obviously they must have been inoculated by now against Mme de Kostrowitzky's strange behaviour, and probably did not even bother to question it. Guillaume in particular was out to enjoy his holiday to the full. It was characteristic of him to try to extract every germ of enjoyment and profit from the present moment, partly out of the fullness of his uncommon vital energy, partly too as a conscious process in the writer's storing up of "copy." In an age when people did not travel so freely, the stay in the little Ardennes town could serve both as valuable experience, and source of background material.

From early morning he was out, walking on the moors, observing or assimilating or findings words for his impressions of this, to him unique, scene. Often he was seen scribbling away seated on a large rock called La Pierre du Diable. He would stop and chat to anybody he met, the villagers, the customs men, the smugglers, and then afterwards write down in his notebooks the peculiarities of the local dialect, and the stories they told him about the gossip of the place and the traditional enmity between the Walloons and Prussians. Amongst his many projects at this time there was even a novel on this subject. But, however far he wandered in search of local colour, he always made sure that he was back at the *pension* for his meals, large Belgian meals that were made even larger by dishes of the fungi that he loved gathering on his walks, and which he insisted were edible despite the Constants' protests. Then they were not far from believing that he must be something of a sorcerer, a special kind of *frisson* that he loved to induce.

In a similar melodramatic way he put himself over to the young village schoolmaster whom he would spend hours bewildering with his tales of divination and sorcery and the most sinister kinds of magic. His most prized possession was a

mildewed book on demonology that he had recently picked up
on the *quais*, and he often used to read aloud from it and make
comments, obviously convinced for the moment that he too was
a magician and prophet.　This same schoolmaster still has some
poems of Guillaume's signed with a sort of cabbalistic swastika
near the signature.

Even at this stage, the infinite variety of his charm was
astonishing.　With some mimetic flair he seemed to be able
to turn on just what was needed by his various audiences.
Witchcraft for the schoolmaster: for the villagers, as he sat
with them smoking his pipe on the bench in the village street
or hung about in the *estaminets* of an evening, talk of the high
life of the Côte d'Azur; and then for the little court of pretty
girls which began to form around him, elaborately gallant
compliments, acrostics made-to-order on their names—so
much more difficult than mere poems—and malicious comments
on the loutish young men of the village.　However they got
their own back one day when, at a rehearsal of their amateur
dramatic society, Guillaume who was behind a partition overheard them laughing with the girls about the penniless
"Russians" and the patches on their trouser seats.　He appeared,
pale and outraged and so impressively angry that everybody
dispersed.　Later he saw the girls and made a violent scene:
one woman of Stavelot says to-day: "He was really furious.　It
was the only time I saw him annoyed, because he was always
charm itself."[5]

These touchy, tempestuous outbursts that follow the
pricking of an inflated sense of honour were to occur again and
again in his life: they were obviously due to the tension of the
whole equivocal family situation, and possibly to the fact that
this was the one basic, emotional complex of his life which he
chose not to exteriorise fully in his writing.　At any rate he
was too busy with the whole process of living to brood too long
over one set-back, and, as was fitting for a young man on
holiday, he set about paying particular court to the undoubted
belle of the village, Maria Dubois, daughter of the chip shop
owner, who had recently been chosen to pose in local costume
for the souvenir postcards, and who figured prominently in the

[5] Christian Fettweis, *Apollinaire en Ardenne*, 1934, p. 44.

displays of folk dancing as an expert at the "maclotte," the Stavelot jig. At first he used to haunt the chip shop; later, when he had no more money for this particular food of love, he had to lure Maria out on to the moors and up to the Pierre du Diable. At first she was cold and reserved, then she seemed to lend herself more to his insistence, but even so the impression left in the many verses Guillaume wrote to her, is that despite his attempts to force the pace, her kisses remained as cold and limpid as the waters of the Amblève, and that he himself was never deluded into thinking that this could be more than a holiday flirtation, or a necessary and conscious prodding of his poetic muse.

But while Guillaume was thus savouring without actually tasting the initial bouquet of love, the Constants were beginning to be anxious about their money. The bill had now run into quite a large amount which they had been counting on in order to buy the trousseau for their daughter's wedding. It was quite obvious to everybody in the village that the boys were penniless; Guillaume's one pair of shoes had been mended so often that the shoemaker refused to touch them any more. But Mme Constant had grown so fond of the two boys that she hesitated to press them. At last she told them that they must write to their mother, which obediently they did. Mme de Kostrowitzky wrote back saying that if Mme Constant would send the exact bill to Paris she would settle it immediately. This too was done, but there was no reply. After another week, about 22 Sep., Mme Constant demanded at least an instalment of two hundred francs. Again the boys wrote off to their mother and this time they told their landlady that she would shortly be coming to Spa again, and that while she was there she would come down to Stavelot, pay the bill and take the boys away with her. This letter was not shown, but Mme de Kostrowitzky's arrival was announced for 5 Oct. Mme Constant was fairly pacified by this, and waited patiently for the mother to appear, little dreaming of the plot that was being hatched under her very nose.

On the morning of 5 Oct., when Mme Constant called her two lodgers, there was no reply. She opened the door, and unable to believe her eyes, looked at the empty room and the numerous papers and books strewn about it, which were all that was left of the two young "Russians."

Now, to effect this escape had been by no means an easy matter. The letter which was supposed to announce their mother's arrival had given the boys the first sign, and they had carefully followed out the instructions which it contained. On 4 Oct. they received another letter, by express from Paris, which ought to have aroused Mme Constant's suspicions and which obviously contained the money for their railway fares. But before this, Guillaume and Albert had had to reconnoitre the various possibilities of being able to leave the village, where everybody knew them, without being seen.

The choice of station needed careful consideration. Stavelot was not on the express line to Paris. The next village, Trois Ponts, was too obvious. Finally they settled on Roanne-Coo, some way off over the mountains, where nobody would think of looking for them immediately. Their luggage was the next problem. Separately and on two successive days, the boys tramped over the moors in order to deposit parcels at the station of Roanne-Coo. Then well before dawn on 5 Oct., they crept out of the *pension* carrying their two large cases on their backs and smaller ones in their hands.

Apollinaire continues the description of the adventure in his letter to James Onimus. "Seven kilometres through the woods, a smell of mushrooms from Stavelot to Roanne-Coo, fortunately we didn't meet anybody. Two hours in the freezing cold at the station of Roanne-Coo and then we left for Paris." But then, as always with Apollinaire, the already fantastic is not fantastic enough. At the frontier the guards wanted to arrest him; naturally he imagined that it was because of his escape from the *pension* and was very frightened, but it was in fact due merely to his name. It had sounded to the customs man like that of an anarchist who was on the run. Eventually the boys were allowed to continue and on 7 Oct. joined the "twenty-six year old Olga Karpoff" as her "nephews."

Stavelot and the whole countryside was in an uproar. The Constants, heartbroken because their daughter's wedding would have to be postponed, and furious that their confidence had been so abused, had gone to the police, and then the most improbable rumours began to circulate. Guillaume and Albert and the dandified uncle were international crooks, foreign spies—what else with such a name?—anarchists, professional swindlers. The police got to work: they questioned the station-master at Roanne-Coo who remembered having sold two second-class tickets to two boys. (It is amusing to think that although they were penniless and could not pay their bill, they still travelled second and not third class.) Eventually the affair was handed over to the Parisian police who at last ran the family to earth in December. The three of them were interrogated by the *juge d'instruction*. Guillaume protested with an air of injured innocence and a fair measure of sophistry:

> I cannot understand why we are accused of swindling. It is true that my brother and I had to leave Stavelot without pay-ing our bill. But this was our mother's affair; we live with her, she sees to our needs, and we do not possess any personal means.[6]

Mme de Kostrowitzky was quite up to the situation. "Of course," she said, "they left without saying anything. It would, I imagine, have been most embarrassing to say that I couldn't send the money, and so like the two children [*sic*] that they were, they had to do their best to avoid the brutalities that would have resulted."[7] She went on to explain that it was because of her gambling losses that she had been unable to pay the bill, but promised to settle if the charge of swindling was dropped. Then with all the aplomb in the world she queried certain items and finally succeeded in having the total amount reduced.

From then on proceedings were dropped and the Kostro-witzkys were left in peace.

An ironical sequel to the whole episode is that the town of Stavelot which was so incensed against the swindling Kostro-witzkys now devotes quite a cult to the poet Apollinaire, with a "monument Apollinaire," a "musée Apollinaire," a plaque over the Pension Constant, and a "colloque Apollinairien" each summer. All of which is not inappropriate, because these few

[6] Christian Fettweis, *Apollinaire en Ardenne*, 1934, p. 93.   [7] *Ibid.*

holiday months do in fact appear to bring about the first real
fruition of his budding talent. Until now he has been, like an
able pianist, endlessly practising, albeit with a supple hand
and sure touch. Now, in the middle of these scales and
exercises, suddenly break through tunes that are entirely his
own.

How much Stavelot itself had to do with this development
is open to question. It is an easy job for the critic to pick
out the obvious images, the picturesque references to picturesque sights, the bilberries and ferns, the pine trees, the Elves
of the Amblève and the pearls in its mussel beds, the "maclotte,"
which reappears in the famous poem "Marie" thirteen years
later. Obviously Apollinaire, a child of the south, had never
known country like this. The wildness and melancholy, the
general contrast and strangeness certainly stimulated him.
But it is only in the wonderfully accomplished short story,
"Que vlo vé?" that the actual scene and the village characters
are the real source of his inspiration and fuse with his own brand
of fantasy. In his poetry their role seems to be purely circum-
stantial, and they add little to his stock of important, deeply
experienced imagery. Apollinaire was generally an excellent
judge of his own poetry, and he chose to publish only three of
the Stavelot poems, "L'Adieu" in *Alcools,* and "Elégie du
Voyageur aux Pieds Blessés" and "Fagnes de Wallonie" in
Il y a. Rightly so, because although he must have written
hundreds of verses to Maria Dubois, who later destroyed them
all, it is obvious from the few that he kept and that have been
unearthed, that in the main they were mere suppling-up
exercises, and that the actual subject had no profound importance for him. They are *pastiches* in the Symbolist vein, full
of stale tricks and worked-out images: pale hands, dying roses,
nymphs and fountains and the unidentified "belle," all set in
minor key, punctuated by refrains or repetitions and exuding
an air of decadence and lassitude, which in fact had nothing
in common with the young man's actual experience of courting
his beloved in the fumes of the chip shop, or of calming his
ardour in the cold mountain river. "If I were God and
Maeterlinck"[8] runs a strange entry in the so-called Stavelot

[8] James Lawler, *op. cit.*

notebook. He may never have entirely grown out of the first
wish, and it took him some time to shake off the second.

But technically, Maeterlinck and other Symbolists had
still much to teach him, and it was the perfecting of his craft
as a poet which at this stage really obsessed him rather than
the charms of Stavelot or of Maria. It cannot be too much
emphasised, especially outside France, how complete was his
mastery of this prime essential and at what an early age he
attained it. Rather surprisingly the notebook shows that he
was already experimenting with verse forms which much later
appeared as comparative novelties. There are unrhymed
alexandrines, octosyllables (at the end of his life he rightly
claimed to have given "a new life to the line of eight feet"),
and more exceptionally, the "verset," with which later both
he and Claudel independently made great play. There is also
one poem "Le Repas" in a kind of *vers libre* which he made his
own particularly from 1913 onwards, based on a fluid but almost
conversational rhythm, which swells out here and there into
lyrical exclamations and then fades away on a flat, moral note.
With the alexandrine, naturally enough, he is most at home:
but, what is surprising for a French poet, and most indicative
of his natural bent, he shows that he is primarily concerned with
a marked, rhythmic beat and actually scans lines of Moréas
and Racine as anapaests, "Aŭ sĕul sōn / dĕ ša vo͞ix / lă mĕr
fu͞it / lĕ ciĕl trĕmble," which really does seem to be a case of
wishful thinking. More appropriate is his assessment of
his own line: "Dĭs-lĕ mōi / mŏn ămo͞ur / ešt-ĭl vra͞i / qŭe tŭ
m'aĭmes."

In fact, this is one of the most interesting features in the
Stavelot notebook: that already amongst all the derivative
snippets, there are so many lines, images, whole passages even,
which he later used in entirely different contexts. One comes
across: "Oui je veux aimer mais vous aimer à peine," which
reappears as it stands in "Marie" in 1912: "J'ai cherché
longtemps sur les routes / Tant d'yeux sont clos au bord des
routes / Le vent fait pleurer les saussaies," which is sandwiched
amongst the Surrealist images of "A Travers l'Europe" in 1914:
"Au bord des fleuves vierges lors nous irons pêcher / Pi-mus
allant par couples en profondes eaux," which turns up in "La

Porte" probably written in 1904. Already there are some of the images of "La Chanson du Mal-Aimé," the "argyraspides," the "dendrophores," the "sept douleurs," the "désirade" ("Quand bleuira sur l'horizon la désirade"), and the mourning Doppelgänger of his own shadow: "Je voyais que rampait éperdument mon ombre," which is to be a constantly recurring image. It is not difficult to understand why: Guillaume Macabre and Guillaume Apollinaire, sun and shadow, the extreme poles between which his temperament was constantly and with astonishing rapidity oscillating, but both, miserable shadow, or fiery apotheosis, viewed with an ironical detachment which gives to his essentially naïve outbursts the curl of sophistication. Another of his favourite images is already fully worked out in the notebook : that of emigrants stretching out their hands in farewell in a wet, autumnal port. The poet as exile or wanderer is a common enough conception, but he had more reason than most to experience this sense of loss and homelessness as one of the basic facts of life.

It is only comparatively recently that the full extent of Apollinaire's borrowing from himself has been revealed.[9] The spirit, as he admitted towards the end of his life, blows where it listeth; often it does not choose to blow at all, and he was a wary enough judge to recognise the vistations and make use of them in later doldrums, or even as propitiatory offerings to encourage further divine gusts. Some critics have implied that this minimises his achievement: the finished products can be the only criteria. Some are obvious patchworks, but one or two of these mosaics are amongst his finest achievements; a fact which, as well as raising many other points about poetic procedure generally, shows yet again how at best he was capable of reconciling two extremes; his natural facility, with controlled, intellectual selectiveness, and organisation.

But then he was an able critic too, even of his own manifestations of quality, and it is the works which he chose later for publication:—"Merlin et la vieille femme," "L'Ermite" and "Le Larron" in *Alcools*, *L'Enchanteur pourrissant* and "Que vlo vé?" which best reveal his preoccupations as he walked

[9] In particular by Michel Décaudin in *Le Dossier d'Alcools*, 1960 (henceforth ited as Décaudin).

alone on the Stavelot moors. His scribblings may be more
directly autobiographical, but perhaps it was the very tension
between the irresistible desire to tell all and the need of his
hurt pride to hold back, which makes these published works
more satisfactory creations, less explicit, but with a far more
poignant impact.

One of the deleted passages from *Le Poète assassiné* once again
comes too near the truth:

> Yet another departure. Love and rest.... I am a traveller
> without a stick, a pilgrim without a bell. And yet I am also
> Travaillin in my loose yellow worker's smock, without belt,
> without purse, hooded. I am he who is indefatigable, he who
> is condemned to travel or to work; he who loves working and
> who has no work, he who is less powerful than any other man,
> he who has nothing, he who does not know how to read or
> write.[10]

A strange claim that last, and he was to reiterate it
nine years later.[11] Untrained, inept, exiled, deprived, yet
perdurable—it was not a situation which was going to help
in his problem with women, and this too was a burning one,
the need to satisfy his feverish desire and his instinctive tenderness ("sheer lust" and "passionate reverence") ideally in one
object. "I have kisses on my lips," says Travaillin to La Fille
in the same text. "Here they are, here, on your hands, on your
neck, on your eyes, your eyes, your eyes. I have kisses on my
lips, here they are, here, burning like fever, lingering to be-
witch you, kisses, maddened kisses, on your eyes, your fore-
head, your cheek." But the girl simply pushes him away.
"Go away, your kisses smell of vomit."

From this, as well as from some of the poems of this period,[12]
it would seem that, uninhibited and pagan as he later appeared,
at this stage "sheer lust" was a burden to him, and that naturally enough for a young man with a conventional, religious

---

[10] *Le Poète assassiné*, 1959, p. 273.

[11] Décaudin, p. 205.

[12] Cp. The Manuscript of *La Porte* with the line "Je t'ai pris mon péché ô ma
mère; cp. also "Je ne sais plus ni si je l'aime Ni si l'hiver sait mon péché." *Le
Guetteur Mélancolique, Oeuvres poétiques*, 1956 ; cp. also "Vae Soli," *Le Guetteur
Mélancolique, Oeuvres poétiques*, 1956, p. 523.

schooling it was followed closely by disgust and guilt. After the sunlight, the shadow. There are moments when he appears to be quite obsessed by it, but as he was mercurial and resilient enough to get over his obsessions quickly and find temporary solutions, or smother them with irony as he does with this whole complex about being poor and having to work, it has, I think, not been emphasised enough as the source of the particular atmosphere of these early works, compounded of febrile yearning, concupiscent solitude, violent outbursts of obscenity and even sadism, layered with a lyrical tenderness.

But in fact he was more devious and ambitious at this stage than to want merely to plait together into verse the strands of his own emotions. One can easily identify the figure of Merlin, magician or poet enslaved by a woman, or the Hermit with his troublesome flesh and his sense of sin and resulting blasphemy, or the thief, the exiled poet caught in petty larceny in a strange land. But Apollinaire was already deeply involved in a more central and life-long concern: poetry as poetry. What is poetry and what must it be about? What is fit subject-matter for poetry in the modern world and what form must it take? A question to which, vociferating loudly his Q.E.D.s, he found many successive answers in the course of his life, but no definitive one, and manfully ("I am Travaillan, the indefatigable") refused to believe that the negation implied in this could ever be the only final reply. In fact in "Le Larron" and "Merlin et la vieille femme" he was already feeling his tangled way towards some sort of personal "Art poétique," the sort of stance he must take, as he was to do later in each of his major works. The critics who have accused him of being too derivative, or of merely shouting louder than most on the bandwagon of innovators, can surely not know these earlier works, which, although they are badly flawed with wilful obscurity and forced erudition, with vulgarity pushed beyond the limits of the possible, and still very conventional in form, are nevertheless highly original and serious in their content. Mme Durry is the critic who has best seen this, and her analyses of these two poems are most perceptive.[13] While pointing out that "Merlin

[13] Durry, pp. 208-33.

et la vieille femme" is so obscure that it is impossible to pin down one meaning to it, she ably demonstrates that this union of Merlin at the crossroads, in springtime, with Morgane, his equal, his "très ancienne Mémoire," and the resulting birth of a son who, haloed in fire, shall march towards Rome, reveals the young poet's decision to tap the whole past of myth and legend and eventually Christianity for his subjects. I should only like to add that there would seem to be a much more egocentric and characteristic, if not clearly formulated attitude: that he the poet is both Merlin, and his even older female memory; that not only has he the male powers of creating with his mind but he can let his particular poetic intuition right down into the well of the collective unconscious; that he too, the poet, is on a level footing with Christ, able to lead mankind to salvation: and finally that through him time and space are annulled and he is at the centre everywhere at all moments. An audacious conception; no more so, admittedly, than Rimbaud's, but Apollinaire at least stuck to it and did his best to bear it out all his life.

"Le Larron" is a more accomplished poem in itself, and more accessible, because it is visually more exciting and musically sweeter, and also because its aim is more specific. It again represents the poet, this time the poet of Christian tradition shipwrecked in the weird, richly jewelled, bizarre, splendid, pagan world, but turned away from its possibilities of happiness because he represents a religion of suffering and loneliness, a shadow amongst their light and fire. Mme Durry makes the valid point that this is a way of saying that the *Parnasse* is not enough: regretfully the modern poet has to acknowledge his inheritance of Christianity whether he likes it or not, and he cannot take refuge as the Parnassians had done in the classical myths. It is also one young man's personal expression of a modern as well as an ancient myth, that of the Golden Age, Paradise Lost, a happy, guilt-free, primitive childhood followed by adult suffering and disgust and awareness of sin. It also could be taken as giving one of the first glimpses of his very characteristic Janus-like attitude, a regret for all that is splendid and rich in the past, and yet a rather chastening and unwelcome awareness that this can no longer suffice.

The allegorical form was an obvious enough choice for him to repeat it both in poetry and prose. It enabled him to prowl around and sniff at the dead weight of his own worries (the decaying corpse of the Enchanter), while yet executing many weird, fantastic steps on the way. *L'Enchanteur pourrissant* is a rare example of the fantasy which he later claimed was " his way of interpreting nature":[14] and in both senses of the word for there has been no re-edition since 1909 of this strange, esoteric, little work. At first sight the lyrical prose and the dream-like scene appear obviously Symbolist, the whole work possibly too dated for the modern reader. Underneath these paraphernalia of the epoch there are marked signs of Apollinaire's own strong individuality and of ways of thinking which, when he elaborates them years later, appear to be cornerstones of a new æsthetic.

It is the culmination of his adolescent bookishness, the essence he had reduced from the bubbling wine of centuries of myth and legend and by-ways of history. Round the tomb of Merlin, put to sleep for ever by the fairy Vivian, Apollinaire brings together in one fabulous night all the strange, mythical figures that had been to-ing and fro-ing in his mind for years, all hypertrophied creatures, either more or less than human, winged monster and magician, saints and vampires, druids and demons, sphinxes and hermits, founders of cities, a gigantic superknight made of bronze, prophets and the men who never died. From out of all time and all lands they are assembled, and the Enchanter, immobile in the centre of this motley fantasmagoria, listens to their clamour, to the yearnings and complaints of their ambitions, to their declarations of love, to their obscene jokes, and finally, as in a collective orgy they rape and kill St Angélique, to her "last voluptuous death rattle" rising above the grunts. For as usual, there is the naïve peppering of sulphur and black magic, of sadism and scatology ("What is the rarest thing in the world? The excrement of the Pope"), and blasphemy. For this extraordinary night is a "Noël funéraire" complete with false Magi.

It has been customary to stress the undoubted, dream-like character of the work; and this primarily because when it was

14 Preface, *Les Mamelles de Tirésias*, *Oeuvres poétiques*, 1956, p. 866.

published in book form in 1908, Apollinaire added a final
chapter called "Onirocritique." This is quite a separate piece
obviously written under the influence of Nerval and Jarry,
and it became one of the milestones in the literary history of the
time, even, so it has been claimed, a starting-point for Surrealism. But this must be regarded as an addition and not as an
integral part of the work.

Dream or no, the fluid vision of *L'Enchanteur pourrissant*,
unlike that of most earlier Symbolist pieces, has many concrete
stepping stones: food inevitably, the delicacies the creatures
deposit on Merlin's tomb and his craving for the staff of life,
good plain bread ("dough," Apollinaire said once, obsessed
by the need to knead, "is like a woman's flesh");[15] the stink
of the corpse, the itching of the worms in it, and the red trail
of blood that is the last sign of Vivian, the fairy, when she returns
to her palace in the lake and abandons the rotting cadaver of
her lover. "Pourquoi," as an old lady once said to the Gon-
courts, "sommes nous faits en viande?" The immature male
from time immemorial seems to think that women are more
so than men, and takes this as a personal insult to himself.
This would certainly appear to be one of Apollinaire's own
reactions at the time; gratuitous references to menstruation
abound in his early poems, although they are certainly not
unique in French poetry, and have a more heartfelt ring than
his formal, stilted attempt to find images for the differences
between the sexes. "But I was aware of the different eternities
of men and women"—a stereotyped stance over and against
"the eternal feminine."

A more æsthetic preoccupation which emerges from
L'Enchanteur pourrissant, as it had done from "Merlin et la
vieille femme," is the conception of himself as the creator,
ubiquitous in time and space, a magician able to conjure up
a whole turning world from his still centre. This is one of his
most important and constant ideas; throughout his whole life
he never ceases to grapple with the problem of portraying it
most effectively. It is this obsession with portraying the
multiform aspects of life simultaneously which later propelled
him into some of his more audacious inventions. At first sight

[15] *Tendre comme le souvenir*, 1952, p. 178.

the experimental poems of 1912 onwards might seem far removed from his adolescent vision of Merlin in the tomb; but the principle of "simultanisme" which inspired them, already informs the whole of this early work. Like Merlin he felt that he was " Guillaume Apollinaire qui fut à la guerre et sut être partout."[16]

Here, like Proust, but reaching further back to finger the whole fabric of man's collective story, he attempts to gather round him the folds of time, condensing memory into the fourth dimension of dream. Later, for his aspiration knew no bounds, he will further claim to have torn aside the veil of the future.

L'Enchanteur pourrissant stands successfully as a complete work in itself. Recently [17] it has become clear that it is to be linked with the various autobiographical essays which Apollinaire was obsessively trying out at this time, and which he finally condensed into *Le Poète assassiné*. After the departure of Vivian, the Enchanter in his tomb is visited by two young men, both of whom could, along with Nyctor and Claude Avray, be further manifestations of Apollinaire himself: Travaillin, the poor wanderer, and Raoul the rich, young man, possibly represent the fulfilment of his wishes at that time. It would seem to be a fair measure of his egocentricity, this peopling of the world with fragments of himself, a megalomania of the imagination.

Another curious fact which emerges from this manuscript episode is that the young girl who repulses Travaillin's advances has all the traits of the heroine of *Le Poète assassiné*, Tristouse Ballerinette, who has always been taken to be the split image of Marie Laurencin, not to appear in Apollinaire's life until 1907. She sings snatches of old tunes as Marie sang folk songs: she is thin and dark. "She was dark-skinned and her shining, mobile eyes were like birds with brilliantly-coloured plumage. Her hair was short, but as thick and as dark as a forest at night."[18] Perhaps the two Maries were alike in more than name: he certainly associates them in the famous poem "Marie." It would not however be so surprising, if a man's

[16] "Merveille de la guerre," *Oeuvres poétiques*, 1956, p. 272.
[17] Michel Décaudin's edition of *Le Poète assassiné*, 1959.
[18] *Op. cit.*, p. 270.

E

tastes and desires were borne out sooner by his imagination than they were realised in his life.

L'Enchanteur pourrissant, a lyrical allegory, is a piece of poetic prose. Like his poems of the same period it is cloud and chaos pierced here and there by the beams of a powerful but still immature talent. "Que vlo vé?" the Stavelot short story, is, like the Piedmontese stories, quite a different matter; and judging purely on his completed work at this time, a critic would have been justified in predicting for him a greater future as a short-story writer than as a poet. Here is, straightaway, his authentic and highly original tone of voice, pitched first to the note of fantasy and faery, for Que vlo vé? is the divinity of the Ardennes, "companion of the wild boars, cousin of the hares and squirrels, and the wind shook his soul as the East wind shakes the orange berries on the mountain ash." But his poetic guitar which is "a shred of the wind that is always moaning through the Belgian Ardennes," also crudely sounds "more hollow than the devil's fart" when it has none of the local gin "to piss out." This god is also a flea-ridden tramp who nightly gets drunk in the pub with the filthy-tongued, belching peasants and Guyame the poor poet with the gift of ubiquity, whom Guillaume the poor poet lovingly includes as a painter might fit a self-portrait into a corner of his picture. For all his divine affinities Que vlo vé? is finally to meet his match in "le babo," sexual champion of the village "expert comme pas un à faire pimpan dur et longtemps."

It is a unique blend, this tracery as delicate as frost-fingers woven out of the muck of the village. Que vlo vé? and the "babo" both want to "aller schlof" with "la Chancesse," and this village Helen, who is to launch them incontinently on to the waters of Lethe, is an old barmaid. "They went into the house of the Chancesse. She was telling her rosary, seated, with her legs wide apart. Under her bodice her tits seemed to tumble down like an avalanche."

Like her ageing bosom, the action now begins its inevitable, downward momentum. The men drink and joke, a paraffin lamp hums, Guyame goes out to relieve himself at the door, and while so doing apostrophises the moon and stars: "What a lot of golden balls in the clear sky this evening! Good God, the sky is full of luminous testicles and we call them stars, planets, moons." At which the "babo" proclaims that he has three testicles and it is he who will "schlof" with la Chanchesse. Que vlo vé? squares up to him and the fight is on.

It is an extraordinary scene, the Chancesse is irradiated with beauty, the kettle hums, Guyame celebrates the battle with a fairy invocation:

> Honour to the heroes, whose blood is flowing like the Waterfall at Coo. Listen! listen! oyez-ve! The elves are coming up from the Amblève. . . . One of them is weeping because he has broken his little glass slippers. . . . Listen! listen! the wind is soughing through the alders. Beautiful Chancesse, let us dance while the fight is on.

And as the blood cascades he and the Chancesse dance a jig, the kettle sings interminably and Que vlo vé? ploughs up the flesh of the wretched "babo." If there is such a thing as naïve sadism, this surely is it. Sitting in a pool of blood the "babo" cries out: "Nenni je ne ferai pas pam-pam avec la Chancesse. Ah! Que vlo vé? voilà que j'ai mal aux couilles!" Then, under Que vlo vé?'s knife he flops like a fish into death, gasping out still in the Stavelot dialect: "Aïe! Aïe vo direz-ve à ma Mareye que je lui envoie on betch d'amour." Que vlo vé? deaf to pity, goes on cutting him up, cutting and cutting through flesh until the arm comes away from the socket and he puts it in his breast-pocket like a buttonhole. The five fingers hang like five petals and as he embraces the Chancesse, the nails tickle her face. The blood flows out through the door, and the still boiling kettle hisses out a prayer for the dead.

But Que vlo vé? is off to the moors in the clear night, and the macabre and grotesque are caught up into poetry:

> Now the Amblève was near and its waters ran cold under their mantle of alders. The elves twinkled their little glass slippers on the pearls that cover the river-bed. The wind took up the sad sigh of the guitar. The voices of the elves floated across the water and from the bank Que vlo vé? could hear them chattering:

> —Mnieu, mnieu, mnieu.

Then he went down into the river and as it was cold, he was
frightened of dying. Fortunately the voices of the elves came
nearer:

—Mnié, mnié, mnié.

Then, "nom di Dio?" once he was in the river he suddenly
forgot all that he had ever known, and learned that the Amblève
communicates underground with Lethe, because its waters too
make you lose all consciousness. Nom di Dio! But the elves
were chattering so prettily now, nearer and nearer.

—Mniè, mniè, mniè . . .

And everywhere roundabout the Elves of the "pouhons,"
those springs that bubble up in the forest, answered them.

Much is revealed of Apollinaire in this strange little story.
He was obviously so completely confident of dominating his
subject and the short-story form, that he could allow himself to
show the quirks and extreme contrasts of his true nature,
the naïve fantasy and greedy appetites, the tenderness and the
cruelty, the obscenity and ridiculous exaggeration of horror
dear to the schoolboy, alongside a mature irony and the delicacy of a skilled artist: and all this in swift succession, discontinuity planed into harmony. There is an amusing moment
when it seems that even he doubts whether he will pull off
such a monstrous amalgam. This he proclaims is the difficult
moment of the story (it is just before the fight); he will need
all his courage to surmount it, even Apollo his usual patron is
out of breath and will want the help of Hermes the thief who is
worthier than he to sing of the death of Que vlo vé? But it is
in fact only the roll of drums to celebrate the mountebank's
most difficult trick, when all along he has known that he
will most brilliantly succeed. Apollinaire may have equalled
"Que vlo vé?" but he never wrote a better story.

The difference between his two levels of achievement in
prose and in poetry at this time is not difficult to explain.
He was obviously still very muddled over the whole subject
of what his poetry was to be about, picking his way through the
debris of his overcrowded mind. Egocentric, and self-obsessed,
his was in fact going to be a very personal, subjective kind of

poetry, needing a history of violent emotion undergone and suppressed in order to burst out and then strike the real note of its greatness. The short-story form, nicely objective, was less exigent. Indeed for such a tautly strung, precocious youth it must have been a release to turn outside himself, to use all that he had observed around him with such a fresh, amused eye, in order to sublimate his own unresolved tensions.

IV

Annie and the Rhineland

La porte de l'hôtel sourit terriblement
Qu'est-ce que cela peut me faire ô ma maman
D'être cet employé pour qui seul rien n'existe
Pi-mus couples allant dans la profonde eau triste
Anges frais débarqués à Marseille hier matin
J'entends mourir et remourir un chant lointain
Humble comme je suis qui ne suis rien qui vaille
Enfant je t'ai donné ce que j'avais travaille

THERE is no certainty about the date of this poem "La Porte":[1] it may have been pieced together later out of isolated lines, but there can be no doubt about the situation it portrays; the argument with the exasperated woman in the ghastly, fourth-rate hotel room, the prospect of a fourth-rate job as only outlet for the Mediterranean morning hopes, and the distant hum of poetry in the young man's mind, the submarine sadness of a northern winter, and the whole Travaillin complex of being no good at anything. But, whether he did not try very hard, or was too choosy, or jobs were scarce, by Christmas he had still found nothing. "A difficult winter," he wrote later to James Onimus, and this was an understatement. "We got to the point of thinking we'd have to eat bricks." It must have been at this point of desperation that at last he fetched up in a publicity agency copying out wrappers

---

[1] *Alcools, Oeuvres poétiques,* 1956, p. 87.
"The hotel door smiles terribly
What can it mean to me o my mother
To be this clerk for whom alone nothing exists
Coupled pi-mus swimming in the sad deep water
Fresh angel fish [angels] that landed in Marseilles yesterday morning
I hear a distant song die away again and again
Humble as I am who am worth nothing
Child I have given you what I had work"

for four sous an hour:

> which is the worst job imaginable amongst a lot of crooks, broken-down lawyers, adventurers back from the Gold Rush. There I am with all the riff-raff they don't even want for the Travsvaal, mingling with the starving plebs. Then at the end of the month when I've earned my 23 francs 50, I clear out. It's the lady of the place herself (mistress of Galezot) who pays me along with all the dead-beats, and she has to burn Armenia paper in order to smother their stink. This is the worst of my memories.

The voice of the little boy in the sailor-suit and blond ringlets seems to echo through the lower depths. There was never any Bohemian nostalgia for dirt in his nature, but a marked preference for health and cleanliness.

Again jobless and penniless, dragging about Paris with the stench of poverty still in his nostrils, and the hope in his heart of pushing open some side-door into journalism, he met an acquaintance from Monaco, Esnard a failed lawyer and hack-writer who happened to have a commission for a serial story in the newspaper *Le Matin*. He already had one young man ghosting for him and suggested, to Guillaume's delight, that he should also lend a hand. An absurd, breathless gallimaufry emerged. *Que Faire*, although Apollinaire was quite proud of it and boasted that it had been copied by other serial-writers, has no literary merit: but it does show the wide range of his fantasy and invention. There are duels and Duchesses and talking gorillas and a sort of de Sade hero, an expert criminal who violates the heroine while she is dying in a welter of blood, and a hilariously funny scene when the gorilla irrupts into a spiritualist seance: most interesting, although here Apollinaire may have been completely under the influence of Wells and Verne, there is a phrenologist who with his brain surgery has made the gorilla talk, and who proposes to turn the hardened criminal into an honest citizen. Apollinaire was always fascinated by the possibilities of science; some of his short-stories could be called science-fiction and there are certainly one or two space poems; and his premonitions about future developments like this version of leucotomy have often been fulfilled in principle.

Which is more than were his financial hopes over *Que Faire*. By May it had come to an end and Esnard was conveniently forgetting to hand over Guillaume's share of the money. The young man, despite his frugal diet of herrings, found one way to revenge himself. He promptly slept with the fifty-three year old Esnard's young mistress. He then took up shorthand, for he was forced once again to think of an office job. In July through an advertisement in a newspaper he found himself installed as "secretary" at twenty-five francs a month in a very dubious little office with the impressive title of "La Bourse Parisienne," a sort of investment agency but with no capital backing. There could hardly have been anybody less suited to manipulating investments than Apollinaire. The Stock Exchange was obviously far less real to him than Merlin and the forest of Broceliande. Although he pretended later to competence about such matters and Gustave Kahn once actually followed his advice, he would have been quite capable of inventing companies of his own if he had felt like it. The Constant Insurance Company might have filled a gap!

At his first appearance at the Bourse Parisienne the same magic operated as had done on the first day at the Collège Saint Charles. Immediately he won a friend. However miserable the background of his life might be, however dejected his moods of solitude, once in company the charm, the high spirits, the desire to be liked, and also a certain opportunism—for how else does one get on in life?—took over. This time it was René Nicosia, a younger boy, who at once invited him home, and who then, because Apollinaire opened his eyes to a "new world unforgettable in its originality," became his inseparable companion. Guillaume was soon going there every day for his meals, and his mother too became a frequent visitor. Nicosia's account of Apollinaire is interesting.[2] After the event he is by no means so whole-heartedly enthusiastic as Toussaint-Luca. At the time he was definitely under his spell and drank in Apollinaire's elucubrations in kitchen, museum, or café; later he seems to have questioned his motives and decided that the friendship was not disinterested. The Nicosias had a fine library which Apollinaire made full use of, and René's uncle

[2] René Nicosia, "Apollinaire familier," in *La Table ronde*, 1952, p. 102.

was a director of Olympia and gave the boys free tickets for the music halls and reviews. He also promised to consider the play Guillaume had written about his flight from Stavelot, *A la Cloche de bois*, but the manuscript has never been seen again. In any case, whatever the Nicosias could offer, Guillaume certainly gave good value in return, even if his rollicking high spirits helped to cause at least one nocturnal scandal. Nicosia's final summing up of his character is rather niggling and so reveals his own:

> Jolly, naïf, unaffected, unambitious about money, (with his looks he could easily have found a widow who would have relieved him of his money difficulties) everything interested him and he found the most hair-raising situations amusing, a creature full of originality and whimsy, but at heart with the soul of a child, and so slightly ridiculous.

To underline this he describes a grotesque lecture which he claims Apollinaire once gave to five people (including Albert and Nicosia), in which he explained that the Venus de Milo had lost her arms because she had fallen out of a train.

In the poem "La Porte" the lines which read "Qu'est-ce que cela peut me faire ô ma maman / D'être cet employé pour qui seul rien n'existe," had originally, and disconcertingly, been the exact opposite: "D'être cet employé pour qui seul tout existe."[3] It is a Pascalian duality. The "misère" and the "grandeur," the flat disgust or the joy when suddenly the imagination seems to undo the envelope of the world. It is a sad comment that this power of creativeness carried into everyday life should be regarded as "childishness." One has been told, on the other hand, who are the inheritors of the Kingdom of Heaven.

At this moment in his life Apollinaire seems to have felt keenly the need for a substitute family-circle. During the course of the summer of 1900 he made another friend, Ferdinand da Molina, whom he had met in a bar near the Gare Saint Lazare. Mme de Kostrowitzky had recently moved to the rue Victor Massé; and Molina like Nicosia took Apollinaire home and made him feel one of the family. He obviously was uncomfortable in his own home and probably even ashamed of it. Albert

[3] Décaudin, p. 142.

Molina, Ferdinand's younger brother, has said[4] that Guillaume did not approve of his mother's guests. The Molina family sounds charming; they were Portuguese Jews, and the father was a dancing master at Saint-Cyr. There were several children, including a pale, pretty girl of sixteen, Linda, with whom Apollinaire inevitably became infatuated.

When he first crossed the threshold, Ferdinand da Molina noticed that "his piercing eyes seemed to be summing up in an amused kind of way the sort of *milieu* into which he had fallen," an intelligent, warm-hearted Jewish family which readily adopted the young man. And just as readily he gave of his best, helped the mother to cook (and there is one treasure that he failed to give to the world; *Guillaume Apollinaire's Cook-book*), wrote the younger brother's essays only to get a "Zero, what a farrago of nonsense!" for his pains, told the younger sister fairy stories, courted Linda as he had done Maria with gracefully-turned verses, and assisted the father with a book which he was writing on *La Grâce et le maintien français*. To James Onimus Apollinaire later wrote of this as if it were his own, but in this letter, written in a period of depression, he is obviously boosting his own achievements, and Ferdinand's brother is probably right when he says that Guillaume merely helped, by correcting the proofs and writing the Preface. When he was in Portugal, M. de Molina had officiated in the synagogue, and Apollinaire who was already fascinated by the lore of religion, and had at least dipped into the Cabbala, plied him with questions about Jewish rites and customs and history. He even went one step further, and began to take Hebrew lessons, whether from M. da Molina himself or through his offices, is not known, but with the certain intention of gathering background material for his short stories, or even possibly the novel, *La Gloire de l'Olive* which he started at this time and which, as he boasted to Onimus, was going to cause quite a stir in the world. Later, for the novel was never his *forte*, he had the good sense to lose the manuscript in a train. The short story which was born at this time out of a similar curiosity about the by-ways of religion had a happier fate and eventually gave its title to his first published volume of stories *L'Hérésiarque et Cie*. Like all his

---

[4] Albert Molina, "Apollinaire familier," in *La Table ronde*, 1952, p. 94.

stories it is curious and original, although Mme Durry has
convincingly linked the subject with Anatole France's *Thaïs*.[5]
The actual heresy is curious enough; that the whole Trinity
died at Golgotha, God the Father in the person of the good
thief, and the Holy Ghost in that of the bad one. "Love
eternal, which once it was made flesh, craved to be like human
love which is infamous," and so had one day violated the sleeping Virgin Mary. The tone of the story is even more curious.
It takes a mature acceptance of the ridiculous complexity
of human nature, an assured irony, to pass from obscenity—
the Heresiarch mortifies his flesh in the most peculiar ways
and expresses himself in crude Piedmontese—through ribaldry
—the heresy reveals itself in a silly ditty—to a naïve gravity
about the sincerity of his faith. "The truth is the Heresiarch
was like all men, because we are all sinners and saints if not
criminals and martyrs." The young author had already learned
this the hard way, not only from his own extreme nature but
from his nearest and dearest.

But despite the achievement he shows in this story, he had
still made little material progress in the literary world. When
he took "L'Hérésiarque" to the offices of *La Revue blanche*,
he was told to leave it, and did not hear again until they actually published it a year and a half later. His one important
contact was still Léon Cahun of the Mazarine who occasionally
invited him to his home. In his letter to Onimus he does some
name-dropping about the journalists whom he has met there
and says that just before his death Cahun predicted to all and
sundry that the young man "would become something."
But for all that, when it became obvious that the Bourse
Parisienne was needing even Apollinaire's meagre salary
for its speculations, and he was once more out of work, the only
way he could find of actually earning money by his pen was to
write a pornographic novel. This was the first of a series:
in fact Apollinaire was eventually to become quite the professional pornographer. "Professional" here is the important
word: there is no question of any of these novels or the " clan-
destinely" published poems having literary merit, except that
they are written grammatically and spelt correctly which is more

[5] Durry, p. 184.

than most of the *genre*: Apollinaire wrote them according to
the classic formulæ in order to make money. The fact that, as
M. Sartre would say, one gets the kind of prostitution one
deserves may be relevant to Apollinaire himself, but not to the
intrinsic worth or lack of worth of the books. He was not like
de Sade, trying to prove any point or show men to themselves,
but merely making a pensum into a lark, as is obvious from the
edifying title, *Mirely ou le petit trou pas cher*. It was simply an
easier and more amusing occupation than adding up figures
or copying out wrappers at four sous an hour amongst a crowd
of smelly tramps; and "le rire hénaurme" of Flaubert's
Garçon, or of Le Père Ubu is never far away. In fact the
devising of Guillaume's licentious conceits was to give him and
his friends many an occasion for that kind of laugh throughout
the years. The fact that sometimes he went too far even for
this *genre* is characteristic. Whenever he embraced a cause he
was nothing if not thorough. In *Les Onze mille verges* he boasted
that he would outdo de Sade, and the enormities become so
enormous that they cancel each other out, and after all the
impalings and disembowellings nothing is left but the blood
and excrement of the silent charnel-house. In the patterns of
his imagination he could never bridle a certain curve reaching
out to the Apocalypse. It is significant that for many years he
was to work on a novel called *The End of the World*.

Meanwhile his own behaviour was on a very different plane.
From the moment he had entered the Molina household he
had begun to court Linda with a particularly precious,
affected gallantry which caused a certain amount of amusement in the family. He would gaze at her with spaniel-like
eyes, shower her with gracefully-turned, melodious verses in
which he referred to her as "une Madone," "une pâle Infante,"
or—after Baudelaire—"la très Bonne," "la très Douce";
in short, he treated the sixteen-year-old schoolgirl like the
poet's lady he had made in his imagination. It was an
exaggerated, overwhelmingly elaborate parade which only
embarrassed Linda, although she was a kind-hearted girl
and did her best not to hurt him. In fact Guillaume was not
very deeply involved. There was possibly one moment in
the early summer when he was caught up in his own game and

came to believe sincerely in what had begun as a literary pose. Momentarily he even toyed with marriage. The whole family was leaving for Cabourg where M. de Molina had a job for the season as dancing-master at the Casino, and the prospect of Linda's prolonged absence, and possibly, too, that of the whole family which had come to seem like his own, undoubtedly brought his feelings to a head.

> Lorsque vous partirez, je ne vous dirai rien,
> Mais après tout l'été, quand reviendra l'automne,
> Si vous n'êtes pas là zézayante, ô Madone
> J'irai gémir à votre porte comme un chien.
> Lorsque vous partirez, je ne vous dirai rien.[6]

At Cabourg he pestered her with letters, semi-declarations backed by an entrenchment of involved irony, until at last she made it quite clear that she could only ever be his good friend. Then after the gentle Symbolist invocations ("Votre âme est une enfant que je voudrais bercer"), the specious conceits ("La force du miroir trompa plus d'un amant / Qui crut aimer sa belle et n'aima qu'un mirage"), the poems which show more of his skill in versification than the depth of his feeling, comes a violent outburst of revenge. The theme of "Adieux" is pure Ronsard. "Lorsque grâce aux printemps vous ne serez plus belle," he the despised poet will make her immortal: but it is laced by the characteristic Apollinaire whip-lash of thwarted desire:

> Car l'endemain viendront des chevaucheurs encore
> Moustachus et câlins ou brutaux à souhait
> Qui, joie! seront vainqueurs, Ma Joie, vainqueurs encore
> Par la caresse lente ou même à coups de fouet,[7]

---

[6] For this and for all the Linda poems, cp. "Les Dicts d'amour à Linda" in *Il y a, Oeuvres poétiques*, 1956, p. 320.

> "When you go away, I shall say nothing to you,
> But after the whole summer, when the autumn returns,
> If you are not there, lisping, o Madonna,
> I shall go and howl at your door like a dog.
> When you go away, I shall say nothing to you."

[7] "For the next day yet more riders will come
> With their moustaches and cajolements or brute force if you will
> Who, joy! will be conquerors, My Joy, and conquerors yet again
> With their slow caresses or even with the lash of the whip."

and held in equilibrium between two extremes, the black pit of melancholy:

> Intercalées dans l'an viendront les journées veuves,
> Les vendredis sanglants et lents d'enterrements,
> Des blancs et de tout noirs vaincus des cieux qui pleuvent
> Quand la femme du diable a battu son amant,[8]

and the soaring craft of his poetic ambition:

> Et pourtant c'est bien vrai je n'eus aucun désir
> Sinon téter la lune, ô nuit au seul tétin
> Et creuser à jamais mon logique Nazir
> Malgré l'amour terrestre aux baisers florentins.[9]

The firm resolution which emerges, "Non, je ne veux aucun de ces coeurs que l'on donne . . . ni de l'amour humain qui fait trop d'embarras," shows that the main hurt was to his pride. To Ferdinand da Molina he had said, "If you unite your strength to my intelligence we will do great things."[10] Madonnas come and go. The constant was "Et la rage et le doute et le nom des poètes."

The fact that at this same time he had already begun the parade of seduction, the dumb-show of devotion, the eloquent, brown velvet glance, with another girl who was to prove one of the great loves of his life, only underlines his "rage," for life as well as glory: "Moi qui sais des lais pour les reines, / Et des chansons pour les sirènes," is an already formulated refrain in one of the Linda poems.

When the Molinas had left, Guillaume went back to the Nicosias for company. Once again he was out of work, although he had made two small steps forward in the literary world. Marius and Ary Leblond of *La Grande France*, to whom he had been introduced by an acquaintance from Cannes, had

---

[8] "Interspersed in the year there will be widowed days,
Fridays that are bloody and slow with funerals,
Overcome by the white and the jet black of rainy skies
When the devil's wife has beaten her lover."

[9] "And yet it is true indeed that I had no desire
Except to suck the moon, o night with one pap
And to hollow out for ever my logical Nazir
In spite of earthly love with its Florentine kisses."

[10] Albert Molina, *op. cit.*

accepted two of his poems, "Ville et Coeur" and "Epousailles," for publication in September; and he was turning out some political and financial articles for a small review called *Le Tabarin* edited by Gaillet, the other ghost writer of *Que Faire*. But neither of these offered much money: and when Mme Nicosia suggested that he might act as tutor to a little girl to whom she was giving piano lessons, Guillaume jumped at the opportunity. A hundred francs a month for a mere two hours each morning must have seemed a princely wage.

The little girl was the daughter of a Frenchwoman, Mme de Milhau, the rich widow of a German Viscount, who unfortunately for Guillaume as it at first seemed, was planning to go back to Germany in the autumn taking only an English governess with her. However she must have been pleased with him as tutor because she then changed her mind, called Guillaume to see her and asked him if he would like to go too. He later said that he accepted because the English governess was pretty. He undoubtedly would have accepted anyway. Life in Paris was not holding out immediate rewards: there would be a journalistic market for his articles on Germany and if Stavelot had proved a stimulus to his pen, how much more inspiring to a poet would be the romantic background of the Rhineland.

For it was there that the Milhaus had their two houses, and there to Bad Honnef on the banks of the river itself Guillaume went with the Viscountess in her de Dion Bouton at the end of August, while the English governess accompanied the other half of the family, Gabrielle and the Viscountess's mother by train.

The little town of Honnef itself was a banal enough watering place and of no particular interest to Guillaume who had been bred in similar surroundings: but the Milhaus's house outside the town was what he considered "romantic" with gables and a weathercock and cypresses framing a magnificent view out over the river, the unique river with its constant bustle of steamers and ferries, its vine-covered slopes, and ruined castles and enough legendary creatures infesting its crags to satisfy even the mythomane Apollinaire. Apart from supernumerary elves and mermaids and Rhine maidens, there was of course the Lorelei, and the shade of Roland the Paladin who had ended his days on the towering rock of Rolandsbogen on the opposite shore from Honnef, after his wife Hildegunde, hearing false news of his death at Roncesvalles, had taken the veil in the convent of Nonnenwerth on an island further down the Rhine: there was Siegfried who slew the dragon on the Drachenfels, whose vineyards now yield the red wine called Drachenblut: there was even a patron saint for Wilhelm Apollinaris de Kostrowitzky, St Apollinaris, Bishop of Ravenna. In 1164 the ship bearing his head to Cologne was miraculously prevented from continuing its journey until the sacred relic had been placed in the chapel there near Remagen, the Apollinariskirche, where it is still preserved in a sarcophagus in the crypt. Remagen is the source of a mineral water which was called "Apollinaris Wasser."

It is hardly surprising that the first poem that Apollinaire produced on his arrival should show a marked advance on all others up to date. He was in the first stages of infatuation with Annie Playden, the pretty English governess, he was excited by the "romantic" surroundings, the autumn sunshine was mellow, the wine good, and by dint of sheer application and practice he had arrived at a stage of considerable technical proficiency. He was in fact at this moment so completely confident in himself that instead of using conventional or derivative themes, as he had done until now in his poetry, he chose instead for "La Synagogue" the sort of original subject matter which he had hitherto treated in prose, his amused, sympathetic observation of local lore and piquant characters; in this case the two old Jews, Ottomar Scholem and Abraham Loeweren, who in their green felt hats are walking together along the Rhine to the synagogue, and shouting and cursing at each other so violently that "Old Father Rhine has to turn his head to smile." And the cause for so much anger? Simply that on the Sabbath they are not allowed to smoke while the Christians walk by with their cigars alight, and that both are in love with Lia "aux yeux de brebis et dont le ventre avance un peu." And yet once in the synagogue, when they kiss the *thora* (it is the "fête des cabanes"), they will forget their differences, smile at each other and loudly and gravely join in the psalms, calling as it were on a Leviathan to arise from the deep and destroy the heathen. In the synagogue they are united against the rest of the world.

All the effects which Apollinaire had achieved with such apparent ease in his short stories are here conveyed in even more lapidary manner. The authoritative brushing in of background colour and movement, the "feurtres verts," the "synagogue pleine de chapeaux," the tying together of the strands of earthiness and faery: "Bâtard conçu pendant les règles ou Que le diable entre dans ton père / Le vieux Rhin soulève sa face ruisselante et se détourne pour sourire," the ironical sympathy for his simple souls, in which he encompasses his own simplicity, the use of local colour and dialect (here the line "Hanoten ne Kamoth bagoim tholanoth baleoumim" is apparently[11] not a direct quotation from a psalm but a perfectly grammatical phrase of his own, result, no doubt, of his Hebrew lessons in Paris), and even the swiftness and suspense and surprise climax of his narrative—all these are conveyed in five four-line stanzas. He was an incomparable versifier who knew how to manipulate rhythm most supply, and, as he proves here, with considerable originality. For despite a normal enough beginning of alexandrines with an *a b a b* rhyme scheme, the lines soon grow uneven, swell out to great length for the men's imprecations, are telescoped again for the alexandrine of their mutual smile, and then lift into the great diapason of the psalm:

Ils déchanteront sans mesure et les voix graves des hommes
Feront gémir un Léviathan au fond du Rhin comme une voix
   d'automne
Et dans la synagogue pleine de chapeaux on agitera les loulabim
Hanoten ne Kamoth bagoim tholanoth baleoumim[12]

It is quite obvious that Apollinaire's point of departure was the rhythm and swell of the Hebrew psalm, including but

[11] Décaudin, p. 181.

[12] "They will sing flat and out of time and the deep voices of men
Will make the Leviathan in the depths of the Rhine groan like a
   voice of autumn
And in the hat-filled synagogue they will wave the loulabim
Hanoten ne Kamoth bagoim tholanoth baleoumim"

F

drowning the off-beat dissonances of individual voices: through it he has achieved a very individual *vers libre*, fluid but strongly rhythmical, without necessarily having read Laforgue's translation of *The Leaves of Grass* which it resembles. It is not unreasonable to suppose that his studies of Hebrew—even if these were only primary he would be bound at least to consider the psalms—and the creation of this poem in order to give the impression of the psalm-filled synagogue, opened his eyes to the possibilities of the *verset* which he used later to such effect: and this at a date when he knew nothing of Claudel, and Blaise Cendrars was still a small boy, these being two writers by whom some critics have claimed that he was influenced in this respect. In such a complex person as Apollinaire the fact that at times he was derivative does not preclude a very real originality, and this is certainly one aspect of it.

At Honnef he could hardly have had time to do more than write this poem, for the Milhaus had only halted there. Their real destination was the other house, Neu-Glück near Oberpleis some twenty kilometres back from the Rhine, in the Westerwald on the foothills of the Siebengebirge. The countryside was wild and deserted. One could walk for miles in the woods and along the roads without meeting anybody, and even the post office was an hour's walk away. But the house, set in a dense wood of fir trees was a riot of vulgar colour. Like all the houses in the district, it was timbered in black and white, but some of the beams had been painted red, and dotted with bright rosettes. Inside it was clean, respectable, rich, with Bourbon lilies in honour of Mme de Milhau's French descent sculpted on the gratings of the basement. The new young French tutor did equal honour to his employer and everybody was impressed by this charming, erudite, young man with the exquisite Gallic manners. One cannot help but feel that, adaptable as always, he enjoyed playing up to his role.

However he was not allowed to forget that essentially he was a subaltern. He was stuck in a tiny room, badly lit and badly heated, with a view from one window of the black regiment of fir-trees and from the other of the few, miserable farms that made up the hamlet. This however did not seem to worry him unduly. His poet's imagination was stirred as it had been at Stavelot by the strangeness of the scene, the sadness, quintessence of all northern autumns, and the trail of melancholy legend lingering in a peasant's song. A little poem of *Alcools*, written at that time, "Automne," conveys this admirably, with its pointillist picture of mist and misery:

> Dans le brouillard s'en vont un paysan cagneux
> Et son boeuf lentement dans le brouillard d'automne
> Qui cache les hameaux pauvres et vergogneux[13]

its forlorn tune:

> En s'en allant là-bas le paysan chantonne
> Une chanson d'amour et d'infidélité
> Qui parle d'une bague et d'un coeur que l'on brise[14]

and the poet's childish cry of joy at the "ingenuous miracle," the beauty of his own perception of it all.

> Oh! l'automne l'automne a fait mourir l'été
> Dans le brouillard s'en vont deux silhouettes grises[15]

As at Stavelot, he was fascinated by the peasants and would spend long hours drinking with them, and even sometimes wake up the next morning in the ditch. He would watch the children running to and fro from the village school, and he made friends with one of the local young men, Johannes Dachs, and most important of all, he was busy falling in love with Annie, the governess.

"Les Colchiques," another highly successful poem of *Alcools* written at this first moment at Neu-Glück, combines his awareness of the lovely but doomed autumn countryside with a clear-sighted sense of the slow, inevitable process of sinking into infatuation, the sweet bitterness of abandon:

> Et ma vie pour tes yeux lentement s'empoisonne

---

[13] "Into the mist goes the knock-kneed peasant
And his ox slowly in the autumn mist
Which hides poor shameful hamlets"

[14] "As he goes away the peasant hums
A song of love and infidelity
That tells of a ring and a heart that is breaking"

[15] "Oh! the autumn autumn has made summer die
Into the mist go two grey silhouettes"

It is strange that even from the beginning their affair wore this air of doom, for Annie from what one can judge from photographs and accounts in later life, seems to have been a jolly sort of girl, with grey eyes, fair hair, a delicate complexion, a round face, and a dimple in her chin. But she was obviously more complicated than she looked. She came from a strait-laced Puritanical family of Clapham. Her father was an architect with the reputation of being very strictly religious, and Annie was enough imbued with his example to start a Sunday school as soon as she arrived at Neu-Glück. But she must already at home have given signs of other rather different tendencies. Once her brother had seen fit to warn her that she could not go out "with eyes like that."

At first for Guillaume there were plenty of diversions from what he too thought were "cursed eyes." With the Milhaus he paid a visit to another family seat at Krayerhof in the Eifel (in fact it was not very far from the Ardennes); from there he went on foot to the lake, the Laacher See, and the convent of Maria Laach. They all passed through Bonn where he made use of an introduction to a French university lecturer, and then to Cologne: from there, always eager to explore and see as much as he could, he went alone to Dusseldorf where he stayed with a schoolmaster whom he had met through the Milhaus. Immediately after this the family left again for Honnef where they stayed for November and December. And it was there that Guillaume's elaborate courtship, the gifts of poems and flowers and amethysts and baroque pearls, the insistent, velvety gaze, the long kisses in the romantic garden above the Rhine seem to have won Annie over entirely.

It is a favourite sport among biographers to conjecture whether the two lovers actually slept together. This must remain conjecture but everything seems to indicate that they did. In the letter to James Onimus dated July 1902 Apollinaire himself says crudely: "Je pars le 22 août 1901 depuis je vois toute l'Allemagne et couche avec la gouvernante, anglaise 21 ans, épatante des nichons et un cul (!)." This is vague enough, could of course be only the young man's boast. But fourteen years later, summing up all his affairs for the girl who was then about to become his *fiancée*, he still insists that this was the only *raison d'être* of his feeling for Annie: "I was infatuated with her physically, but otherwise we had nothing in common."[16] It is indeed difficult to imagine the obsessive, passionate young man putting up for months with daily converse with a girl who spoke pidgin French, and he no English, and who in no way understood him as a poet, without their affair advancing physically. The poems themselves seem to speak unequivocally. During all this early period Annie appears only incidentally. In fact in "Rhénane d'Automne" which he wrote in November at Honnef the verses which refer to the presence of the beloved were those he had already written at Stavelot. "Les Sapins," "Schinderhannes," the interesting "Les Femmes" which is a real precursor of his later "poems—conversation," and which he wrote that winter at Neu-Glück, are inspired purely by the picturesqueness of his surroundings. It is not until later in the spring when she, through fear of his intensity and through her own guilt, begins to resist him, that hints of the true nature of their relationship begin to appear. And this is a normal pattern in Apollinaire's life. While he is being fulfilled with a woman he does not feel it necessary to write about her. Only when he is frustrated either by absence or her resistance does he then find it imperative to unload his accumulated charge of emotion and repressed desire. This happened with Annie, with Marie, with Lou, and with Madeleine: and his wife Jacqueline appears in only one poem as a charming presence. With Annie it is only in 1903 that his past desire, his rage and jealousy, and his nostalgia pour out vehemently and directly in the magnificent "Chanson du Mal-Aimé," the images of which would alone seem to be convincing proof of the intense, physical nature of their relationship.

There is, however, one revealing if only glancing hint of this earlier, in the spring of 1902 when Annie was no longer so complaisant, when already doubts, guilt, fear, resistance, and frustration were worrying them both. It would appear that the couple had had their fortunes told by a gipsy and had learned that their destinies lay apart.

[16] *Tendre comme le souvenir*, 1952, p. 70.

La Tzigane savait d'avance
Nos deux vies barrées par les nuits
Nous lui dîmes adieu et puis. . . .
De ce puits sortit l'Espérance

L'amour lourd comme un ours privé
Dansa debout quand nous voulûmes
Et l'oiseau bleu perdit ses plumes
Et les mendiants leur Ave

On sait très bien que l'on se damne
Mais l'espoir d'aimer en chemin
Nous fait penser main dans la main
A ce qu'a prédit la Tzigane[17]

That second verse condenses in the remarkable image of
the cumbersome, lolling bear led by the gipsies, the whole
sense of a delicate idyll erected into heavy, guilt-ridden sexuality
—Annie's guilt, but also Guillaume's for he too had not been
without his own share of shame for the sensuality he felt he
had derived from his mother. "Je t'ai pris mon péché, ô ma
mère," runs a line in the manuscript of *La Porte*.[18] The
premonition of being poisoned by those violet-ringed eyes is
being fulfilled. Nor was his translation of Brentano's *Die
Lorelei* foreign to this line of thought. "Je suis lasse de vivre
et mes yeux sont maudits / Ceux qui m'ont regardée, évêque
en ont péri." It has been suggested [19] that he may in this
premonition have been influenced by Heine and his "amours

[17] "The Gipsy knew beforehand
    About our night-crossed lives
    We said farewell to her and then . . .
    Out of this well rose Hope

    Love as heavy as a tame bear
    Danced erect when we wanted
    And the blue bird lost its feathers
    And the beggars their Ave

    We know full well that we are damning ourselves
    But the hope of loving on the way
    Makes us think hand in hand
    Of what the gipsy foretold"

[18] Décaudin, p. 142.
[19] *Op. cit.*, p. 184; also Pierre Orecchioni, "Le Thème du Rhin dans l'inspiration de Guillaume Apollinaire," 1956, p. 57.

maudits." This could have been possible at the beginning when he was playing with the idea of falling in love, and acting the part of lover.

Once really caught in the trap of his own emotions there was no longer any question of acting. It became a real obsession for him. Back in the snowy isolation of Neu-Glück there was no escape. The two were thrown together the whole time, both young, both the family's subordinates, and throughout the long winter evenings they would sit together in the sitting room, Annie playing the piano and singing, Guillaume reading his way through the Milhau's library, and as a diversion painting her portrait in water-colours. Then he would tell her the stories he had read or made up, and make her teach him English and read Shakespeare. Over-elaborate in court-ship, in possession over-tyrannical, he demanded a complete submission of her personality to his, and the sudden switches from tender gallantry to violent desire and even more violent rage if he was rebuffed were too much for the conventional young English girl. She began to be terrified by his demands especially as the Vicomtesse, suspecting what was going on, kept reading her sermons about men and how they could ruin a woman's life. The more the poor, bewildered girl retreated into prudence and prudery, the more inflamed Guillaume became, and then even more terrified she. It was a vicious circle from which by the end of February he was wise enough to seek escape. The Milhaus were planning to spend two months in Munich at Easter time and Guillaume asked for time off to make a trip through Germany before joining them there. The situation between the two young people had become so charged that Mme de Milhau thankfully let him go.

But Guillaume rarely in any of his actions had only one motive in view: not single, not double but multi-minded. He may immediately have been driven away by the impasse with Annie: but he had certainly not lost sight either of his duty to himself as poet and story-writer, or, on another plane, of the necessity to make a career for himself as a journalist. New sights and places were a potent stimulus to his poetic muse, a fertile matter for his stories, but also a source for *rapportage* which might win him a hearing in some of the big

reviews. Already *Tabarin* and *La Grande France* had published
little notices, such as "The State of the Roads in Germany,"
or the performance of the *Red Cockrel* of Gerhard Hauptmann
in Berlin. Throughout the year *La Grande France* continued to
publish his articles on Germany. He had already, before he left
Paris, held out a bait for *La Revue blanche* with his story
"L'Hérésiarque," which suddenly in March it was to publish
without his knowing. This was obviously a spur to him, and
during his roundabout trip through Germany he was to produce
a spate of his characteristic *contes*, most of which appeared
gradually through the year in this same review. In April he
sent in to *La Plume* a piece about Russia and proposed his
services as a regular contributor on Germany, but without
success.

He was in fact determined to use Germany as a sort of
trump-card to win his way into the highly competitive world of
journalism. But his reaction to the country generally was
characteristically Latin and blinkered. Berlin he thought "a
ghastly though convenient city," German drama was often
stupid, all German works of art looked as though they had
just been turned out of a factory, you had really to be mad
about music to be able to listen to it in the hideous hangar of
the Beethoven-Halle at Bonn.[20] Obviously he was not. It
seems strange that a poet with such a sensitive ear to the music
of words, who even composed his poems on the basis of a
musical tune, should have seemed so impervious to real music.
Visually his taste was very developed and it was the ugliness
of some aspects of Germany which he could not forgive.
Taste, wit, intelligence, these were what he admired in the
French; and then also the qualities he was not born with but
strove to have, classic restraint and order, ideals of the French
themselves for precisely the same reason. He, a foreigner, is in
fact all his life the most conspicuously pro-French of writers,
never ceasing to claim the French heritages as the apogee of
civilisation, and then second in place the Italian. In fact his
cultivation of the pan-Latin spirit becomes a real emotional
prejudice, and achieves chauvinistic proportions during the
War.

[20] "Le Pergamon à Berlin," in *La Revue blanche*, 15 May 1902.

It seems a little surprising that with his appetite for visual works of art he should ignore altogether the whole world of Baroque architecture and art, for he went to some of the finest centres, Dresden and Vienna and Munich. Perhaps this was a blind spot in his knowledge. It is, of course, in all these places primarily the picturesque, the folk-lore, the strange customs of the people, not the static lines of stone and cornice which excite him as a writer—proof, if it was wanted, of the truism that you see in a place only what you yourself bring. For instance, in Cologne, his first stop, it is not the Carnival which figures in his completed poems, much though that must have fascinated him for he had always loved his childhood Carnival-times in Rome and Nice, but the towering Gothic cathedral, and the picture of the gentle Virgin with the Bean Flower by Meister Wilhelm: the blonde Madonna reminded him of Annie, and the cathedral symbolised his own over-leaping ambition, his statement of his own value as a poet as opposed to his recent dependence and enslavement as a lover. In the midst of a mediocre poem full of the faults he so easily fell into at the time—puns, crudeness, involved erudite references—this sense of his own power soars forth in char-acteristic, megalomaniac voice.

> Mes durs rêves formels sauront te chevaucher
> Mon destin au char d'or sera ton beau cocher
> Qui pour brides prendra les cordes de tes cloches
>   Sonnant à triples croches[21]

and the pretty girl is temporarily exorcised.

There is possibly another clue to the particular stage of rage and frustration he was in when he left for Cologne. He was obviously fascinated by the story of St Ursula martyred by the Huns with eleven thousand other virgins, and buried in the cathedral. The "ribambelle ursuline" crops up again years

---

[21] "Le Dôme de Cologne," in *Le Guetteur Mélancolique, Oeuvres poétiques*, p. 543.

> "My hard formal dreams will ride you
>   My golden-charioted destiny will be your handsome coachman
>   Who for reins will take your bell-ropes
>   Ringing out in demi-semi-quavers"

later in the poem "Cortège," dragging with it a definite under-
tone of grievance against women.[22] The haunting phrase
"Les onze mille vierges" too must have struck him, for, again
much later, it appears transformed grossly into *Les Onze mille
verges*, an extravagant novel which fully lives up to the pornographic promise of the title and which if the virgins had been
able to turn in their graves would have caused an earthquake
in Cologne. Who knows if it was not the gentle English girl
who set off this whole train of thought.

It is she anyway who still haunts him when he writes his
story about Hildesheim, and the description of Ilse the heroine
of *La Rose de Hildesheim* not only tallies exactly with the photographs of Annie at the time but takes precedence over the
fairy-tale setting. Her mother had even been English:

> Her pale blond hair had golden lights and gave the im-
> pression of moonlight. Her body was graceful and slim.
> Her face was bright, warm, laughing, she had a dimple in her
> plump chin and her grey eyes, although they were not very
> beautiful, suited her face and fluttered like a bird's wings.

But as he moves further away, and becomes more and more
taken up by his surroundings, the need to write about Annie
fades. In Prague he is so enchanted by the street scene, the
Jewish quarter with the clock whose hands move backwards,
the Hradschin, and the amethyst which figures a mad face
looking just like his own, that he allows his fantasy to take wing,
and as in the euphoria of his first arrival in Paris he saw all the
great literary figures of the day in every passer-by, so now in
the story, "Le Passant de Prague," he spices his nocturnal
wanderings with an encounter with the Wandering Jew,
one of those magical, mythical figures like Simon Mage and
Merlin, who with their larger-than-life capacities always spurred

---

[22] "L'odeur d'un petit chien ô Corneille Agrippa m'eût suffi
Pour décrire exactement tes concitoyens de Cologne
Leurs rois-mages et la ribambelle ursuline
Qui t'inspirait l'erreur touchant toutes les femmes"

As M. Décaudin points out, Corneille Agrippa was the author of a treatise
De Nobilitate et præcellentia fœmini sexus, 1509, a sentiment which here at least,
Apollinaire is far from sharing.

on his own imagination, itself in quest of the superhuman. It is the thrill of the supernatural striking through the most basic human situation, the eternal old man copulating non-stop through the centuries. In typically Apollinairian fashion he presents what is almost a metaphysical yearning towards possessing all time past in his own eternal present in this the most palpable of all ways. The piquancy of such a conception obviously fascinated him, because he returns to it again in a strange and amusing story written in 1912, "Le Roi Lune." Here he describes a machine which enables the wearer to make material, and to possess physically, any character at any moment of history. The antics that ensue and the *graffitti* that they inspire constitute one of those "by-ways of history" which Apollinaire was expert in evoking.

The procedure of letting fantasy take over from the matter-of-fact as he wanders about a strange city, obviously follows one of the inevitable patterns of his thought. In "La Chasse à l'Aigle" he tells of his meeting with a strange creature who wears the mask of an eagle and whom he watches being hunted down. It is the heir of Bonaparte.

In the outlandish villages of the Danube Valley, reality itself had a sharp enough taste even for his palate. "L'Otmika," the traditional rape by which the young peasant wins his bride, has all the mixture of savagery and naïvety which excited him in "Que vlo vé?" and "Les Pélerins piémontais." With his usual bold splashes of colour he reproduces the erotic "danse de la croupe," the weird food, the old gipsy who knows the arts of depilation and restoring virginity, and weaves them into one of his swift-moving, direct narratives.

Munich, where he joined the Milhaus and Annie again, although it also left Bacchanalian memories of the Beer Festival which he was to use in *Le Poète assassiné*, inspired him in a very different vein. Perhaps this was due to a renewal of the idyll with Annie: for "L'Obituaire" is a lyrical piece of prose, so lyrical in fact that later by a mere changing of the disposition of the lines he turned it into a poem: "La Maison des morts." This apparently cavalier treatment of poetry has been criticised. In fact it is probably a case of what at first was intended to be an experiment about the nature of prose turning out to be an experiment about the nature of poetry, an extending of limits in both directions. But it is an essentially poetic fantasy. In the Munich cemetery he and Annie had seen the dead bodies that are shown there behind glass cases before inhumation. This is the "point de départ," not for a "danse macabre" in the Lenore vein but a delicate arabesque, a Watteau-like "bal champêtre" of phantoms, where a diamond angel breaks all the windows and the troupe of the dead pair off with the living and dance lightly to "one of those refrains with absurd, lyrical words, which undoubtedly are the remnants of the oldest poetic monuments of humanity." This reference to folk-song and ballad and nursery rhyme and meaningless ritual refrains as part of a whole ancient poetic inheritance is important. Apollinaire never ceased to tap it as one of the fertile sources of his own poetry. It could well be that he had been made more acutely aware of the possibilities of the folk-song through his recent acquaintanceship with German ballads and Lieder. Certainly the reference to the broken ring in "Automne" must be connected with "Der Zerbrochene Ringelein" of Eichendorff. It would be interesting to know at what stage he became conscious that he was composing his own poems on a musical air. Later he described this as his method of composition and the actual tune has been noted down from the one he hummed to Max Jacob.[23] Dr Mario Roques[24] has also ingeniously discovered a basis of the popular songs of the day for the rhythm of some of the poems, in particular his translation of "La Loreley": "A Bacharach il y avait une sorcière blonde" which has the same rhythm as "A Parthenay il y avait une tant jolie fille," a favourite song at the time.

"L'Obituaire" ends on a curious note, curious at least for Apollinaire who was always so much of this world that he spared little thought for the next. The living who have fallen in love with the dead find that this is an unhoped-for happiness, and are thereby transformed into superhuman beings. "For, is there anything so elevating as the love of a dead person?

[23] Marie-Jeanne Durry, " Un Secret d'Apollinaire," in *Le Flâneur des deux rives*, Dec. 1954, p. 13.
[24] Mario Roques, "Guillaume Apollinaire et les vieilles chansons," 1949, p. 142.

One becomes so pure thereby that eventually one is fortified
for life and no longer needs anybody." This seems again to be
an attempt to tap time, the poet's sense of harnessing his own
imaginative powers to the chariot of the past so that his own
present knows no reins. If he identifies himself with the
past he becomes timeless, can thus withstand its erosions. It
is also yet again, for this identification with "le souvenir"
and "la mémoire" is one of the functions of poetry, an
affirmation of his own strength as a poet, as opposed to his
need as an ordinary human being for another's love,
and perhaps too a premonition that that love will soon be
dead.

And once again, now that he was constantly in Annie's
company, the infection had set in, with its accompaniment
of inflamed demands, scenes swollen with violence, and the
temporary balm of reconciliation. Honnef and its romantic
site semed to act as a catalyst for them: in the autumn it had
brought their courtship to a head; now the flowering spring
countryside inspired them to the extremes of emotion. In her
reminiscences[25] Annie tells of a day when they climbed one
of the nearby mountains and the scene was so beautiful and
the day so fair that they knew together a rare moment of
ecstasy. She also recalls the occasion on top of the Drachenfels
when, after deploying as many mirages as his favourite fairy
Morgane on top of Mont Gibel about his fortune and his
family, he asked her to marry him. As she looked like refusing,
he promptly threatened to push her over the edge unless she
agreed: which naturally enough she did, only to retract once
they were on flat ground.

Nevertheless there must have been many moments of
pleasure in this lovely Rhineland spring, even if they were
backed by the poignant sense that all would soon be over, for
this was a period of intense poetic inspiration for Apollinaire
and the major part of his "Rhénanes," which themselves form
a large group in *Alcools*, was written then.

It was indeed often "the end of love," as he once put it,
when the breath of absence heightens the bloom of present

[25] Quoted by Robert Goffin in *Entrer en poésie*, 1948 (henceforth cited as Goffin),
p. 137.

enjoyment, that proved one of the finest stimuli for his love poetry:

> Les pétales tombés des cerisiers de mai
> Sont les ongles de celle que j'ai tant aimée[26]

It is an almost perverse savouring of what is now pleasurable but is going to cause pain: and then comes his retreat into the self-defence of irony:

> Mon verre s'est brisé comme un éclat de rire[27]

But irony was too slight a weapon to combat the full misery when it broke, and even poetry too fragile a vessel to hold it. The summer months at Neu-Glück when Annie finally rebuffed him were a torment during which he was not only incapable of working—he even ignored requests for more stories from *La Revue blanche*, which would normally have delighted him—but also feared for his reason. "I'm heading for a complete nervous breakdown,"[28] he wrote at this time, a fear which he also echoed in "Le Passant de Prague" after seeing his own likeness in an amethyst. "I was pale and unhappy, because I who am so afraid of going mad had just seen this crazed portrait of myself."[29] It seems as though he had for the first time in his life really been himself surprised by the violence of his emotions, and wondered if he could ever control them. And during that summer he did behave as if he were a little unhinged. He became insanely jealous for no good reason over Annie and the village schoolmaster. Like a hurt child he even appealed to the far-away James Onimus for consolation, and this in a letter otherwise full of bravado and boasting:

> Since then I have been so lazy that for two months I haven't replied to a letter from the editor of the *Revue blanche* who is trying to wake me up a bit. I am terrified that I am being cuckolded and I'm miserable. Console me.

---

[26] "The fallen petals of May cherry-trees
   Are the finger nails of the woman I have loved so much"

[27] "My glass broke like a peal of laughter"

[28] Letter to James Onimus, *Les Lettres Françaises*, 13 Dec. 1951.

[29] "Le Passant de Prague," *L'Hérésiarque et Cie*, 1936, p. 15.

Obviously when the time came to decide whether to go back to Paris or to stay on with the Milhaus for another year— for they were quite willing to have him—he chose to leave. The situation had become a stalemate: this state of apathy and self-pity had diminished him in every way. He had just enough strength of will left to make the break and creep back to Paris where Albert at least, always the solid member of the family, had managed to find a good regular job in a bank. It was hardly a triumphal return, but the lowest, downward curve of the graph after the inspired apogee. And yet in his career as a poet this short year had been a remarkable period. In it he had stored up the fat off which he was to live for the next five years.

V

Le Mal-Aimé

WHEN he arrived back in Paris he held himself erect like a Prussian ramrod. His poetic baggage too, now obviously bore the label *Made in Germany*. Apart from the Rhineland subject matter of his collection of "Rhénanes" there is the strong, rhythmic beat of the *lied*, the sweet sentimental sadness and a certain detached irony akin to that of the German Romantics. These were obvious enough influences, but in fact they had merely underlined his own bent. They had certainly helped him to find his own characteristic tone of voice away from the all-pervading influence of Symbolism. There is no evidence that he studied widely or profoundly in German literature, although he learned to speak German fluently if not completely accurately. But the collection of German books that he brought back is a typical hotch-potch, consisting of volumes of folk-songs and hymns, of stories, mainly erotic and scatalogical, Sacher-Masoch alongside charming handbooks with such hygienic titles as "Wie nämlich mit Kot und Urin die meisten Krankheiten geheilt werden,"[1] which makes nonsense of the theory that he did more than dip here and there in the by-ways of German literature, or sought for more than what offered itself to his superficial curiosity.

For his stories the main contribution of the country had been picturesque: for his poetry, the overwhelming and ill-starred love affair with Annie. Charming and accomplished as the "Rhénanes" are, they pale in importance beside the two great poems "La Chanson du Mal-Aimé" and "L'Emigrant de Landor Road" which, two years later, were the final, æsthetically triumphant outcome of all the desire and tears and frustration and rage of that year in Germany.

Unlucky in love—his mother may have done all the card-playing—but now a few tricks of a different nature were to fall into the young man's hands. Talent, if you want to live by your pen, is never enough. Apollinaire gave the appearance

[1] Cp. list given by Ernst Wolf in *Apollinaire und das Rheinland*, 1937.

of being very deft at literary strategy, but in fact, like most opportunists, he expended a considerable amount of energy before he knew any immediate reward. In the early days his progress in manœuvring himself into the right tactical position in the literary world was slow and hard-going. That autumn particularly he felt that he was getting nowhere: after all his efforts to be introduced to recognised men of letters he had succeeded only in meeting Gustave Kahn whom, with the usual fastidiousness of his aristocratic background, he thought filthy in his personal habits. "I am still rather isolated," he writes to Onimus, but doggedly he kept on with the one line of attack which was essential to a young writer in those days, publication in the small reviews. After the summer's idleness he was obliged to send to *La Revue blanche* "Trois histoires de châtiments divins," which even he himself thought childish and not up to the standard of his previous ones.[2] By the end of the year he was back to his old form with the publication of "La Rose de Hildesheim" and "L'Otmika" and also the poem "L'Ermite." About this he was particularly pleased because *La Revue blanche* rarely published poetry. He stopped contributing to *La Grande France* because they did not pay him for the articles on Germany and he was badly in need of money. Nor did *Le Tabarin.* But *L'Européen* instead accepted his *rapportage* on Germany and there he became a regular contributor.

The real moment however when both chance and the *Zeitgeist* joined hands to set him on exactly the right track was in April 1903. The review *La Plume,* following the tradition of the Hydropathes and the Chat Noir, had just reintroduced their Saturday evening gatherings, where poets known and unknown would gather and declaim their poems aloud, the readings alternating with songs and piano pieces. The ones which gained the most applause were then bespoken by Karl Boës, editor of *La Plume,* for the review. But in fact if a young man had the nerve to get up and say his party piece well, the audience alone could give him an excellent *entrée* into the literary world. On the other hand if he was an impostor they could be merciless. They were a mixed collection, hard-core Symbolists like Stuart Merrill, René Ghil, and the strange

[2] Letter to James Onimus, *Les Lettres Françaises*, 13 Dec. 1951.

G

poetess Marie Kryzinska who had been one of the pioneers of *vers libre*, others younger than these who were going to found reviews of their own and become influential figures like Paul Fort with *Vers et prose* and Eugène Montfort with *Les Marges*. And even when a writer became well known it was always of vital moment to have an outlet for his poems and articles. There were journalists like Fagus, Félix Fénéon, and Charles Henry Hirsch, who could extend invitations to other famous literary rendezvous such as the Closerie des Lilas under the ægis of Jean Moréas, where yet again the circle of contacts would be widened. And there was, like nobody else, the eccentric genius Alfred Jarry who of all present was to have the greatest influence on Apollinaire's actual work. In fact these rackety "Soirées de la Plume" held in the cellar of a café in the place Saint-Michel, and apparently a free-for-all, could prove to be an "Open Sesame" to literary fame.

Naturally Apollinaire knew the importance of the occasion and rose to it. Everybody who has ever known him insists on the impression of complete authority that he gave. He imposed his personality, but with charm, good humour, and a certain grace. Even in those days when he was comparatively thin, he moved as though he knew that he was essentially a fat man, bearing already the weight of his destiny if not of flesh. "A great man," says Mme Sonia Delaunay. "I see nobody to-day who can even be compared with him."[3]

That evening in the cellar the great man got up very nervously, made a deprecatory grimace, with almost feminine coquetry, but once at the piano began to declaim with sudden violence the "Rhénane" "Schinderhannes," the *tableau vivant* of the Brigand and his band feasting before going out to assassinate a rich Jew.

When he came to the last verse:

> On mange alors toute la bande
> Pète et rit pendant le dîner
> Puis s'attendrit à l'allemande [4]

---

[3] In conversation with the author.

[4] "Then they eat the whole gang
Fart and laugh during the dinner
Then get mawkish in the German way"

he complacently dwelled on the word "pète" and then bellowed out the last line of all at the top of his voice, "Avant d'aller assassiner." His enthusiastic living the part was infectious. The applause was deafening. Obviously gambling on his capacity not merely to "épater le bourgeois" but also to make the *avant-garde* sit up, he chose to go on with "L'Ermite" which had the dubious merit of containing lines like:

> Vertuchou! riotant des vulves des papesses
> Des saintes sans tétons j'irai vers les cités [5]

"What a case!" people murmured. "Whoever is it?" It was in fact more his personality than his poems which brought the house down. As always happened, the physical charm worked like a magnet and his contemporaries were irresistibly drawn to him. Two of the young men who rushed up in wild enthusiasm, and spent the rest of the night with him wandering round Paris, were to remain life-long friends: André Salmon, also a poet and later a fellow art-critic, and the curious Jean Mollet, who was so devoted to Guillaume that he later became his general factotum, secretary, valet, cook, and was rewarded by the honorary title of Baron. Amusingly, as if Apollinaire really had the regal right to confer such honours, he is still to-day known everywhere as "le Baron Mollet."

This was the beginning of a whole way of life, of meeting and eating, and drinking and talking and rambling the night long through the streets of Paris. Soon the high-spirited younger group led by Apollinaire and Salmon and backed by Jarry began to sabotage the Soirées de la Plume. "Too Symbolist" was the war-cry, and then inevitably somebody would leap up and begin to declaim Corbière's "L'Elegie du fils de Lamartine et de Graziella." It was here in the early summer of 1903 amongst this little band of dissident spirits, that the real break-away from Symbolism began to take shape. Inevitably when a new century begins young men who come of age with it feel that it is theirs to fashion. By the very arbitrariness of the calendar a new era is proclaimed. Apollinaire, aged

---

[5] "Vertuchou ! tittering over the vulvæ of female Popes
And saints without tits I shall set out towards the cities"

twenty-three, announced in one of his chronicles in *La Grande France* in April—that is at about the same time that he attended his first Soirée de la Plume—that the nineteenth century was dead, that it has been "admirable but often depressing," and that it "was now making way for enthusiasm, for a healthy vigorous, true, universal literature"; that the twentieth century could be harmonious and classical like the seventeenth, just as the nineteenth had been akin in its grandiose endeavours to the sixteenth. And he, who is known for his quicksilver bounds and *volte-faces*, is still saying precisely the same at the end of his life in "L'Esprit nouveau." Vigour seems to be the key-word of his personal ideal, a robust, optimistic, life-praising classicism after the charnel-house of the *fin de siècle*. Nobody could really criticise such an aim: it remained, however, to be put into practice. And for this it needed its own organ, a review where the young men who shared the same ambitions would be able to express themselves freely. This became an even more pressing need in the course of the summer, because *La Revue blanche*, where not only Apollinaire but many of the others had been finding a home for their elucubrations, suddenly collapsed. When they heard this terrible news, the little band was desperate. Apollinaire it was true, with his flair for seizing an occasion, had begun to spread his net more widely; he appeared regularly in *L'Européen*, and had recently joined *La Revue d'Art dramatique et musical du siècle* with a literary gossip column. *La Plume*, following up the promise of the soirées, published the poem "Avenir" in May and "Le Larron" in August. He even managed to find a home for two short stories, "Le Giton" and "La Rose de Hildesheim," in the Greek review *Le Journal de Salonique*. But these episodic appearances were not enough. It was necessary to make a combined frontal attack, an appearance in force.

Apollinaire was the real guiding spirit in the founding of the new review. The role of editor and animator always held a potent fascination for him, and with his infectious personality and talent for friendship, he was admirably suited for it. He was never happier than when he was allowed to assume the duties of a "chef d'école"; and even at this early stage, his friends, Salmon, Nicolas Deniker, Mécislas Golberg, Paul

Géraldy, Arne Hammer, instantly recognised his authority and rallied round him. Soon they were having "soirées" of their own, sometimes at the Flore, but more often at the restaurant of le père Jean near the Odéon; and as they demolished the food and drink that they had not paid for— le père Jean, in the amiable tradition of the restaurateur of yesteryear, had a system of *petits papiers* which he collected religiously from them and then destroyed indiscriminately whenever they gave him any token money on account— Apollinaire definitely shone as the leading spirit. They might laugh at him, for he had his funny, rather childish ways, but if he said, as once he did, "Come along, I know a marvellous new café," although they all knew that he knew no such thing and that they would be better off where they were, they found themselves trooping off after him, a latter-day Pied Piper, and ending up according to his whim in a miserable dump in the rue Christine, which he later made famous in the poem "Lundi, rue Christine."

However if Apollinaire impressed his little band of satellites, it was Jarry who impressed himself on Apollinaire, Jarry who was too privately eccentric ever to found a school in his life-time, but who overawed everybody by his extraordinary willingness to let literary fantasy invade his real life. Not only had he shocked the literary world by creating one of the strangest characters in fiction, "le père Ubu," but he then went on to identify himself with his creation and impose this fantasy character in actual fact. Even in the hour of his death in the workhouse he was still expressing himself in the mock pompous manner of Ubu: "Nous trépasserons . . ."—"We shall die on such and such a day," and promptly did so. It was he who was the real "case," not the young Apollinaire who was much too full-blooded and normal in his appetites ever to impose on himself the apparent self-mutilations of a Jarry in the service of art. It was Jarry who consistently drank absinthe mixed with red ink, whereas Apollinaire tried it only once, and Jarry who did succeed finally in poisoning himself with his self-imposed diet of no food and too much drink, whereas whatever food or drink Apollinaire swallowed, it seemed to transform itself immediately into life-embracing energy. An account of

Jarry's life is a mixture of squalor and pathos. He lived entirely on his own with absolutely no known emotional relationship with woman or man: he literally starved himself to death: when the floods rose and inundated his little shack on the banks of the Seine he merely climbed up and slept on the table; he then emerged, still dripping, for his nightly tour of the cafés: he always carried a revolver and occasionally really used it to the terror of the *bourgeois*, pregnant women, and children. After one of these scenes, "Was that not," he said, dead-drunk, but still in the tones of Ubu, "as splendid as literature?"

And yet Apollinaire, and many others, admired him and found him a delightful companion. To Onimus in July 1904 Apollinaire wrote that Alfred Jarry and Charles Henry Hirsch "who are exquisite, are my most sincere literary friends." From the first time that they met, they had been friends, and had spent the whole night walking up and down the boulevard Saint-Germain talking of heraldry and heresies and versification and puppets.

Jarry's influence, not only on Apollinaire, but on the whole of modern literature—and perhaps, incidentally, on modern pictorial art—is enormous. The complete abolition of logic and representation, the installation of the absurd, the counter-point on the theme of incongruity, the celebration of shock-tactics, the erection of fantasy and dream into solid sky-scrapers, the crowning of laughter and the ridiculous, these guiding principles of Surrealism and, even more recently, the theatre of the absurd, are all there fully developed in Jarry. Apollinaire, with his razor-sharp intuition, was quick to see his real quality as well as his utter originality. In an article written after Jarry's death in 1909 he gives a most penetrating analysis of this singular creature.

> Jarry's monkey-tricks did the greatest harm to his reputation. . . . Alfred Jarry was a man of letters in the rarest of fashions. His smallest action, his pranks, are all literature. That is because he was steeped in it and in that only. But how admirably! Somebody once said in front of me that Jarry was the last burlesque writer: which is false! At that rate, the majority of fifteenth-century writers and a large part of sixteenth-century ones would be nothing but burlesques.

This word cannot describe the rarest products of humanist culture. We have no term to describe this particular kind of gaiety of spirit in which lyricism becomes satirical, and satire working upon reality so overreaches its object that it destroys it and climbs so high that even poetry can barely reach its heights, while triviality meanwhile is an integral part of taste, and by some inconceivable phenomenon, becomes necessary. These debauches of the intelligence in which the emotions play no role were permitted only during the Renaissance, and Jarry miraculously, was the last of these sublime debauchees.[6]

As well as illuminating the particular nature of Jarry, this passage reveals much of its own author, and his powers as a critic, which were considerable but very individual. In this as in everything he is very much the poet, proceeding by intuition, almost by his senses, sniffing out the particular flavour and scent of a work, holding the weight of it, letting his antennæ grope around it. And always there is this awareness of the past as stretching around and about the present, clothing it. It is in no way an intellectual method, but rather acute beams of perception shining into dark corners; and the judgment of posterity has more than justified his sensibility and fundamental right-headedness. Even at his first meeting with Jarry in 1903, Apollinaire was well aware that some of the characteristics which Jarry embodied might be necessary to a new "humanist culture." His own heroic period of intense innovation from 1912 to 1914 could also well be described as "a debauch of the intelligence."

For the moment this was only a premonition: he had not fully worked out the implications to be drawn from Jarry's work. But he was so dazzled, that for a while he copied slavishly. During 1903 and 1904 he was engaged on a composite work called *Le Jim-Jim-Jim des Capussins*, which apparently was pure Jarry. It was never published and the manuscript has not yet been unearthed, but it almost certainly furnished the material for the beginning of the chapter "Dramaturgie" in *Le Poète assassiné*, and also much of *Les Mamelles de Tirésias*, a play which did not see the light of day until 1917,

[6] "Alfred Jarry," in *Il y a*, 1949, p. 176.

when it was still regarded as a piece of *avant-garde* scandal. As in the Preface Apollinaire used the word "surréel" to describe his Jarry fantasy, it might mistakenly be thought of as contemporaneous with the first manifestations of Dada. Time and time again what seems to be most obviously new in Apollinaire, and what through him most helped younger poets to find their own path, can be traced back to this moment at the turn of the century and to what Apollinaire first saw exemplified in Jarry and shared with him.

In the meantime, in the summer of 1903, Apollinaire was gravid with his brain-child, the new review. He had by now managed to follow his younger brother's example and find a job as a bank clerk, which at least took care of his daily bread. For his nightly mental sustenance there were the endless discussions and plans; where would the review have its headquarters, what would be its title, what its aim, and above all where would the money come from? By October all the problems were solved. The review was to be called *Le Festin d'Esope* because it would "publish works of every description, literature of the imagination and of ideas" and not be the organ of any one school, taking merit as its only criterion. Guillaume Apollinaire was the editor, André Salmon the secretary, and Jean Mollet the business manager, and the offices were to be Salmon's flat in the rue Saint-Jacques. They had hoped to share the office that housed *L'Européen* where their friend Arne Hammer was in charge. Guillaume had already adopted this locale to the extent of returning there from whatever corner of Paris he happened to be in when he wanted to use its comfortable lavatory. But Arne Hammer knowing their *sans-gêne* and lack of any sense of property—they would simply requisition all the copies of other reviews sent to *L'Européen*—refused point-blank. As for the money, nobody ever knew where that came from except that Apollinaire had talked of some mysterious mother's boy. His also was the less successful idea of inventing advertisements to encourage genuine ones. Thus came into being "la Bière Burton" invented by Lord Burton, sincere friend of His Majesty King Edward VII.

At any rate his progeny survived all these labour pains and flourished well. The first number which appeared in

November contained "Que vlo vé?" and a charming poem by Salmon, "Féerie." *La Plume* gave it an avuncular welcome:

> *Le Festin d'Esope* such is the title of a new literary review which first came out in November 1903 and which is edited by our friend Guillaume Apollinaire. And from the pen of Guillaume Apollinaire himself there is a harsh and violent short story *Que vlo vé?* into which he weaves most curiously the Flemish dialects. Our best wishes for its success.

One of the regular features was Apollinaire's "Notes du Mois," a spicy gossip column which ranged over an extraordinary variety of topics, from Isadora Duncan to a "nouveau Transcontinental asiatique." This was a *genre* that he much favoured, and in which with his gourmandising curiosity he excelled, mixing his own characteristic anecdotes with pieces of information that seemed equally fantastic.

It was also one of the most reliable ways in which he managed to earn his living in journalism, particularly in the *Mercure de France* with his "Anecdotiques," which appeared regularly, except for an interval during the War, from 1911 until his death.

He took the opportunity of publishing many of the poems he had so far completed. There was, for instance, a mediocre poem "Passion," inspired by the gaunt crucifixes of the Ardennes moors, and then two little poems later to appear in *Alcools*: "L'Adieu," and "Le Retour," which was changed to "La Dame."

These two last are interesting examples of how Apollinaire could modify and transform his own work. "L'Adieu" had first appeared as part of a long poem entitled "La Clef," (which also furnishes single lines for poems of such late date as "A travers L'Europe 1914") a diffuse, bizarre poem in dialogue form with a Laforguian ring of irony, and certain Surrealist images—"Tant d'yeux sont clos au bord des routes." "L' automne est plein de mains coupées." There it ran:

> J'ai cueilli ce brin de bruyère
> Mets le sur ton coeur pour longtemps
> Il me faut la clef des paupières

> J'ai mis sur mon coeur les bruyères
> Et souviens-toi que je t'attends[7]

In the version of *Le Festin d'Esope* the third line is altered to the more ordinary "Nous ne nous verrons plus sur terre."

In 1912 Apollinaire unearths this little strophe for the review *Vers et prose* and makes two further modifications.

> J'ai cueilli ce brin de bruyère
> L'automne est morte souviens-t'en
> Nous ne nous verrons plus sur terre
> Odeur du temps brin de bruyère
> Et souviens-toi que je t'attends [8]

and this is how it eventually appears in *Alcools*. It is the fourth line "Odeur du temps brin de bruyère" which is the really inspired invention, and which brings the whole little poem together into its particular minor key. It is as if the rest had been waiting there for years in embryo, and now with this one flash of illumination has sprung into the shape for which it seemed always to have been intended.

"Le Retour" goes through a similar metamorphosis. In *Le Festin d'Esope* it appears with only one line changed from "La Clef."

> Toc, toc . . . "Il a fermé sa porte.
> Les lys du jardin sont flétris . . .
> Quel est donc ce mort qu'on emporte?"
> —"Tu viens de toquer à sa porte."
> —"Et je suis veuve, aux pieds meurtris."[9]

---

[7] "I have gathered this sprig of heather
Put it long against your heart
I need the key of eyelids

I have put the heather against my heart
And remember that I am waiting for you"

[8] "I have gathered this sprig of heather
The autumn is dead remember
We shall not see each other again on earth
Perfume of time sprig of heather
And remember that I am waiting for you"

[9] "Toc, toc. . . . 'He has shut his door.
The lilies of the garden are withered. . . .
What is this corpse that they are carrying away'
—'You have just knocked at his door.'
—'And I am widowed, with bruised feet.' "

The change was in the second line and is fairly insignificant
"Et ses yeux pleins de pierreries." But in the final version
of *Alcools*, again there is another "trouvaille" and the few lines
are given a special resonance, indeed are lifted on to a different
level altogether.

> Toc toc Il a fermé sa porte
> Les lys du jardin flétris
> Quel est donc ce mort qu'on emporte
>
> Tu viens de toquer à sa porte
> Et trotte trotte
> Trotte la petite souris[10]

Such a confrontation explains nothing; if anything it
makes even more mysterious the detours and the lightning
flashes of poetic inspiration.

It would appear that already at this stage Apollinaire
was contemplating the publication of a volume of poetry,
for four of the Rhineland poems—"La Synagogue," "Les
Femmes," "Schinderhannes," and "La Lorely"—were announced as part of a volume to be entitled *Le Vent du Rhin*.
The other big event of *Le Festin d'Esope* was the publication of
L'Enchanteur pourrissant in five instalments.

Other regular contributors included Mécislas Golberg,
John Antoine Nau, Ernest Raynaud, Paul Géraldy. Jarry
was represented by a fantasy called "L'Objet Aimé" which,
with its characters who fall down dead and then keep popping
up again, definitely points to *Les Mamelles de Tirésias*. There
was also an enquiry about the state of the modern orchestra
with replies from Ernest Newman, Edward Dent and Romain
Rolland; and a translation of Hebbel's play *Judith*.

In the midst of all the success and excitement that accompanied the birth of *Le Festin d'Esope*, Apollinaire did what
seems superficially to be a very strange thing. One would
have imagined him completely caught up with this very full

---

[10] "Toc toc He has shut his door
   The lilies of the garden are withered
   What is this corpse that they are carrying away

   You have just knocked at his door
     And trot trot
     Trot little mouse"

life in Paris; one would have thought that in the eighteen
months that had passed since he had left Germany, he might
have consoled himself with other girls than Annie, and that the
memory of her would have dimmed. But in fact just the opposite
seemed to have happened. More and more in her absence
had his love crystallised and the possibility of her refusal faded.
Now in November he went off to London with the express
intention of asking her to marry him. It is possible that he
chose just this moment of small triumph because it had given
him the necessary amount of self-confidence to sweep her away
with his overbearing will.

There was also an entirely practical consideration. He
could have hardly afforded the trip if he had had to stay in a
hotel: but in recent months he had been in correspondence
with an Albanian living in London who edited a review called
Albania. Faïk beg Konitza had invited Apollinaire to stay
with him and Apollinaire jumped at this opportunity of com-
bining business with pleasure. Faïk beg Konitza was one of
those weird characters who seemed to crop up in Apollinaire's
path with such frequency that one might even think that he had
the powers of sorcery that he claimed and could magic them
out of his imagination. Certainly his account of his stay [11]
with the Albanian seems to bear little relation to fact, from the
very *entrée en scène* at Victoria Station, when Faïk beg Konitza,
having promised to make himself known by sporting a white
orchid in his buttonhole, Apollinaire perceived a whole platform full of men wearing white orchids in their buttonholes.
When he arrived by taxi at his friend's house in Hampstead,
he found him just leaving to buy his white orchid. The rest
of the account continues on the same note of fantasy to the
accompaniment of strange nasal Albanian folk tunes played by
Faïk beg Konitza on his collection of ancient wooden instru-
ments. He seemed also to have a curious talent for pro-
crastination. His review managed to be several years late,
the numbers for 1901 emerging in 1904; and meals in Oakley
Crescent followed a similar pattern so that Apollinaire never
saw any of the museums or art galleries in London because he
would always arrive just at closing-time.

[11] Note by Michel Décaudin in *Le Poète Assassiné*, 1959, p. 244.

He did, however manage to see Annie: but only after great difficulty. Contrary to his confident expectation, she had been so alarmed at the idea of introducing him to her family that at first she simply refused point-blank to see him. A Catholic, a foreigner and a poet, nothing could have been more unconventional and different for the narrow-minded English *petit-bourgeois* family to accept; and the inference in that circle if she actually brought the young man home would be that he wanted to marry her. However Guillaume was so insistent, that she eventually did so. Immediately he turned on his notorious charm to the full, but the Puritanical Playdens were amongst the few people in the world who were impervious to it. Only the younger sister, Jenny, was wooed over to his side with presents and blandishments. However, mere civility demanded that at least Annie should be let out to show him the sights of London, the Tower and the Houses of Parliament, as long as she was back at an early hour. But Guillaume was left in no doubt that he was not a welcome visitor.

Annie's conduct throughout this whole period appears highly ambivalent. During this first visit she rebuffed him enough to make him go back to Paris feeling that he had been betrayed and in his desperation to write some of the bitterer parts of "La Chanson du Mal-Aimé." On the other hand she left enough hope for him to go back to her the following spring, and the two cards and a letter which have been discovered from her hand all bear witness to her feeling of tenderness for him and to some sort of mutual understanding, as for example this touching little piece of broken French written after the supposed final rupture of the second visit: "Merci pour carte chère Je pense à toi N'oublier pas ton photographie pour moi Mille baiser. Penser à moi. Bonjour à ton mère Annie."[12] It is all rather mysterious, and one can only think that the poor girl was genuinely as much in love as he, but terribly torn between this alien creature and everything else that she had ever known before, home, family, religion, moral scruple. Also, she herself may well have been a little terrified of his obvious strangeness, by the brutality of his eroticism and feared to choose him as a husband—possibly with reason.

[12] Décaudin, p. 100.

At any rate, when he went to London again in May he was even more determined to make her marry him: but her apparent blowing hot and cold during these three weeks at last proved too much for Apollinaire's highly strung temperament and excited him to quite violent extremes, which eventually brought the situation to a totally unexpected conclusion. The Playdens had now reached the stage of actually refusing him entrance. One day when they tried to shut the door in his face he attempted to force his way in. He began to utter threats of physical violence which terrified them all. It was a question now of merely getting rid of the importunate suitor in order to save their skins. And so merely to have some peace and respite, the distracted girl was persuaded by her family to tell him that she had been offered a job as governess in America and would soon be leaving Europe. But when she attempted to break the news to Guillaume she realised that he would never believe it unless it actually were true, and incredible though it may seem, caught up in the effects of her own lie, she then went off to a domestic agency and actually arranged for just such a job straightaway. It is a fantastic story, for she did in fact sail for America a short while after his departure and has stayed there ever since. It is indeed an exemplar of Apollinaire's extraordinary strength of character and single-mindedness, the creative intensity of his will-power, that he could so shape her whole life (nor was she the only woman he so affected): also of this violence of his emotions which at times drove him to something near madness. Annie herself says[13] that she will never forget the look that he gave her when he left from Victoria, an extraordinary look with eyes that had gone thick like velvet. On his return he wrote her a postcard containing nothing but this quotation from Oscar Wilde—in English of course—"For each man kills the thing he loves." She must, poor girl, have been relieved once she was safely on the boat for America. But even then the fear that he had engendered still lived on, for her family steadfastly refused ever afterwards to let him have her address.

Back in Paris, Apollinaire tried to console himself in time-honoured ways, by the febrility of constant company, by drink,

[13] Quoted by Goffin, p. 138.

by other women, "par floppées, par ribambelles."[14] André Salmon has described him as having a special taste for high-class tarts.[15] He would follow a splendid-looking creature in the streets, appear for a while with her in tow, then announce in kingly fashion, "I'm tired of her. I shall repudiate her." From one repudiation to another, he was not for another three years to find anybody who could fill Annie's place.

Of more profound consolation was poetry. At last, now that it was all unquestionably over, the time was ripe, the need imperious, to force the whole mangled mixture of emotion into the shaping mould of art. For him this kind of exorcism was the only possible way to recovery; and, incidentally, to scaling his particular Everest as a poet.

"La Chanson du Mal-Aimé," the composite poem which he finished piecing together after his final return from England in the summer of 1904, is his most popular poem, and with good reason. From the marvellously resonant first line, "Un soir de demi-brume à Londres" which for so many French people has come to hold the very essence of London, two things are obvious: first, that one is in for an exciting narrative—and Apollinaire did in fact think of calling it "Le Roman du Mal-Aimé"—and secondly, that one will be propelled through the course of it by a strong musical beat. "Et je chantais cette romance," runs his little prologue, and it has indeed the merits of a song, enslaving the reader with its rhythm and melody. But popularity apart, it must be judged as a major work. Although it was pieced together out of heteroclite chunks written at different times dating back even to Linda, it has that inevitability of the real work of art, gives the impression of having always existed in exactly this form, as if the artist has merely had to draw aside a veil to reveal it.

The process of composition seems to have been the opposite of what he has been doing until now. Instead of having to trick out undefined or trivial emotions, or to repress complexes that he thinks better buried, in order to produce a finger-nail scratching of a poem, this one has imposed itself upon him. He is not trying to do or to be anything, not seeking to run away

[14] Letter to James Onimus, *Les Lettres Françaises*, 13 Dec. 1951.
[15] André Salmon, *Souvenirs sans fin*, VOL. I, 1955, p. 161.

from anything; he takes no stance as a poet, but simply expresses himself as honestly and directly as he can, clutching at poetic expression as at a lifebuoy in the sea of his otherwise disintegrating personality.

This does not mean that "La Chanson du Mal-Aimé" is an hysterical cry from the entrails. Technically he was canny enough by now to know that when it comes to writing poetry there is a right moment to catch at the balance between emotion and control. He is never submerged, always aware of where he is going. As opposed to the Symbolist poet who takes a simple object and lets it swell into an almost impenetrable forest of symbols, he starts from a maze of violent and complex feelings, of contradictory swiftly-succeeding states of mind, and lights them up into a kinescope of finely interrelated images, which swing vertiginously from the past in myth and history ("le sage Ulysse," "l'époux royal de Sacontale"), to men's future as dead spirits let loose in the universe ("nageurs morts suivrons—nous d'ahan / Ton cours vers d'autres nébuleuses"), from the poet's own immediate unhappy past, to a more distant fulfilled love, and which eventually pin him down in his own person in the present moment.

Many critics have implied that Apollinaire did not make his great leap into modernity until he wrote "Zone" in November 1912. On the contrary, it would seem that here in 1903-04 he is, simply by being most true to himself, already intensely modern. The lack of any fixed centre, dispersal of personality, discontinuity, plasticity, the sum total of self being the total of successive states of mind, these particular fundamental facts of modern man form here the very basis of the poem, in short the whole story of the "mal-aimé." And the method that he uses to tell it is precisely the method which modern poetry was to develop with increasing single-mindedness from 1912 onwards. This is not to say that Apollinaire had invented it— Rimbaud, if anybody, was the real Cortès. although Nerval and Baudelaire and Lautréamont had already embarked on the voyage of discovery—but he swings effortlessly from one little constellation of images to another with no regard for logic or time, hauling himself along on the thread of emotion alone.

More original and equally topical is Apollinaire's own cavalier treatment of time which has appeared more than once before. And the date of this poem is well before the appearance of any of the volumes of *A la Recherche du temps perdu*. The poet is able to project himself at will into past, future, or present: all for him are co-existent, a great source of being. All history contributes to the sum of his present personality: he is the centre of the world, not, like Rimbaud, the "voyant," but a sort of sun, a vivifying force round which the earth turns. It is this conception of the poet's role which drives him to try to achieve "simultaneity" and which justifies his high pitched moments of megalomania, omnipresence, and prophecy.

In the very first strophe, the essential feature of the love affair emerges. Against a Dickensian background, the poet, pushed by his distress to the point of schizophrenia, comes face to face with his Doppelgänger, the self who has loved, and realises that it is a "mauvais garçon" leading him on in spite of himself. Guilt and shame, the note had been struck in a muffled way in previous poems. At his own violent, hectoring jealous nature? At an exasperated eroticism pushed to brutality, even sadism? Or just at a normal physical fulfilment demanded by him against her scruples and religious convictions? This for the moment is to remain a mystery. Whatever the cause, love has turned bad, guilt sets the tone. And the immediate identification with the first of his King figures, the incestuous Pharaoh, unjustly pursuing the Hebrews, bears out this implication. And yet, for every feeling bears its opposite within itself, even so his voice swells out in a hyperbole of pride at the majesty and strength of this unique love:

> Que tombent ces vagues de briques
> Si tu ne fus pas bien aimée
> Je suis le souverain d'Egypte
> Sa soeur-épouse son armée
> Si tu n'es pas l'amour unique[16]

---

[16] "May these brick waves fall
If you were not well loved
I am the sovereign of Egypt
His sister-wife his army
If you are not the unique love"

H

Veering back again into disgust, he sees the mist as bloody, the gas lights are like wounds, the beloved too has disintegrated schizophrenically and her double, reeling through the evil fog, is a drunken whore with a scar on her neck. ("For each man kills the thing he loves.")

With one of his characteristic *volte-faces*, Apollinaire now jumps from all this murk and his own split personality and the false, perjured face of his love, into an illuminated picture of precisely the contrary, of the happy Kings, Ulysses and Doushmanta, with faithful wives who waited years for them.

> J'ai pensé à ces rois heureux
> Lorsque le faux amour et celle
> Dont je suis encore amoureux
> Heurtant leurs ombres infidèles
> Me rendirent si malheureux[17]

This image of himself, or rather the self who has loved, as a shadow split away from him, is to be one of the main *Leit-motiven* of the poem. It is surely more than a mere fascination with chiromancy or an adoption of the Peter Schlemihl theme. Instead it would seem to be a real neurotic symptom, the classic last defence of a personality strained to the utmost by suffering, an attempt to externalise the pain, push this sinister black double out of the self. Later in the heart of the poem Apollinaire returns to it, comes to closer grips with it, nearly becomes one of its victims, "its mad priests." For that way assuredly lies madness. Now at this initial moment he manages to push it away in a loud outcry of distress; "Qu'un ciel d'oubli s'ouvre à mes yeux." May a whole heaven of forgetfulness blot out the hell of my memories. But again just the opposite happens. Instead of amnesia it is the precise detail of her kisses which comes to him: and neatly then Apollinaire the poet knits together his two main images so far: shadow and kings, so as to lead back into a complex web of memory.

[17] "I thought of these happy kings
When the false love and the one
Whom I still love
Jostling their faithless shadows
Made me so unhappy"

Pour son baiser les rois du monde
Seraient morts les pauvres fameux
Pour elles eussent vendu leur ombre[18]

First there is his recent numbed paralysis of feeling, no doubt throughout the last year of her absence, which he evokes by the image of the martyrs of Sebastopol, who as a reward for their mute fidelity were frozen into the ice they lay upon: then he probes further back into the chattering dialogue (again the split), with his obsessive, guilty memory:

Mon beau navire ô ma mémoire
Avons-nous assez navigué
Dans une onde mauvaise à boire
Avons-nous assez divagué
De la belle aube au triste soir[19]

a verse of particular beauty and pathos, possibly because of the recollection of the childish song in "mon beau navire," which emphasises a whole naïve aspect of his suffering— "Surely this can not be happening to *me*." It is here too that Apollinaire's link with the folk-song tradition is evident, in the repetitions and the rhythm of the refrain. He then swings forward again to his present decision to have done with it all: "Celle que j'ai perdue / L'année dernière en Allemagne. Et que je ne reverrai plus." And immediately—again it seems an inevitable effect of his lack of balance—from that decision he is swept right into the heart of a recall of their moments of ecstasy, with one of the ballad-like refrains that are a feature of the poem:

Voie lactée ô soeur lumineuse
Des blancs ruisseaux de Chanaan
Et des corps blancs des amoureuses

---

[18] "For her kiss the kings of the world
Would have died the poor notorious ones
For her would have sold their shadows"

[19] "My pretty ship o my memory
Have we sailed enough
In a sea that is bitter to drink
Have we rambled on enough
From lovely dawn to sad evening"

Nageurs morts suivrons-nous d'ahan
Ton cours vers d'autres nébuleuses[20]

which, with its images of the Milky Way, and the luminosity of
stars, the milk and honey of the Promised Land, evokes the
milky whiteness of her naked body, and a physical experience
of such ecstasy and splendour as might in that moment have
seemed to transcend even death, "vers d'autres nébuleuses."

At this memory of the height of his sexual prowess his mood
is again turned inside out, and a confident, even flippant,
young man sings "à voix virile" the joyful aubade which he
had in fact written the previous spring in Munich, and which
is totally different in tone, a precious, superficial conceit in
which, entirely in command now, he manœuvres the gods to
their sprightly rendezvous, and lets them fall down into
bathos "Les grenouilles humides chantent."

It is fascinating to see with what skill Apollinaire slips
this piece of foreign material into the seams of his story,
stitching it up with his transition from these gods who have
now all died, along with love "Le grand Pan l'amour Jésus-
Christ / Sont bien morts," back to himself, humble, miserable
speck, weeping in a courtyard in Paris. Then, the next leap
into self-assertion is tremendous, with that other refrain which
had also existed previously:

Moi qui sais des lais pour les reines.

But this claim to bestraddle time by means of his poet's gifts—
another of his themes here announced although not yet
developed—is short-lived. Once again he falls back from
the heights into a dead world, he alone alive worshipping
idols: "Je reste fidèle et dolent." The analogy with music
becomes more evident. A theme is announced—fidelity,
then the variation fans out—the reply of the Zaporogue
Cossacks to the Sultan.

But it is yet another example of the double face of each

[20] "Milky Way o luminous sister
Of the white streams of Canaan
And of the white bodies of amorous women
Dead swimmers will we still toil
After your course towards other nebulæ"

of his emotions that the image which now takes up the theme of fidelity is just the opposite of what one would expect, a defiant refusal spat out in sadistic obscenity:

> Poisson pourri de Salonique
> Long collier des sommeils affreux
> D'yeux arrachés à coups de pique
> Ta mère fit un pet foireux
> Et tu naquis de sa colique[21]

Some people regard this as an intrusion into the lovely lyricism of so much of the rest of the poem. But in fact the revelation of his own nastiness and cruel violence is essential to this poem which has a story of personal catharsis to tell. It is one of the stages in his confession, one of the reasons for his burden of shame.

The pendulum continues to swing: the lead weight of violence and revenge now soars upwards again into the ecstatic "Voie lactée " refrain, from out of which, as if ecstasy were its native element, guilt arises. The woman is a whore, but splendid like a panther: falsity and beauty combined. Stars are her eyes, but there too in this trembling flow, with which he repeatedly evokes their excitement, lie damnation and sin:

> Ses regards laissaient une trâine
> D'étoiles dans les soirs tremblants
> Dans ses yeux nageaient les sirènes
> Et nos baisers mordus sanglants
> Faisaient pleurer nos fées marraines[22]

It is as if the poet catches himself in his own trap: whenever he is led back through images of whiteness and stars and the river scene which obviously accompanied their happiness, to a too-precise recalling of their caresses, the

[21] "Rotting fish of Salonica
Long necklace of the ghastly slumbers
Of eyes that have been torn out with a pike
Your mother gave a liverish fart
And you were born of her colic"

[22] "Her glance left a trail
Of stars in the trembling evenings
In her eyes sirens swam
And our kisses biting and bloody
Made our fairy godmothers weep"

tenderness he has been trying to stifle is reborn. He may earlier
have pronounced his farewell: now with all his being he yearns
for her. He has prayed for a heaven of forgetfulness to swallow
him up; now the memory of her is his only support. "Si
jamais revient cette femme / Je lui dirai Je suis content."
But all the contradictory and ambivalent emotions that he has
successively explored amalgamate now into a great flood which
overwhelms him and drags him down into a state near to
madness. In a striking image he conveys this sensation of
total lack of control, when everything in and around him has
become fluid:

> Mon coeur et ma tête se vident
> Tout le ciel s'écoule par eux
> O mes tonneaux des Danaïdes[23]

and cries through it, a child suddenly in his distress, as a
young soldier cries out to his mother in his death agony:

> Comment faire pour être heureux
> Comme un petit enfant candide[24]

Now his mind races on with maniac rapidity flickering with
the white images of his love ("ma colombe, ma blanche rade,"
the "marguerite" which he has "exfoliated"), and which are
always far away beyond his reach. He is as if possessed: evil
spirits trample on his raw nerves. And he slithers down into a
state of complete neurotic uncertainty, surrendering utterly
to the split in his personality. Again in self-defence he is
having to push all the suffering part of his being outside himself,
and he sees it now not merely as a "mauvais garçon," but as
some cruel divinity demanding sacrifice, served by mad priests,
exacting victims. Suffering is one of those false gods whose
death he has celebrated; so too is his own guilt, which links
up with his first theme now in the form of a shadow, his
old serpent, always glued to him, and always tracking him

---

[23] "My heart and my head empty themselves
The whole heavens pour through them
O my sieves of the Danaides"

[24] "What must I do to be happy
Like a little innocent child"

down. This identification of his shadow and the serpent is revealing. The serpent, the tempter, in Apollinaire's imagery often conveys the idea of a guilt-ridden sensuality: in the first version of "Le Larron" for example there was this verse:

> Ceux de ta secte adorent-ils un signe obscène
> Belphégor le soleil le silence ou le chien
> Cette furtive ardeur des serpents qui s'entr'aiment
> Car il est bien d'être obscènes quand on s'aime[25]

And this "shadowy wife," this whole furtive burden of sensuality has been taken out, aired in the sun, had its day. Now he is approaching the real kernel of the affair. Throughout the poem he has been hovering round it, touching lightly, then swerving away from the open wound that he has not yet dared fully to explore, the confession which alone will bring catharsis. In this ante-chamber of madness he approaches the memory of Annie circumspectly again, evoking her nakedness and also the countryside which framed their love in further images of whiteness. "L'hiver est mort tout enneigé / On a brûlé les rûches blanches.... Mort d'immortels argyraspides / La neige aux boucliers d'argent," until he reaches out to the final image which sparks off the whole confession that lies so heavily on his heart:

> Et moi j'ai le coeur aussi gros
> Qu'un cul de dame damascène[26]

a remarkable image which is quintessentially Apollinairian. Critics have talked of it as a use of shock tactics, as though he had particularly used it here to surprise, and make the reader sit up. But often too much is made of the poet's conscious manipulation of an anonymous reader: a writer writes what he can. In this mysterious operation he explores the labyrinth of his own mind as best he may. An image appears: he is

[25] Décaudin, p. 150.
"Do those of your sect adore an obscene sign
Belphegor the sun silence or the dog
That furtive ardour of serpents making love
For it is good to be obscene when one loves"

[26] "As for me my heart is as heavy
As a lady's damascene arse"

lucky and most skilful when he can catch it, and draw it into the light. Here this one of his heart as heavy as the opulent forms of Aphrodite Callipyge swelling through tightly-drawn silk or with the skin like tightly-drawn silk, then pierced and penetrated by the seven swords of sorrow, with its powerful erotic implications, condenses the whole wealth of his desire, in turn tender, crude, flippant (the characteristic defensive pun on "damas" and "damascène"), even sadistic, but in any case totally overwhelming.

It engenders a sort of physical excitement which finally enables him to bring to light the physical stages of the love affair in the episode of the Seven Swords, and so purge himself of them. It is these which have in fact been the real, prime cause for his descent into the ante-chamber of madness.

> Sept épées de mélancolie
> Sans morfil ô claires douleurs
> Sont dans mon coeur et la folie
> Veut raisonner pour mon malheur
> Comment voulez-vous que j'oublie[27]

This precise, erotic interpretation of the apparently hermetic allegory, first put forward by James Lawler,[28] seems to me the only possible one. In fact, contrary to Michel Décaudin,[29] who thinks that Lawler is too precise, I think that he is not precise enough. A large portion of Apollinaire's poetry is purely erotic; and this is not a reference to the schoolboyish, dirty verses he published "sous le manteau," which are to be classed with his pornographic novels, but his love poetry generally, which just cannot help spilling over into what are commonly regarded as details too intimate to be published: at least one considerable volume is and is likely to remain in this case.[30] In fact, for this man whose emotions were

[27] "Seven swords of melancholy
Smooth-edged and bright sorrows
Are in my heart and madness
Wants to argue for my undoing
How do you imagine I can forget"

[28] James Lawler, "Les Sept épées," in *Le Flâneur des deux rives*, 1955, p. 10.
[29] Décaudin, p. 105.
[30] Unpublished poems and letters to Lou.

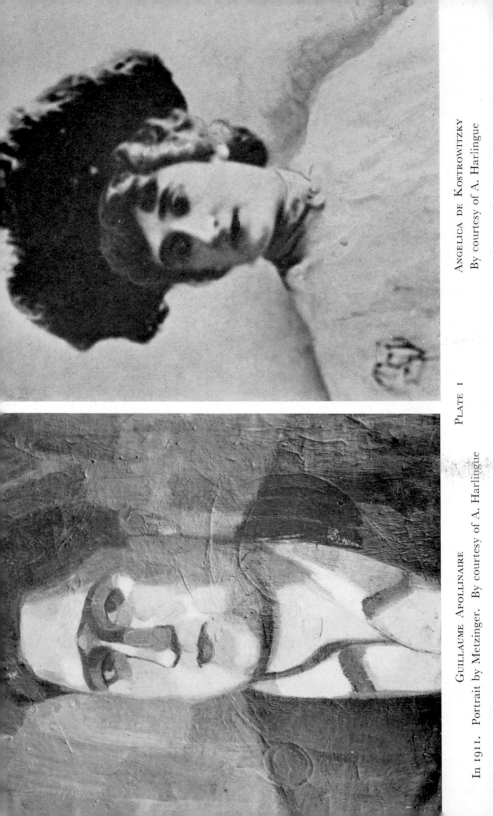

GUILLAUME APOLLINAIRE

In 1911. Portrait by Metzinger. By courtesy of A. Harlingue

ANGELICA DE KOSTROWITZKY

By courtesy of A. Harlingue

PLATE I

Apollinaire et ses amis

PLATE 2   1909. Painting by Marie Laurencin. By courtesy of A. Harlingue

GUILLAUME APOLLINAIRE

In 1912. By courtesy of A. Harlingue

PLATE 3   GUILLAUME APOLLINAIRE

C. 1912. By courtesy of *Paris Match*

Guillaume Apollinaire and André Rouveyre
In 1914. By courtesy of A. Harlingue

Plate 4

passionate, whose senses greedy and exigent, who felt that poetry was the finest manifestation of the life force, and that he was living at his highest peak only when he was loving, eroticism was the most powerful of all the stimuli that impelled him to write poetry, and an awareness of this highly-charged, explosive content is essential to any understanding of his work. But for a man who could be so expansive about these matters when writing fiction, he had a very complex attitude towards revealing his own personal experiences. As was proved abundantly in his confessions about his early life, he was torn between the need to unload his burden of intense emotion and the circumspect suspicion that he must not reveal himself too openly. (This, ironically, he was to do most abundantly in later love poems, but in fact none of these were intended by him for publication as they stood.) Hence the veil of mystery and obscure imagery. He was not naturally a hermetic poet: when he appears to be so, it is because he is up to his trick of confessing something intimate but covering it up in private language. More particularly so when it came to sex, for most people tend to invent their own private language as lovers. Again, the puns, the hidden meanings, the erudite references, the whole game of virtuoso, verbal play, always formed part of his poetic stock in trade. They are akin to the artifices of the medieval poet, the anagram and the "trovar cluz," and show just how much of a craftsman in poetry he felt himself confidently to be. It must also have given him amusement and even release to be able to refer to specific, sexual details with impunity because of the cleverness of his disguise. It might have given him even more to watch our clumsy, partial attempts at unmasking him.

This episode of the Seven Swords is a perfect example. It is the core of the poem, the reliving of the traumatic experience: therefore he has decked it out into an obscure allegory, which we are still having difficulty in interpreting. And naturally and logically the more obscure the passage the more intimate the detail.

Each sword has a name, a fanciful invention of Apollinaire's own, but with undoubted implications. The first has presented few difficulties: Pâline, as Lawler presented it, is a mixture of "pâle" and "câline": it is silvery white and trembling, and obviously represents the girl as a virgin, vowed to a destiny which is both bloody and Ghibeline (anti-religious). The setting, for this was inseparable in Apollinaire's memory from the various stages of the affair, is a wintry, snowy sky, which indeed was the Neu-Glück background for the beginning of their affair.

The second sword has proved more recalcitrant. It is called Noubosse. I would suggest (and in such a case one can do no more) that this is a reference to the female sex. The analogy to "un bel arc-en-ciel joyeux " need not be too remote, and the name could have something to do with Mons Veneris, which would then lead by association of ideas to "Les dieux s'en servent à leurs noces."

The next two lines have seemed really inexplicable:

> Elle a tué trente Bé Rieux
> Et fut donée par Carabosse[31]

The general implication is clear. The final effect of this particular sword is pernicious ("tué" and "Carabosse," the evil fairy). But who are the Bé Rieux and why are there thirty of them? Lawler has suggested that they are simply the Bel-Rieurs, handsome, laughing young men; Décaudin has brought forward the quarrelsome band of medieval knights called the Berruyers. In neither case can this possibly be a reference to any past lovers that Annie, twenty-one, Puritan, and obviously a virgin, might have had. It might however evoke the number of times that they had slept together; more probably even the number of times they had not managed to sleep together because she had repelled his advances and so quenched his ardour—"Bé Rieux": although it does seem rather odd and far-fetched in this case to have kept count. But the specific number of thirty could well have come into Apollinaire's mind through an analogy between this female Judas and the original traitor who sold his master for thirty pieces of silver. (In late imagery, Apollinaire does actually identify himself with Christ.)

---

[31] "It has killed thirty Bé Rieux
And was bequeathed by Carabosse"

The gift of the evil fairy Carabosse is easier to explain. Carabosse decreed that the Princess Aurora should, at the age of sixteen, prick her finger and die. This "evil gift" was then transformed by the good fairy into a hundred years sleep. Apollinaire here could be admitting that Annie's treason has left him as bereft and as dazed as a somnambulist, that she has emotionally put him to sleep. And indeed five years later as he looks back at this period he does characterise it as "a sleep," "a bad dream."[32] In this case his choice of image reveals an accurate premonition of the future and this short stanza is a good example of the way in which he condenses a wealth and subtlety of emotion—past, present, and future—into one very precise evocation.

The third sword is the most difficult of all to decipher:

> La troisième bleu féminin
> N'en est pas moins un chibriape
> Appelé Lul de Faltenin
> Et que porte sur une nappe
> L'Hermès Ernest devenu nain[33]

It has already been established convincingly[34] that Lul de Faltenin was Apollinaire's private name for the penis (phallum tenens). The composite word "chibriape" formed from "chibre" and "priape" has obviously the same meaning, as does Hermès. Lawler accordingly dismisses this as a simple reference, following logically after Noubosse, to the male sex. But why then is this particular priapus "bleu féminin" and why does Apollinaire use the expression "n'en est pas moins"—it is nevertheless, although feminine, a "chibriape"? One explanation could be that it is a reference to what is specifically, if vestigially, male in the female anatomy, and its part in the whole amorous by-play. This, as a prelude, would also

[32] "Et je me suis endormi," in the manuscript of "Les Fiançailles," Décaudin p. 205.

[33] "The third of a feminine blue
Is nevertheless a *chibriape*
Called Lul de Faltenin
Which is borne upon a cloth
By the dwarfed Ernest Hermes"

[34] René Louis, "Encore Lul de Faltenin," in *Le Flâneur des deux rives*, 1955, p. 7.

fit into a chronological sequence, leading to the real, successful consummation with the fifth sword, the unequivocal Sainte Fabeau ("beau phallus").[35]

But even this possible explanation does not clarify the next line "Et que porte sur une nappe." This "chibriape," whatever it may be, is carried on a cloth (like a sacred Grail Lawler suggests, but in the circumstances this would seem to be going a little too far) by a phallus (Hermès) which has been erected (the only possible derivation of "Ernest" seems to be the German "ernst," "serious," "full of ardour"), and is now dwarfed. The manuscript, although also obscure, does help to throw an added light if not on the actual details which are obviously too personal to emerge clearly, at least on the whole emotional complex suggested by the stanza:

> Et que porte sur une nappe
> Devant l'antipapesse un nain[36]

The dwarf is obviously part of the same image, but "antipapesse" introduces a whole aura of anti-religion, of Annie's religion which is anti-Catholic, of pornocracy—the rule of the prostitute, even possibly of black magic. It is redolent with a sense of guilt and evil, of a conflict between sensuality and religious scruple. The conflict may have existed between the two lovers because of Annie's resistance, or within the minds of each one, but in any case it seemed in the early, difficult stages of the affair to end in fiasco.

The fourth sword is different in that it is characterised entirely by details of scenery, of a green, golden river at evening, with women bathing and boatmen singing. It is called Malourène, almost certainly a combination of "malheur" and "reine." The image of river scenery occurs more than once

[35] In an article on "La Tzigane," which has appeared since this went to press, in *Guillaume Apollinaire 1963*, (*Revue des lettres modernes*) Mme Durry suggests that in this affair with Apollinaire, Annie was, and remained, a "demi-vierge." I think that this was undoubtedly true for some long time, and that this is the implication in the third verse. Despite the references to "l'ami aux si douces mains" and "un cyprès sur un tombeau," I am less convinced that she remained so, and still maintain that the fifth and sixth verses celebrate some kind of fulfilment, even if this was only temporary.

[36] "And which is carried on a cloth
By a dwarf before the Antipopess"

in the poem, and each time it seems to evoke a particular
plenitude and fulfilment but always with this same implication
of "malheur" or damnation for the man. (There are also
sirens swimming in the water.) Perhaps this particular episode
which obviously refers to Honnef in the spring, and to a physical
advance in their affair, figures the moment when Apollinaire
found himself really losing his foothold, more in love than he
could cope with, feeling that this was a sort of damnation. There
is too in this verse, I think, an intention of conveying the
tenderness, the specific fluidity, the rocking movement of the
whole act of love. This would be a suitable progression for
here indeed in the fifth sword is the supreme moment, Sainte
Fabeau an unambiguous picture of the triumphant male sex,
and "beau" is echoed again in "la plus belle des quenouilles."
(There is another rhyming echo in this last word which might
also not have been absent from Apollinaire's mind.) It is "un
cyprès sur un tombeau," erect over a recumbent form, and
again is identified with the setting, the garden at Honnef
which was witness each night to the final, flaring climax:
"Et chaque nuit c'est un flambeau."

The sixth, and now there is no need to invent a special
name, is simply "métal de gloire," the successful lover who has
triumphantly proved himself, "l'ami aux si douces mains" at
the moment of his departure at dawn.

Emerging now from the private labyrinth is the seventh
sword, presenting apparently no problem of interpretation:
it is a woman, a rose, significantly no longer a marguerite—
and Apollinaire was to harp on this distinction between the
virginal lily and the rose at length with Madeleine. But the
rose is dead. And here in fact seems to be the whole key
to this extraordinary complex of emotion, the explanation of
this sense of guilt which has been weighing on him abnormally.
In some way Apollinaire seems to have felt that he had actually
killed the thing he loved, not merely symbolically by seducing
a virgin, or awakening her senses sinfully, although Annie's
conscience may have presented it in this light, but also, by his
own impossible behaviour, his jealousy, scenes, and over
exigent demands, actually killing love. Possibly he had even
had moments of actually intending to kill her. It is this, not

merely his own sexuality, which has induced the whole involved sense of guilt, this that he has needed in his roundabout
way to confess. Now having done so, he makes a characteristic
ironical pirouette, and lets the door be closed on his love.

> Merci que le dernier venu
> Sur mon amour ferme la porte
> Je ne vous ai jamais connue[37]

After thus reliving the whole experience in the space of
time from white winter to the season of dead roses, he has
freed himself enough, regained enough balance to see his individual plight against the backcloth of the destiny of the whole
human race. The "voie lactée" refrain, summing up once
and for all the essence of the affair swings him now with its
"d'autres nébuleuses" into a sort of cosmic dance, senseless
and led only by hazard.

> Les démons du hazard selon
> Le chant du firmament nous mènent
> A sons perdus leurs violons
> Font danser notre race humaine
> Sur la descente à reculons[38]

The tone has settled down to quieter resignation. With a
consummate ease which is a fine proof of his masterful technique,
he now gathers up the threads of all his past themes—except
that of the shadow which has been successfully exorcised by the
episode of the Seven Swords—restating them together in a
balanced, harmonious finale. This contemplation of the whole
human race has led him back to his kingly figures, standing
out in the wastes of history, but now they are contrasted with
him, not because they are happy and have faithful wives, but
because they have succumbed to the madness and eventual
suicide which he has just, but so nearly, surmounted. They too

[37] "Thank goodness that the latest comer
Shuts the door on my love
I have never known you"

[38] "The demons of chance lead us
According to the song of the firmament
With vanished notes their violins
Make the human race dance
Backwards down the slope"

have "ces grelottantes étoiles de fausses femmes" in their
beds, and here he draws together all the images that have
throughout the poem symbolised his love—whiteness, swan,
siren, star, trembling movement, "vacillent les lucioles,"
"des vents qui tremblent," and the green and gold river scenery
it was set in—a lake, and "baracols chantants," a ruined castle.

In another transition of acrobatic ease, the body of the mad
King Louis of Bavaria floats to the shore, its unseeing eyes
fixed on "le ciel changeant." Like a film shot this then pans
back through the changing sky to another part of it, which
burns in summer heat above Paris. And now the architecture
of the poem is being completed. "La Chanson du Mal-Aimé"
began with a city scene, alien London in autumn fog. It ends
with the other city to which he has come home, "mon beau
Paris" in the height of the summer: and the introduction of a
new image, the sun, strikes the note which eventually will
round off the whole story. "Juin ton soleil ardente lyre brûle
mes doigts endoloris." The sun here is his poet's lyre. Martyred
he may be, alone and lost, but still he is a poet. In three
lapidary verses he then condenses a whole evocation of anguish
set in a modern city. From the Laforguian:

> Les dimanches s'y éternisent
> Et les orgues de Barbarie
> Y sanglotent dans les cours grises[39]

he goes out into the noisy, drunken, flashing night.

> Soirs de Paris ivres du gin
> Flambant de l'électricité
> Les tramways feux verts sur l'échine
> Musiquent au long des portées
> De rails leur folie des machines[40]

---

[39] "Sundays last for ever there
And there the Barbary organs
Sob in the grey courtyards"

[40] "Paris evenings drunk
With the burning gin of electricity
The trams green lights upon their spines
Musicate throughout the trolleys
Their machine madness"

The tramways are alive like monsters ("l'échine"), the noise they make ("musiquent") is a strange neologism of music, they are a mad parody of man. The final image which draws the veil over the city is surprising: peripheral, grotesque, inconsequential, it nevertheless represents the last wave of regret and nostalgia petering out:

> Les cafés gonflés de fumée
> Crient tout l'amour de leurs tziganes
> De tous leurs siphons enrhumés
> De leurs garçons vêtus d'un pagne
> Vers toi toi que j'ai tant aimée[41]

The café is swollen with smoke, as his own heart has been swollen with love. And then, as if he were choosing to end not with a bang but a sneeze, it fizzes out like a soda siphon with a cold in the head. This again is Apollinaire at his most characteristic and his most modern at the same time. "Leurs siphons enrhumés" is pure surrealism.

But this offbeat cacophony is not the last word: there are more tricks still in the hat, yet one last *volte-face*. The "ardente lyre" has not been forgotten, source of all his strength, and the last chord of all swells out in the major affirmation of the "Moi qui sais des lais pour les reines" refrain. The poet, even if he is unlucky in love, can outsing the sirens.

[41] "The cafés swollen with smoke
Cry out all the love of their gipsy fiddlers
Of their sneezing soda siphons
Of their waiters dressed in loin cloths
Towards you you whom I have loved so much"

VI

Montmartre and Le Bateau Lavoir

AT this stage in his life, Apollinaire's behaviour would seem to exemplify the split in personality that he makes much of in "La Chanson du Mal-Aimé." He may have been driven to distraction by Annie; his friends, however, found him the merriest and most riotous of companions. Despite his private disarray, he was beginning to feel that he was known and appreciated as a writer. The *Festin d'Esope* managed to live for ten months, quite a long span for a small review. He was accepted by older established figures like Moréas and Remy de Gourmont. He was admired and looked up to by his contemporaries. He had managed to acquire various outlets for his journalism: *La Démocratie sociale*, *l'Oeuvre*, *Le Soleil*, *Messidor* and the faithful *Européen*, where he turned his pen to all manner of subjects, and if the subjects were lacking simply invented them, as was the case with an article announcing the conversion of the Kaiser to Catholicism, which was fortunately censored in the bud. He had even scaled the august heights of the *Mercure de France* with an article on Anatole France's *Thaïs*,[1] a subject which had undoubtedly influenced him in "L'Ermite" and "L'Hérésiarque."

Once again he was in difficulties about a regular job. The bank where he had been working had gone bankrupt: but one of its employees had had the bright notion of starting a sort of financial journal offering advice to investors. Naturally enough it was Apollinaire who became editor of the *Guide du rentier*: on the analogy of the article on the Kaiser it seems rather surprising that he escaped being sued by hordes of misguided *rentiers*, but at any rate he was adaptable enough to make his advice sound good, and as there seems to be a strong element of fantasy and myth in the whole business anyway, his extra drop in the ocean of speculation passed unnoticed.

---

[1] *Mercure de France*, Jul. 1904.

Perhaps the most important fact of all in his life at this time was the widening of his circle of friends, and the encounters that he made in this year 1904 were to have a most profound effect on the course of his life. In January Mme de Kostrowitzky had moved from the Saint-Lazare district out to the more salubrious suburb of Le Vésinet, where she set up house again with Jules Weil. Guillaume and Albert were both dependent enough on her financially to go too, although she complained that Guillaume went home only to sleep, eat, and have his clothes washed. At any rate it was there on the banks of the Seine at Chatou, in the cafés that Maupassant had made famous that Apollinaire met Derain and Vlaminck and their coterie. Soon, as usual, he was one of the hilarious, leading figures, appearing in a rather strange boating costume, and getting up to all manner of pranks in a canoe, a ribald Pantagruel capable of overturning tables at the Sunday riverside banquets. He was known as the leader of "la bande à Guillaume," "Guillaume's gang." As Willy the wit christened him, "un vrai bouc-en-train."

This was his first acquaintance with the world of painters: and at this moment it was already beginning to be undermined by revolutionary, new theories. Apollinaire, who was always loyal to his friends, continued throughout his life to maintain that Derain was not only, with Matisse, the originator of the Fauves, but with Picasso the father of Cubism. In an article written in 1912 and intended to sum up the whole involved history of Cubism, he situates the real beginning of the new movement in art with the encounter in the autumn of 1902 between Vlaminck and Derain and their mutual interest in negro art.

> Maurice de Vlaminck's taste for primitive, negro sculpture, and André Derain's meditations on these bizarre objects, at an epoch when the Impressionists had at last delivered painting from academic chains, were to have a great influence on the destiny of French art. . . . That same year [1905] André Derain met Henri Matisse and out of this meeting was born the famous school of the Fauves, to which a great number of young artists destined to become Cubists belonged.
>
> I note this encounter because it is useful to clarify the role

of André Derain, an artist originating from Picardy, in the evolution of French art.

The following year he became friendly with Picasso and this friendship had for its immediate effect the birth of Cubism.[2]

However much Derain may first have opened Apollinaire's eyes to what was afoot in the world of plastic arts, the really momentous meeting was with Picasso. This was arranged by Mollet, who deserves to be remembered if only for this one deed. He took Picasso into one of the bars near Saint-Lazare that Apollinaire used to frequent on his way out to Le Vésinet. There sat Apollinaire, majestic, enthroned between two negresses with cartwheel hats and a red-haired English jockey, holding forth in affable discourse about the various merits of German and English beer. Without pausing he winked at Picasso. It would be tempting to follow Apollinaire's example in tracking down moments of conception and to say that in that wink modern poetry was born. The meeting was like that of two crowned heads on a latter-day Field of Cloth of Gold. Both the young men, neither more than twenty-four, were profoundly conscious of their own importance. Both had precociously and brilliantly served their technical apprentice-ships, both knew that this was the moment when art must turn up a new path, without yet knowing precisely which one, both had assumed the mantle of sovereignty in their respective fields. Their friendship represented the junction of the two main branches of the *avant-garde*, Apollinaire's clan from the left bank, and the Montmartre crowd headed by Picasso and Max Jacob (who had almost immediately been dragged along to meet Apollinaire and who was seduced instantly, this time in the middle of a speech about Nero, as Picasso had been), and eventually including Derain, Vlaminck, Braque, Mac Orlan, Carco, Modigliani, and the sculptor Manolo. They were to become one of the most formidable artistic coteries ever to have existed, formidable and unique because of the close mixing of the two elements, the pictorial arts and litera-ture. Rarely in the whole history of art have the most gifted poets and artists of the day been so closely united, or influenced

[2] "Les Commencements du cubisme," *Le Temps*, 14 Oct. 1912.

each other so mutually and so fruitfully. It was a very particular moment in the history of art, and they were a very particular group, without whom we would not be seeing or feeling or expressing ourselves in quite the same way as we do to-day. Whether one regards the era they ushered in as a new Renaissance or the prelude to a new artistic Dark Age, it has certainly been a revolution and they alone have been responsible for it.

They were all in their varying ways extremely clever, gifted young men, one or two were even geniuses. And what is more, they knew it. "You've heard of La Fontaine and Molière and Racine," said Max Jacob, "well now that's us." He might have been nearer to the mark if he had invoked Raphael and Cézanne, for in this revolution the pictorial arts led and are still leading the way, but by and large time has proved him right. It was in fact a gathering of the *élite* such as any generation might dream of.

The real story, of course, is what went on behind the closed doors of studio and attic. The people who talked most and made most noise about the new theories were, inevitably, the hangers-on. "Défense de parler au pilote," said Picasso one day, irritated by words, when what mattered was his own solitary, obstinate work, his coming to grips with purely plastic problems which could be solved only by more and more audacious and intensive plastic experiments. The theorising came later. At that moment in 1904-05 he had still to work through what Apollinaire called his "mystic harlequins" of the Rose Period, stacking up his huge canvases and scattering the floor with drawings in the strange wooden shack in the rue Ravignan which was known as Le Bateau Lavoir and which soon became as it were the head office of the whole *avant-garde*.

Much has been written about the days of the Bateau Lavoir, all no doubt slightly coloured by a nostalgia for a period which did not know world wars, and by a romantic tendency to turn these essentially serious young men into a crowd of layabouts raging up and down the streets of Montmartre, letting off revolvers, roaring imprecations and eventually tumbling down the Butte in drunken stupor. Apollinaire apparently once stumbled into a dustbin and rolled down a staircase in it as if it were a bob-sleigh. They had, it is true, enormous high spirits and obviously, like most exceptional people, a great deal of energy. Most of them had to do a normal hard day's work—Apollinaire had found another job in a bank, Max Jacob worked in a department store, Salmon was a journalist. They still could talk and joke and discuss their theories all night long, and also produce their own original, creative work.

They certainly had another mentality from their counterparts to-day. They were not in any way commercially-minded. There was just no question of their ambition envisaging large sums of money. Enough, indeed more than enough, if they could eat, drink and keep warm. Poverty was their native element: whether they liked it or not, they did not bother to waste their time questioning it. If they were not exactly content to live in squalour, to have no possessions, to have to steal the flowers for their vases from the cemetery, they accepted it as the normal way of life. Apollinaire, for instance, with his rather fastidious tastes about cleanliness and comfort and his mother in the background feeding him up or washing his linen, was always laughed at as being rather *bourgeois*. Having seen Verlaine die in the extremes of poverty and watching Jarry and Moréas go the same way, they simply brushed aside the dangers of malnutrition and alcoholism.

Their disinterest in material things, their total absorption in art seems in some ways most admirable. On the other hand they were extremely ambitious. They knew their own worth and aimed for another kind of reward—La Fontaine, Molière, Racine. They were exclusive, completely inward-turned and without a thought for what was happening outside their own close confines. Politics, a social sense, interest in world affairs, these things were quite foreign to them. The War, of course, was going to change all that. They also, being so tightly knit, engendered a special kind of spite and malice, that particularly devastating French wit which spares nothing and nobody. Apollinaire, with his rather florid Italianate behaviour and his naïve pomposity, came in for his fair share of it. When they gathered in the Montmartre cafés at night and the poets among them began to declaim their verses, he was always greeted by the outcry "Still too Symbolist," a criticism which he took very much to heart. Max Jacob in particular could be really waspish. Not only was there the great joke and song about "la mère d'Apollinaire," but they used also to make fun of his mannerisms. One of these was his habit of signing his letters "Ma main amie Guillaume Apollinaire." Soon everybody began to sign their letters in this way, for instance Max Jacob would write "La main amie de Guillaume Apollinaire, Max Jacob." Other variations developed. "Snowglove, la main sanglante de Guillaume Apollinaire" became Max Jacob's visiting card. Then, as they were all avid fans of the great thriller writer of the day, Fantomas, signs of a bleeding hand were soon being painted over the walls of Montmartre, enough to make poor Utrillo have one of his attacks of *delirium tremens*.

Not only did they have their private jokes, they also had a language of their own, rather like Jarry's Ubu talk with a special tone of voice and burlesque emphasis. Max Jacob was a great raconteur and mimic. Toussaint-Luca recalls[3] a particular evening which began at the Closerie des Lilas and ended up in the small hours in some quayside bistro where Apollinaire declared that the *patron* had just murdered his wife, and insisted on waking him up to tell him so. Max Jacob rounded off the occasion by taking up a broomstick in the deserted dawn and exchanging with it the "Rodrigue as-tu du coeur?" speech from *Le Cid*.

But despite the malice and the gossip and the intrigue which were inevitable in such a confined and clever circle, they generated a particular feeling of solidarity. They were a group and if necessary they would defend themselves and each other against the rest of the world. Apollinaire, in particular, was remarkable for his loyalty and the way in which he seized every occasion to push his friends. Obviously this solidarity gave them a very valuable sense of security which would seem to be an important factor in their development. It gave them a whole background of confidence, a spring-board which made possible the leap forward into the totally new. Talents working in isolation could never have

[3] Toussaint-Luca, p. 46.

inaugurated such a revolution as theirs; and one of the striking facts about the invention and growth of Cubism was the working together of such formidable founding fathers as Picasso and Derain, and Picasso and Braque, which latter combination had the well-known effect of making their works of a certain period appear interchangeable.

Their influence on Apollinaire in this way was considerable. Inevitably a man of his mercurial temperament could never be pinned down to one group, and this trait was to prove an essential in his zig-zag progress through life. At the same time that he was letting off his high spirits in Montmartre, he warily saw to it that he kept in with the Closerie des Lilas writers and the older generation. Nevertheless he was definitely one of the younger group: despite the jokes at his expense they were all in their way very fond of him. He would arrive always late, always in a hurry, with his pockets stuffed with reviews and his usual load of anecdotes and stories and fantastic theories which Max Jacob usually managed to cap. They would talk for hours about astrology and sorcery and palmistry and how the universe is like an onion with its innumerable layers. Apollinaire's great belly laugh, his huge appetite, his inexhaustible fantasy, his way of seizing on an idea and stretching it to absurdity made him very popular. But he in his turn was probably more bowled over by their company and their scintillating talk of new theories than he ever openly admitted.

Most particularly was he affected by Picasso. Indeed Picasso, more by the size and force of his genius than by his ideas which he may not ever have elaborated at length with Apollinaire, their nature being primarily of a plastic order, was the greatest single influence in his life. Apollinaire made no secret of it. From 1905 onwards he never ceased to extol Picasso in his articles, and this in fact was the real beginning of his career as an art critic. *Le Festin d'Esope* had died a natural death in the summer of 1904, and Apollinaire could not rest until he had created a successor. The main requisite was of course to find a backer, but as he seemed to have the gift of seducing men with money into parting with some of it for these purposes, he soon found a certain Henri Delormel

who helped him to start *La Revue immoraliste*, a brave new title
which unfortunately hardly lived up to its name. The second
number became *Les Lettres modernes*, and then apparently everybody lost interest or else no more money was forthcoming,
and Apollinaire's second review had had its day. *La Revue
immoraliste* contained, as well as poems by Max Jacob and
André Salmon, Apollinaire's first article on Picasso, an un-
ambitious entry into the field of art criticism with a description
of the painter's subjects.

> People have said of Picasso that his works show a precocious
> disillusionment.
> I think the contrary.
> Everything fascinates him and his incontestable talent seems
> to me to serve a fantasy which mingles the delicious and the
> horrible, the abject and the delicate.

The following month he produced another longer article
on Picasso for *La Plume*. This reveals more clearly his way of
apprehending a work of art. It is, and was to remain, purely
intuitive, the poet's seizure of the initial artistic experience,
and his translation of it into his own terms. There is no question of any concern with the painter's actual technique. As an
artist himself he simply recognises the quality of another
artist's vision and imagination. "Picasso peintre," the *La
Plume* article, is, if not a poem, at least a piece of lyrical prose
inspired by Picasso. This, is for example, his rendering of the
Blue Period:

> If we had the right knowledge all the gods would awaken.
> Conceived out of humanity's profound self-knowledge, the
> pantheisms that it once lovingly created in its own image fell
> asleep. But, although the immortals slumber, there are eyes
> which reflect human versions of their joyous, divine ghosts.
> These eyes are as attentive as flowers which always yearn
> to contemplate the sun. O fecund joy, there are men who see
> the world through eyes like these.
> Picasso has scanned the human images which were floating
> in the azure of our memories, and which, because of their
> kinship with divinity, give birth to metaphysicians. How
> pious are his skies astir with the soaring of wings, how heavy
> his lighting as if it shone in a low grotto. . . . For the space of

a year Picasso lived through this moist painting as blue as the humid depths of the abyss, and filled with compassion.[4]

Even more revealing is the intrusion of L'Oiseau du Benin (Picasso) into Croniamental, the poet's, life in *Le Poète assassiné*. According to a note in Michel Décaudin's edition, the passage describing it was probably written in 1907 although in the definitive edition, it begins thus: In the first days of the year 1911 a badly-dressed young man ran up the rue Houdon." What is mainly interesting though is his linking of his own creative faculties with his encounter with Picasso, as though in some ways his friend had stimulated their working. As he runs up the Montmartre street

> His extremely mobile face seemed to flit from joy to anxiety. His eyes devoured everything they saw and when his eyelids came together rapidly like jaws, they swallowed up the universe which he was busy renewing ceaselessly. As he ran he imagined in minutest detail the enormous worlds on which he battened. . . . His mouth and his eyes expressed cunning and walking slowly now, he took refuge in his memory and went ahead, whilst all the forces of his destiny and his conscience pushed time aside so as to reveal the truth of what is, what was, and what shall be.

This would seem to be a very accurate presentation of what he considered was the ideal form of poetic creation transcending time.

He then knocks at his friend's door.

> And behind the door the heavy footsteps of a man, who was either weary or carrying a heavy burden, approached slowly, and when the door opened, in the sudden light came the creation of two beings and their immediate union.
>
> In the studio, which was like a stable, an innumerable herd of sleeping pictures lay scattered around, and their shepherd smiled at his friend.
>
> . . . and pushing open the badly closed door, the wind let in strange beings who moaned with little cries in the name of all sorrows. All the wolves of distress then began to howl behind the door, ready to devour the herd, the shepherd and his friend,

[4] *La Plume*, 15 May 1905.

in order to set up in their place the foundations of the New City. But in the studio there were joys of every colour.[5]

Through this visionary prose comes very strongly the feeling of warmth and friendship and fellowship in art over and against a hostile world, which was so vital to a young man like Apollinaire, who always needed affection and love and who had just had it refused him by Annie. But if Picasso did spark off Apollinaire's own creative powers, it was not immediately. For the first three years of this Montmartre period from 1904, after the splendid flowering of "La Chanson du Mal-Aimé" and "L'Emigrant de Landor Road," until late 1907 Apollinaire wrote nothing of moment. Within the gilded framework of nightly sprees and youthful high spirits, lies the depressing image of poetic sterility. The sum total of his work seems to have been the disastrous poem "Palais," which was said to have been influenced by Max Jacob, "Salomé," possibly inspired by Picasso and interesting because of its jumbling of the time sequence and its use of one of those old nonsense refrains that he had noted in "L'Obituaire," and two pornographic works. Admittedly both Picasso and Blaise Cendrars have declared that one of these, *Les Onze mille verges*, was his masterpiece, but Picasso is the man who once said to a journalist: "Negro art? Never heard of it." Even Apollinaire's journalism descended in early 1907 to a rather low level when he joined the scurrilous rag *Je dis tout*. As Moréas declared when the newsvendor shouted its title. "Well you shouldn't."

This sterile period, which in his short life span represents noticeably the biggest trough of all, has until fairly recently, gone uncommented. It has generally been accepted that he was just too busy working in his banking office and writing his pornography. But the time factor never prevented Apollinaire from writing poetry. There were obviously more serious, deep-seated reasons for his silence.

It is with the revelation of the manuscript copies of the big 1908 poems "Le Brasier" and "Les Fiançailles," written when he was safely over the crisis, that something like a complete picture begins to emerge. Michel Décaudin[6] has also

[5] *Le Poète assassiné*, 1959, p. 44.
[6] Décaudin, p. 230.

recently pointed out an interesting reply of Apollinaire's to a questionnaire circulated amongst young writers by *La Revue littéraire de Paris et de Champagne*. He was asked for a "composition significative" and in answer wrote, "I have no significant work and I regret it."

Once he has emerged from the period of silence it is obvious that he looks back on it as a bad dream. Now, what had triggered off the nightmarish sense of desolation and loss and disgust had obviously been Annie's refusal. The first poem really to sound this particular keynote, to knot together images which he uses persistently in 1907 and 1908 to evoke his recent past, is "L'Emigrant de Landor Road," a poem written at about the same time as "La Chanson," although because he externalises his own suffering into that of another character, it does seem to be further removed from the keen misery of the event. Landor Road was Annie's address in Clapham, and the poet fuses her emigration and his own sense of loss in the actual departure of the emigrant. Annie's decision to leave, a piece of news which must have been like the announcement of the end of the world to him, forces its way into the poem, but transformed into the apparently innocuous remark of the emigrant:

> Mon bateau partira demain pour l'Amérique
> Et je ne reviendrai jamais

The poem oscillates less extremely than "La Chanson." Its two poles are the sick autumn scene of the wet quayside, the nauseating sea, shadows crawling about with a slightly obscene movement that is a travesty of love, the shifting, faceless crowd, and at the other extreme an intermittent hope. This hope flickers up in white hands reaching to the sky like birds, and also in the emigrants' vision of a new land significantly linked with poetry, "les prairies lyriques." It is finally summed up when the emigrant looks out to a cruel sea, and craves for "un tout petit bouquet comme la gloire" to cover everything with an immense flowering. Instead the old, obsessive memories go round and round in his head, weaving an endless tapestry; and to put a stop to the incessant nagging, "il se maria comme un doge aux cris d'une sirène moderne sans époux."

It is a truism that a poet's favourite images reveal more clearly than anything else his most deep-seated preoccupations. The sad autumn port, the sea, the shadowy crowd, a repulsive but seductive siren all occur again and again as integral parts of the bad dream, and always in opposition to the sky, birds, light, flowers which are obviously symbols of the poet and his glory. In some way the nightmare has blotted out ambition.

The conflict between the two forms the subject of the strange poem "Lul de Faltenin" which was published at the end of 1907, and which is the first sign in poetry of his emergence. Like the Seven Swords, "Lul de Faltenin" has given the critics much trouble, and apparently for the same reason. It too is mainly erotic. Neither the title, nor the images ("vos terribles bouches muettes," "une grotte avide," "les degrés sont glissants," "J'aime votre pelage" are only some), leave one in any doubt about Apollinaire's intention. It also, on the analogy of Mallarmé's *A la nue accablante tu* (and it was just at this moment that Apollinaire began his collaboration with *La Phalange* a review with strong neo-Mallarmean tendencies), weaves in a parallel and alternate picture of a sunset over the sea. But there is about the whole poem too great a tension, too heavily charged a condensation of imagery for it to be merely a *tour de force* showing how the poet can fuse a Turner landscape with an evocation of the sex act. When Apollinaire is just playing, there is a looseness, a prolixity in his verbal conceits which is the exact opposite of "Lul de Faltenin." It would seem to demand some further explanation.

All the images he uses here are chosen from amongst those potent ones which he evokes again and again in his peotry. In fact his range of imagery was fairly limited, but each one contains within itself a wealth of conflicting, even polar implications—the sea, cruel and blandishing, source of life and yet cause of men's deaths, the sirens, seductive and yet dangerous, fire, light, stars, the blinding consuming glory of the ideal. Now "Lul de Faltenin" represents the conflict that the young swimmer (Odysseus) experiences when he is attracted on the one hand by the sirens, and on the other by poetry and glory. Everything about the sirens is repulsive, they put out their tongues, their breath is fetid, their eyes are "étoiles bestiales" (their attraction is a base simulacrum of the real stars), they are terrible, and avid. His own approach to them is a crawling degradation, a failure to achieve the distant wonder which is so much more worth-while. He tries to protect himself, cries out, blood flows from him, and he admits "le meurtre de mon double orgueil." In the manuscript copy this line was more specifically "l'assassinat de la veille." And yet in some way he feels compassion, even tenderness for them, "Leurs yeux étoiles bestiales / Eclairent ma compassion." When he finally gives in abjectly and descends into their grotto, it appears like an act of self-immolation, "Puisque je flambe atrocement," but afterwards he resigns himself to renouncing the far-away, oblong stars.

Without question, the stars and the distant marvel and the fire represent his poetic ambitions, and the sirens women. But why the extreme conflict, the resistance and sense of abdication when he gives in to them, he who of all poets found love such a stimulus to his muse? He must have been aware, for instance, of the quality of "La Chanson du Mal-Aimé." But could they not instead represent the "grandes grues," that André Salmon talks about, and with whom he sought consolation after the separation from Annie? Their professional patience is even noted, "Dans l'attentive et bien— apprise / J'ai vu feuilloler nos forêts." Now for all his apparent ribaldry and braggadoccio, Apollinaire was at heart fastidious. With prostitutes he definitely felt that he was humiliating himself ("J'humilie maintenant à une pauvre fille au rire horrible ma bouche" he wrote in "Zone"), even though he also pitied them ("J'ai une pitié immense pour les coutures de son ventre"), which is exactly the same combination of feeling as that of "Lul de Faltenin." His own real taste was for the intelligent, well-brought-up, young girl, preferably a virgin, "une femme ayant sa raison."[7]

This would explain the "murder of his pride" as a man, and perhaps generally not enough is ever admitted about the prostitution of men in such circumstances. But Apollinaire's pride is "double." In some way it is connected also with his pride as a poet: and this is impossible to explain logically.

[7] "Le Chat," in *Le Bestiaire ou cortège d'Orphée, Oeuvres poétiques*, 1956, p. 8.

It can only be that the period when he had been drained of emotion into apathy and disgust by the affair with Annie, when he was on the loose in Paris without a specific mistress whom he could love, but dragging himself in the mud of casual encounters, coincided with the moment when he felt that he had been abandoned by his inspiration as a poet; and that he himself blamed first Annie and then the faceless, nameless, other women for his sterility, or at least chose to use them as symbols for this whole episode of the bad dream. It must be a certain comfort to find some scapegoat in one's imagination when faced by the terrifying prospect of creative aridity.

It is only after the crisis is over that he does admit that there was another and more profound cause for it, and that only in manuscript. The first copies of the two big poems[8] of 1908 "Le Brasier" and "Les Fiançailles" reveal the basic reason for his "torment of silence."

> Je n'ai plus même pitié de moi
> Et ne puis exprimer mon tourment de silence[9]

He burns between two nebulæ: that is to say the fire, the creative power is still there, but he cannot release it and so is being consumed by it.

"Qu'ai-je fait," he asks "aux bêtes théologales de l'intelligence?" The whole range of his past subject matter furnished by "intelligence," that is, history, myth, erudition, has deserted him, and with it his extraordinary creative power of making the past live:

> Jadis les morts sont revenus pour m'adorer
> Car ma vie avait le pouvoir de faire renaître l'univers[10]

Then in self-pity he swings to the bad dream, an evocation of the "soirs de Paris ivres du gin." These are the corpses of his days ending up in vomit in the taverns. Suddenly,

---

[8] Décaudin, pp. 173 and 201.

[9] "I no longer have any pity for myself
And I cannot express my torment of silence"

[10] "Formerly the dead came back to adore me
For my life had the power to resurrect the universe"

without warning, comes the essential confession, the real crux of the matter.

> Pardonnez-moi d'avoir reconquis l'ignorance
> Pardonnez-moi de ne plus connaître l'ancien jeu des vers
> . . . J'ai fait des poèmes selon des règles que j'ai oubliées[11]

Here is the admission that the old kind of poetry according to the rules is no longer enough. The cries of "Still too Symbolist" have gone right to the target. The brilliant young man, big fish in the aquarium of Monte Carlo is wondering whether he is not really quite small fry, compared with the towering dynamism of Picasso, the devastating cleverness of Max Jacob, the far-flung originality of Jarry, the charming facility of Salmon. His friends are no longer ready to gape at him in admiration like Toussaint-Luca or James Onimus; now from the heights of their own achievements they are only too ready to ask what he has contributed that is new, world-shaking. And the techniques that he has spent so long mastering must be cast aside. "Mes amis ne craignez pas de m'avouer votre mépris." The fear of his friends' contempt was a very real one. While he was writing nothing, Picasso was already well on the way to *Les Demoiselles d'Avignon*.

Yet he attempts to justify himself. He also has had grandiose ambitions, too grandiose for his powers of expression:

> J'ai rêvé des poèmes si grandioses que j'ai dû les laisser
>   inachevés
> Moi-même j'ai tenté de rythmer
> Parce que mon souci de perfection
> Dépassait mon goût même et les forces d'un seul homme[12]

---

[11] "Forgive me for having regained my ignorance
Forgive me for no longer knowing the old game of versifying

. . . I have made poems according to rules that I have forgotten"

[12] "I dreamed of poems so grandiose that I had to leave them unfinished
I myself tried to put them into rhyme
Because my concern for perfection
Exceeded even my inclination and the strength of one man alone"

And so he simply went to sleep, "Et je me suis endormi." He then spells out in so many letters the cause for his particular dark night of the soul:

> Puis après la fuite et la mort de mes vérités poétiques
> Je m'éveillai au bout de cinq ans.

Much has been written about Apollinaire's "change of front," his apparent switch from tradition to the *avant-garde* in 1912. But the real turnabout in fact took place in his mind during this period of crisis between 1904-07. It was then that against his will he was bludgeoned into a realisation that he would have to refashion entirely his "poetic truths." From now on his poetry was going to be a series of attempts to find new ones; it just happened that those of 1912-14 were more radical than any of the others.

When first he wakes up he is aware only of the same atmosphere of the bad dream—the town is an archipelago, the women's skirts are unkempt, "mal brossées," and the women themselves, if not whores, are unclean, "des accouchées masquées" and "jamais jolies." This same train of thought, the sleep, the awakening into the bad dream, is repeated in the manuscript copy of "Le Brasier" (first called "Le Pyrée). There the crisis has lasted only three years not five:

> Après avoir passé trois ans loin de ma vie
> Me voici de retour et je suis oublié[13]

and the bad dream is presented in exactly the same images as those of "L'Emigrant de Landor Road," the autumn port, mists, a ship departing, a horrible crowd with waving hands.

Here, though, he makes it quite clear that this is now behind him. Not that he has yet achieved any certainty about how he is going to express himself, but the creative spark has been re-kindled. "Aujourd'hui je ne sais plus rien et j'aime uniquement." He is in a state of passive receptivity, knowing that inspiration will soon visit him. "Silencieux je médite divinement." The intensity will surely be enough. And

[13] "After spending three years far away from my life
Here I am back again and I am forgotten"

already he has had visions of new possibilities which with time and patience he may be able to embody:

> Et j'ai le droit de sourire des êtres que je n'ai pas créés
> Mais si le temps venait où l'ombre de ma substance
> Se multipliait en réalisant la diversité formelle de mon amour
> J'admirerais mon ouvrage[14]

It seems inevitable that the precocious young man should have had to go through this maturing process, the realisation that cleverness is not enough, and that the real subject matter of poetry is one's own sweat and tears, and the marrow of one's bones. The real act of homage is not to the rules, but to life itself.

> Puis j'ai reconnu que chaque moment porte
> en soi sa propre perfection[15]

Surely this is the capital realisation for the poet, that he has to live eternity in a moment, open up the present to depths which are normally covered. "Comme la vie est profonde,"[16] he wrote many years later when he might well have been very near to death. This was the truth that he had been learning so bitterly through these lean years and that he was now going to have the task of expressing.

[14] "And I have the right to smile over the beings that I have not created
   But if the time came when the shadow of my substance
   Multiplied itself in a realisation of the formal diversity of my love
   I should admire my handwork"
[15] "Then I recognised that each moment bears
   within itself its own perfection"
[16] Adéma, p. 202.

K

VII

The Phœnix

"How profound life is!" and yet how exquisitely banal at the same time. In 1907 Apollinaire the poet felt that he was being reborn: in 1907 Apollinaire the man had met and fallen in love with Marie Laurencin. In 1907 too he had finally weaned himself from mother and set up house on his own. The Phœnix that naïvely, as he says in his prologue to "La Chanson du Mal-Aimé," he had thought dead for ever had risen from the flames, and with it the source of poetry. For the new love was to issue in a whole period of fertile inspiration. In short "un coup de dés jamais n'abolira le hasard."

The die in this case was thrown by Picasso, who not content with having first dazzled Apollinaire into impotence and then inspired him to new discoveries, now decided that he had met the right woman for him, a young art student who was later to become famous in her own right: Marie Laurencin.

In *Le Poète assassiné*, l'Oiseau du Benin announces to Croniamental:

> I saw the woman for you yesterday evening. . . . She is a real young lady, just as you like them. She has the serious child-like face of those who are destined to cause suffering. And for all her gracefulness, the gesture of hands raised in resistance, she lacks that nobility which poets could not love for it would prevent them from suffering. I have seen the woman for you, I tell you. She is both ugly and beautiful: she is like all we love to-day. And undoubtedly she has the savour of the bay-leaf.[1]

In the manuscript of this part written probably in 1907 the phrase "those who are destined to cause suffering" ran

---

[1] *Le Poète assassiné*, 1959, p. 47.

"those who are made for an eternal love," which reveals with what confidence and hope he embarked on the new affair. It was quite obviously the "coup de foudre." Marie was absolutely ideal for him: she was original and clever and talented enough for him to regard her as a twin soul ("She is myself as a woman," he said delightedly), his Papagena: an idea which is always intoxicating, and always eventually dangerous if the twin soul is young and immature enough to be looked upon at the same time as a Galatea. The Pygmalion complex was very strong in Apollinaire: he always loved the idea of fashioning his own woman, which may have been the reason why some of them ran away from his clutches. For quite a while Marie who was young and inexperienced fitted well into this role. There is a charming little picture of her which shows the pair of them in a boat, she docile, pensive, the plump Guillaume holding forth like a true *magister*.

It is not difficult to imagine her because the odd, triangular face of the women in her paintings was her own. She had creole blood, she was dark and very thin, even angular, and awkward in her movements. Picasso's mistress at the time, Fernande Olivier, paints her portrait with the cattiness of a much more beautiful woman who cannot understand the success of her plainer sister.

A goat-like face, with heavy eyelids, and myopic eyes set too near a nose, that was too pointed and prying and always a little red at the end. Putting herself out a lot in order to appear the naïve creature which she was naturally. Her complexion which was a muddy ivory would go red under the strain of emotion or shyness. She was fairly tall, and her dresses were always moulded tightly to her thin but well-shaped figure. Her hands, long and red as they often are with very young girls, were dry and bony. She had the air of a little girl, who was either vicious or wanted to appear so.

In spite of Apollinaire, who was very much infatuated, and wanted to impress her upon us, she did not immediately penetrate into our intimate circle.

Not particularly natural, she seemed to us to be putting on airs, to be a little stupid, very affected, concerned above all about the effect she had produced. She listened to herself speaking, looked in mirrors at her over-studied, infantile gestures.[2]

Despite this unattractive picture of her, Marie managed to be attractive; although her eyes were short-sighted, her teeth bad, and her face like a goat's, there was about her a distinct and rather strange charm. Guillaume was immediately aware of it. There was something bitter-sweet about her, undefined and undeveloped as yet. Even Fernande admits that she acquired charm later. She evoked in more than one person the image of a figure in a French primitive painting— a Clouet for example, or a noble lady of the sixteenth century. Gertrude Stein says of her: "And it was perfectly true, she was a Clouet. She had the thin square build of the medieval french women in the french primitives,"[3] and Louise Faure-Favier: "The intelligent face of a noble lady of the sixteenth century. It is exactly the profile of the Duchesse d'Este, with the gaily up-tilted eyes of Marguerite de Navarre."[4]

In short she was that specifically French phenomenon, the "jolie-laide," who manages finally to prove that mind can always triumph over matter.

When Apollinaire met her she was still searching for the kind of charm she would eventually have. It is tempting to think that in his taste for this "gamine de Paris," at a time when the vogue was for planturous, female beauty, Apollinaire showed himself as *avant-garde* as in his championing of Cubism, and that with his particular intuition he saw just how she should develop and encouraged her to do so. But of course she might well have done this without him. What she would not have done is to have such a world-wide reputation, for it was Apollinaire who really launched her and never ceased on every possible occasion to extol her at the same level as Picasso, Braque, Derain, Matisse. It is the one case where he let his own interest deform his real judgment of quality, for charming as is her talent, it is too slight ever to be judged on these terms.

There was obviously something quite original about her

[2] Fernande Olivier, *Picasso et ses amis*, 1945 (henceforth cited as Olivier), p. 104.
[3] Gertrude Stein, *The Autobiography of Alice B. Toklas*, 1935, p. 80.
[4] Faure-Favier, p. 57.

even in the early days. When she visited Apollinaire she would take her skipping-rope and skip up the steps. After the Montmartre orgies she would go back quietly to her mother in Auteuil where she lived, as Gertrude Stein said, "like a young nun with an old nun," singing snatches of old tunes. Once, according to Fernande Olivier, they all took hashish. Picasso imagined that he had discovered photography and so had come to an end of his explorations in art, Apollinaire that he was having a fine time in a brothel, whereas the drug had no effect on Marie at all and she simply went home to mother. Whether she was naturally *ingénue* or whether this was part of the act, her role in Montmartre seemed rather that of the child lost amongst sophisticated adults. At the famous party for the Douanier Rousseau in 1908 which seems to have been the quintessence of the riotous living, high spirits, and generous fellow-feeling of those Montmartre days, with Apollinaire presiding and reciting his poems in honour of the old man, and Salmon chewing soap so that he could simulate *delirium tremens*, Marie merely got drunk, fell in the jam tarts, and had to be taken home. Most people found her charming, others, particularly women, were irritated by her. The Spanish poet Ramon Gomez de la Serna who knew her well called her "la froide mais angélique Marie."[5] André Rouveyre in his clever and subtle analyses of several poems in *Amour et poésie d'Apollinaire* takes up the implication of frigidity. This is always a temerarious assumption even when everything seems to point to it. The unquestioned fact is that there is little or no sensuality in the poems that apply to her, even towards the end when Apollinaire became aware that he was losing her, as opposed to the weighty burden of it in the Annie and Lou poems written in similar circumstances. In the peak achievements of 1908 she hardly figures at all, but rather seems to have inspired a supreme sense of self-sufficiency in Apollinaire. He himself in his analysis of his past love affairs to his *fiancée*, Madeleine, in 1915, describes his feelings for Marie thus:

> In 1907 I had for a young girl who was an artist an æsthetic taste which bordered on admiration and still is coloured by this

[5] André Rouveyre, *Amour et poésie d'Apollinaire*, 1955 (henceforth cited as Rouveyre), p. 109.

feeling. She loved me or believed that she did, and I thought that I loved her, or rather forced myself to do so, because I didn't love her then.[6]

Although he is, for obvious reasons, playing down all his affairs, he does nevertheless strike the right key-note for each of them. Annie he admitted he loved "charnellement" although they did not understand each other, with Marie it was a cerebral affair, and her successor, the brilliant *femme du monde* Louise de Coligny who seemed to share with him an exacerbated sexuality, he characterised rightly as "a young woman avid for pleasure." It would seem that as in everything else, Apollinaire tended to see-saw from one extreme kind of love to another.

At any rate in those early days everybody bears witness that he was radiant with pride and joy, that he took her everywhere and showed her off, that he was absolutely charmed by her. Later on came the storms and the quarrels, many and violent, even physical sets to and blows and tears, enough for future biographers to store up a string of scandalous stories. Max Jacob once wrote that he saw her sitting on the pavement in tears with her feet in the gutter.[7] Fernande Olivier witnessed a violent scene from which Guillaume emerged dishevelled and red-faced and after which Marie was not seen again. Given Apollinaire's temperament, his desire for domination, his exclusiveness, his unaccountable moods, this is hardly surprising once his Galatea began to blossom forth and recognise her own strength. Even he himself realised how difficult he must have been, for he makes his Tristouse Ballerinette say: " What miracles the love of a poet engenders! But what a burden too! What sadnesses accompany it, what silences one has to bear!"[8]

Nevertheless for the next five years, despite rows and mutual infidelities, they were together and Apollinaire even moved out to Auteuil to be near her. There is a celebrated picture of them both painted by the Douanier Rousseau entitled *Le Poète et sa Muse*, and although Marie actively

---

[6] *Tendre comme le souvenir*, 1952, p. 68.
[7] Max Jacob, *Correspondance*, 1958, p. 149.
[8] *Le Poète assassiné*, 1959, p. 78.

inspired only a handful of poems and those mainly when the affair was over, she does in this initial stage really seem to have played the role of the poet's muse, awakening him from out of his hibernation, furnishing him with the confidence to take up the most exacting challenge of all for the creative artist: that of creating something totally new.

For this was the heart-breakingly difficult task that these young men had set themselves, the contemplation of which had appalled Apollinaire into his four-year silence, the need not merely to innovate or rejuvenate but to recast completely the old mould. Of all the spurs to their ambition perhaps the spectacular march of science was the sharpest. Even at that stage science was revealing itself capable not only of fulfilling its own specific tasks, but even of taking over many of those which had previously belonged to the arts, already the great miracle worker, the panacea of men's ills, the fulfiller of the old myths and creator of new ones, the inventor of totally new forms, the great stimulus to man's imagination. Technicians and engineers had shown themselves capable of inventing greater wonders than the mind of the poet or the hand of the artist. While science was thus changing the face of the world, artists could hardly go on performing age-old tricks, jumping through the hoop of "l'ancien jeu des vers" or practising jejune juggling with perspective and chiaroscuro. Already by 1908 a painter as ambitious and gifted as Picasso had gone a long way towards abolishing these two outworn conventions, and to experimenting with something to take their place: for destruction is child's play, but how does one take over the god-like task of peopling the waste land? And so advanced did he seem at that time that when he revealed his great picture *Les Demoiselles d'Avignon* to his friends, even they, and this includes Apollinaire, were thoroughly shocked and covered up their embarrassment by being facetious and laughing over what they called "le bordel philosophique."

And what was to be the equivalent of the philosophic brothel in poetry? This was Apollinaire's great and life-long problem. He felt that it was he who was Picasso's literary equivalent, the most gifted of that particular generation: he had always had superb ambitions: he owed it to himself and his "gloire" to be equally radical as a creator. But what can one do with words, which must always remain tied to their meanings, that was the equivalent of what Picasso was doing with forms? From 1908 onwards one witnesses the fascinating, non-stop spectacle of his experiments, his temporary solutions and certitudes, his disillusionments and soothing retreats into "l'ancien jeu des vers," and his apparent *volte-faces*. Some people have accused Apollinaire of not being single-minded enough in his innovations, of being hampered Orpheus-like by a nostalgic backward look at his first love for traditional poetry. This is simply not true. Occasionally he consoled himself in this way, but it in no way hindered his progress forwards. He was always and constantly willing to try anything new even to the point of self-sacrifice and the destruction of his most obvious gifts. It was hardly his fault if the actual material with which he worked proved more recalcitrant than forms and colours and shapes and sounds, a hard fact which has been borne out by the later development of poetry as opposed to the progress into abstraction of the plastic arts and of music.

1908 marks the moment when Apollinaire awakened fully to this particular task. It obviously appeared to him like some revelation and it is in the great poems "Le Brasier" and "Les Fiançailles" that he records this visionary sense of his new role, in terms and images that are often used to describe a religious conversion.

But this, however he interpreted it in poetry, was no sudden "nuit de feu." The convictions had been building up gradually and surely. When at the end of 1907 he joined the ranks of *La Phalange*, a review which had been started by Jean Royère in 1906 and which, although it was mainly characterised as being neo-Mallarmean, gave vent also to talents as diverse as those of Gide and Max Jacob and Jules Romains, Claudel and Marinetti, he followed the publication of "Lul de Faltenin" by an article on Matisse which clearly throws light on his own particular development.

Not that there is anything revolutionary in this essay: he is still an amateur as an art critic and in self-defence even begins: "This is a timid essay." He also makes it quite clear that he considers that there is no connexion between painting

and literature: it seems an important point to underline here
that he was never duped into believing that even if the ends
were parallel the means could be similar, "For Matisse plastic
expression is a goal, as lyric expression is for the poet."

Nevertheless what Apollinaire chooses to record of Matisse's
own dicta is revealing. Matisse has talked to him of the
artist's need for self-discovery, "this perilous voyage in discovery of one's personality. It progresses from science towards
conscience, that is to say towards a complete forgetfulness
of all that is not within oneself. What a task!"[9]

That little exclamation springs from real fellow-feeling.
This is the same voyage that he himself has recently under-
taken and he knows the cost of it.

There is yet one more indication in this "timid" article
of the way in which Apollinaire's thought was going to develop.
"The eloquence of your works," he writes addressing Matisse,
"springs above all from the combination of colours and lines.
This is what constitutes the art of the painter and not as certain
superficial minds still believe 'the reproduction of the object'."
This seems banal enough now. In 1907 it still needed to be said:
and in fact Apollinaire reiterated it the following month in a
long article which he wrote for *La Phalange* on Jean Royère,
making it into the main thesis of his dithyramb in praise of this
poet. The poet because he is a creator is divine. He is all
powerful and his creations stand alone, need have nothing in
common with nature, the handiwork of that other Creator:

> The poetry of Jean Royère is as false as a new creation must be
> compared with the old. What an enchanting falseness! Nothing
> resembling us and everything in our image. . . . But, oh
> triumph of falseness, of error and imagination, God and the
> poet vie with each other in creation.

Now if there is any one guiding principle which has regu-
lated the development of the arts in this century, it is this one,
that the work of art is an autonomous creation and not an
imitation of nature, although it undoubtedly has to use some
of the elements which nature provides. In the realm of
literature it was not new. Baudelaire, Lautréamont, Rimbaud,

[9] *La Phalange*, 15 Dec. 1907.

Jarry, Proust had not ceased to proclaim their belief in the quasi-divine powers of the poet: and Apollinaire from the beginning had assumed them for himself. In the plastic arts, however, it was more revolutionary; only Cézanne had pointed the way. The determination of the artists to recast the world was therefore all the stronger for being pioneer. It was this determination in particular which impressed Apollinaire in the new school of painting, and which made him eager to champion their cause even if he did not always approve of their individual efforts.

But now the time had come for him to manifest his own god-like powers. In February 1908 *La Phalange* published "Onirocritique," which is one of his first conscious attempts at an entirely new creation out of the jumbled-up elements of nature. The result is an Apocalyptic vision of a new world, life as it could be on another planet, or as it could be built out of the ruins of this one. It is freed from mortality, from a sense of time and space, and from the usual divisions of species and the senses. For instance the apple trees and ploughed fields sing and whistle, the narrator is killed but does not even feel it. There are beings of a new kind, a cross between animal and vegetable: monkeys like trees violate old tombs. They mingle with the elements. Out of their mouths shoot forth flames, a herd of trees feeds on the stars, another beast has for its head a whole pearl. Apollinaire was often haunted by a vision of the strange, new beings of the future: in "Onirocritique" he really tries to force himself to conjure them up. For although the title indicates that this lyrical piece of prose is the stuff that dreams are made of, he is in fact, unlike Nerval, deliberately inducing the vision, using it as a method of creation: which is the aspect of "Onirocritique" that fascinated the Surrealists.

To build up the new world he has recourse inevitably to the same limited stock of images of the poems of this period: kings, sailors, stars, sun, flames, shadow, a siren, and also two new ones which are to become significant: a huge ship passing by on the horizon to symbolise his sense of rebirth, and men fermenting in the liquor of wine vats, which well expresses his dionysiac celebration of life in all its aspects, and the sense that runs through "Onirocritique" of his own heady participation in the experience of the whole universe.

Undoubtedly Apollinaire felt at this moment that he was well on his way to finding a new poetic method. In April he was invited to give a lecture on "La Phalange nouvelle" in a series held at the Salon des Indépendants. There, speaking with authority in the name of the young new phalanx, he stated that they were in search of a lyricism both new and humanist at the same time. This definition must have pleased him, because he uses the same terms again in a letter to Toussaint-Luca the following month to describe his own aims in "Onirocritique," in the article on Royère, and in their newest relation, the poem which had just appeared in *Gil Blas*, "Le Pyrée." He himself was always very proud of this poem: even as late as 1915 he declared[10] to Madeleine that with its companion "Les Fiançailles," "the newest and most lyrical and most profound of *Alcools*," it was his best poem.

In *Gil Blas* Gustave Kahn introduced it, but seemed to miss the point of the new trend altogether: "Monsieur Guillaume Apollinaire figures with authority amongst the new Symbolists, amongst the young poets who, whilst they affirm their own personality really belong to Symbolism, that is to say the search for movement and rhythm." If the poem is new and original it is certainly not because of its particular kind of versification. In the article on Royère, Apollinaire had made it quite clear that he considered that there was not much to add to the infinite variety of traditional prosody except *vers libre* which was too often regarded as an excuse for faulty versification. He himself uses his favourite octosyllable in the first part of *Le Pyrée* and then, as he attempts to make his vision clear, expands into his own particularly fluid and rhythmic kind of *vers libre*. This is one of the first poems in which he obviously attaches great importance to the spacing of the words on the page, using in the latter section three single lines to great effect. In this he may have been following Mallarmé's example, but certainly not in the matter of syntax. Syntactically the poem is straightforward. Any obscurity that there is arises mainly from his habit of suppressing the lines of logical explanation and leaving only the images which represent his successive emotional states, for the method is

[10] *Tendre comme le souvenir*, 1952, p. 74.

still essentially the same as that of "La Chanson du Mal-Aimé," the piling-up of images. One critic, Jeanine Moulin, has even suggested[11] that he deleted the explanatory passages in order deliberately to inculcate Rimbaldian disorder. Rimbaud may have been in his mind, but this covering up of his traces was certainly a deep-seated character trait.

The precise story which he is both revealing and not revealing in "Le Pyrée" is that of his own recent past.

> J'ai jeté dans le noble feu
> Que je transporte et que j'adore
> De vives mains et même feu
> Ce Passé ces têtes de morts
> Flamme je fais ce que tu veux[12]

One of the most constant of his themes from now on is his belief in poetry as a religion, and thence his own dedication to it as high priest. This is in fact nothing new, but here his dedication to the flame, his sacrifice of all his dead past obviously signifies a recrudescence of faith, a reaffirmation of all his most ambitious beliefs.

He is at such a high level now that his vision encompasses not merely the past, but the cosmic future,

> Le galop soudain des étoiles
> N'étant que ce qui deviendra[13]

and as in "Onirocritique" other forms of life, animal and vegetable, mingle:

> Se mêle au hennissement mâle
> Des centaures dans leurs haras
> Et des grand plaintes végétales[14]

---

[11] Jeanine Moulin, *Guillaume Apollinaire, Textes inédits,* 1952 (henceforth cited as Moulin), p. 101.

[12] "I threw into the noble fire
That I transport and that I worship
With my live hands into the fire itself
This Past these deathheads
Flame I do your bidding"

[13] "The sudden gallop of the stars
Being only what will happen"

[14] "Mingles with the male neighing
Of centaurs in their studs
And with the great lamentations of plants"

Following his usual pendulum swing he then switches back in a Villonesque outcry to the sordidness of his past life, the unwholesome, debilitating association with women:

> L'amour est devenu mauvais . . .
>
> Les têtes coupées qui m'acclament
> Et les astres qui ont saigné
> Ne sont que des têtes de femmes[15]

And then takes up on a minor note his poet's mission, assumed at first passively,

> Partant à l'amphion docile
> Tu subis tous les tons charmants
> Qui rendent les pierres agiles[16]

but which swells out into the great hymn to fire which begins with sonorous beat and alliteration, "Je flambe dans le brasier à l'ardeur adorable." Here he veritably seems to be seeing himself if not as a god then at least as a saint and martyr glowing like a sun through all eternity with the fire of his faith, and capable as in "Onirocritique" of multiplying himself. "Et les mains des croyants m'y rejettent multiple innombrablement."

Inevitably there is a momentary, downward plunge from his manic height, when he remembers the past, his aberrations and desires:

> O Mémoire combien de races qui forlignent
> Des Tyndarides aux vipères ardentes de mon bonheur
> Et les serpents ne sont-ils que les cous de cygnes
> Qui étaient immortels et n'étaient pas chanteurs[17]

---

[15] "Love has gone bad . . .
  The severed heads which acclaim me
  And the stars which have bled
  Are only the heads of women"

[16] "Therefore to docile Amphion
  You submit all the charming sounds
  That make the stones move"

[17] "O memory how many races there are which breed astray
  From the Tyndarides to the ardent vipers of my happiness
  And are these serpents only the necks of swans
  Which were immortal and did not sing"

This would seem to imply that recourse to myth, use of second-hand materials, such as he had practised it in his early days had led him away as much from the real source of poetry as a concern with the whole sensual and emotional complications of love, which at this stage, he seems to think, did not inspire him ("n'étaient pas chanteurs"). He then makes the categoric statement: "Voici ma vie renouvelée," a rebirth which is symbolised first by the "Onirocritique" image of big ships passing by, and again by the immense flames of martyrdom.

The third and last section of the poem is difficult. Here, again, as in "Onirocritique," he is most ambitiously trying to come to terms with the challenge he himself had thrown down, of rivalling God as creator and fashioning a new world quite out of this world, this time not from the shell of the old one, but with the same virgin materials as God used in the first place, light, fire, stars, infinity, space, endless movement, time.

> Descendant des hauteurs où pense la lumière
> Jardins rouant plus haut que tous les ciels mobiles
> L'avenir masqué flambe en traversant les cieux[18]

This is the divine masquerade which he has conjured up for his eternal delectation and which at first he hardly dares to look at, a theatre beyond our atmosphere built out of the solid fire of the stars by Zamir the worm, without instrument, just as the poet has no instrument but his imagination, and peopled by actors of another species, "claires bêtes nouvelles." This particular vision is one of the most impressive examples of Apollinaire being in advance of his time: for a man who had never been up in a balloon let alone an aeroplane to have this conception of space, of an expanding universe, of whirling worlds, of time being movement and to be able to think up this admirable exact image for the earth seen from above:

> Terre
> O Déchirée que les fleuves ont reprisée[19]

---

[18] "Descending from the heights where light meditates
Gardens wheeling higher than all the mobile skies
The masked future flames as it crosses the heavens"

[19]   "Earth
O torn One that the rivers have darned"

seems really to imply an almost prophetic foresight. But, poor Guillaume, he knows that he can never really sustain such an extraordinary vision. Even here at one of the heights of his ambition and confidence, the melancholy suspicion of inadequacy is his punctuation; for commas the nostalgia for human affection "Nous attendons ton bon plaisir ô mon amie," accompanied by the plaint from out of his adolescent longing "Quand bleuira sur l'horizon la Désirade," and a backward look at the "ville marine" of his childhood, a semi-colon of pity for the poor earth and for himself; and as the final full stop the ironical climax of his descent from space into the small, gnawing secrets of real life: the complex of the great magician being eaten by worms.

> J'aimerais mieux nuit et jour dans les sphingeries
> Vouloir savoir pour qu'enfin on m'y dévorât[20]

Apollinaire is often represented as constantly bending this way and that to the different winds of fashion. Change yes, this was his very nature, but change within the mood itself, from moment to moment, from line to line, not from year to year; and all the big successful poems seem to resemble each other in containing in microcosm as many and as far-ranging shifts of mood as does any total survey of his development.

Although "Les Fiançailles" was not published until November 1908, the manuscripts of this and "Le Pyrée" in some cases overlap, and they obviously spring from the same inspiration: the sleep, the renunciation of "l'ancien jeu des vers," the awakening. Because, however, it is later in date, it does go further in exploring the new method. Like most of Apollinaire's poems of *Alcools* it is a mosaic of pieces written at different moments, but although these first drafts are an invaluable aid towards a full understanding of one poem, it must be judged uniquely on its finished aspect. Like "La Chanson du Mal-Aimé," despite the disparity of its parts, it is very carefully composed. It is dedicated to Picasso and the first section in regular alexandrines strikes the colour-note

[20] "I should prefer to spend night and day in the sphinx settlements
   To strive to know in order that at last I should be devoured there"

blue, a period in his friend's painting which Apollinaire particularly admired, probably because it was the most lyrical and sentimental. These first three strophes also belong to his own early days as far back as 1902: they are melancholy and mannered, very much "Still too Symbolist" with their "oiseau bleu" and verbal conceits, and it soon appears obvious why Apollinaire has used them as his springboard. They are perfect examples of "l'ancien jeu des vers" which he had practised with such craft: and immediately the next section, opening again on an alexandrine, evokes the reaction of his friends towards them:

> Mes amis m'ont enfin avoué leur mépris[21]

This second section takes us with that contemptuous response to his youthful hopes right into the heart of the bad dream, which he here presents as a sort of mock Crucifixion (as the Enchanter's burial had been a mock Christmastide).

> De faux centurions emportaient le vinaigre[22]

It is once again the nightmare city-scene, with its sickly lamplight, its whores and alcohol:

> Les becs de gaz pissaient leur flamme au clair de lune
> Des croque-morts avec des bocks tintaient des glas[23]

The next section swings forward again out of this wallowing mood of self-pity (surely the writer's occupational disease), into the moment when intuitively he knew what was to be done, had had the vision of it, but had not yet found the words to clothe it, nor was sure that he ever would "mon tourment de silence," the mute aspiration ("Un Icare tente de s'élever jusqu'à chacun de mes yeux"), the particular anguish, when all his past, facile cleverness ("les bêtes théologales de l'intelligence") his power of evoking the past ("Jadis les morts sont revenus pour m'adorer") seemed to have deserted him. There is at this point a strange phrase, "Et j'espérais la fin du monde."

[21] "My friends have at last admitted to me that they despise me"
[22] "False centurions carried away the hyssop"
[23] "Gas-lamps pissed out their flame in the moonlight
Undertakers rang the knell with beer-glasses"

Why this obsession with an apocalypse? Here the implication could well be that he had crammed his own brain so full of the past, had had such mighty visions that anything less than the end of the world would seem an anticlimax. This fits in well with his temporary flashes of megalomania and extraordinary sense of creative power, from which, as always, there is the characteristic dying fall: "Mais la mienne arrive en sifflant comme un ouragan," the inevitable deflation and helplessness, possibly even a premonition of his own early death.

This despairing note issues in again the backward look towards the "garden of his memory," that sense of time ruined and the heady fruitfulness of his youth wasted, which always seemed to inspire his most poignant music. Time drops with rhythmic beat like his tears:

> . . . les cadavres de mes jours
> Marquent ma route et je les pleure[24]

Having thus divested himself regretfully of his past and begged, like Villon, for pardon for his new state of nakedness and ignorance he then turns to his present stance, the loving god-like contemplation of life itself. "Je médite divinement."

The next section is a strange interpolation, and has not so far been commented on, although its position in the centre of the poem should indicate that it is a part of his new "art poétique."

It begins casually setting a scene of Sunday leisure:

> J'observe le repos du dimanche
> Et je loue la paresse
> Comment comment réduire
> L'infiniment petite science
> Que m'imposent mes sens[25]

After the staggering claims of pseudo-divinity that he has just emitted he is left alone, trying to analyse just what it means

---

[24] . . . "the corpses of my days
Mark out my path and I mourn them"

[25] "I observe the Sabbath rest
And I laud idleness
How how do I reduce
The infinitely small science
That my senses impose upon me"

to love "uniquement." Again the age-old question: What in fact is his poet's equipment? What is the subject matter of poetry?

And here for elucidation is a passage from the lecture that he gave in the last year of his life, the famous "L'Esprit nouveau":

> Those who imagined the fable of Icarus so marvellously realised to-day, will discover others. They will drag you living and awake into the nocturnal, sealed world of dreams. Into the universes which palpitate ineffably above our heads. Into those nearer and yet further away from us which gravitate around the same point of infinity as that which we bear within ourselves.

This looks very like the programme which during 1908 Apollinaire has already been attempting to follow. The world of dreams explored in "Onirocritique," that of the "universes palpitating ineffably above our heads in "Le Pyrée," and now in "Les Fiançailles" the infinitely small world that we bear within ourselves, of our five senses. Infinitely small, but because of its very infinity akin to the infinity of space. Not without good reason was he so excited by Pascal in the last year of his life. He lets himself sink into himself, reduced only to these five senses, and it is just this kinship that he perceives. Through his senses he is united with nature, the sky, the sun, the seasons, within him is the same spark which is in all manifestations of life in the universe:

> L'un est pareil aux montagnes au ciel
> Aux villes à mon amour
> Il ressemble aux saisons
> Il vit décapité sa tête est le soleil
> Et la lune son cou tranché
> Je voudrais éprouver une ardeur infinie[26]

The staccato rhythm, the emphatic monosyllables underline his hungry desire "Je voudrais éprouver une ardeur infinie."

In anthropomorphic images similar again to those of "Onirocritique" he portrays his hearing as a monster with

[26] "One is akin to mountains to the sky
To towns to my love
It resembles the seasons
It lives decapitated its head is the sun
And the moon its severed neck
I want to experience an infinite ardour"

thunder for its mane and birds' songs in its claws: his eyes swim
in surrealist fashion far away from him to the stars. But then
the inevitable see-saw on which the writer balances has to
swing down again—from excessive confidence into excessive
doubt, the anti-climax of realising his own limits; for the most
beautiful monster of all (we have had the five senses, so could
it be his glory as a poet "ayant la saveur du laurier"?) is left
alone, disconsolate.

And in this mood of self-doubt even the falsest of smooth-
tongues impostors can scare him into thinking that he is no good:

> A la fin les mensonges ne me font plus peur
> C'est la lune qui cuit comme un oeuf sur le plat[27]

other people's false claims to glory (the moon and not his
true sun) frying in their own juice. He himself has been
crucified by his doubt, "Voici mon bouquet des fleurs de la
Passion," but now he is ready to start again, humbly and
modestly, seeking his source of life and of poetry in little things,
even in drops of rain "Ce collier de gouttes d'eau va parer
la noyée." (Here again he forestalls a pronouncement in
"L'Esprit nouveau" that "One can take as one's point of
departure the most banal fact: a handkerchief that falls can be
for the poet the lever that lifts up the universe." There might
even be the same Shakespearian train of association; the drowned
Ophelia, Desdemona's handkerchief.) He is back to the
Travaillin idea, his humble task as journeyman poet, "Des
anges diligents travaillent pour moi à la maison." This is the
natural daily round to which he has been born, even his
religious mission in life, "Toute la sainte journée j'ai marché
en chantant." Then he indulges in seeing a little picture
of himself as a troubadour making his progress through life
singing with a lady watching him from her window:

> Une dame penchée à sa fenêtre m'a regardé longtemps
> M'éloigner en chantant[28]

With this idea of his normal function of writing poetry

---

[27] "Finally lies no longer scare me
They are the moon cooking like a fried egg"

[28] "A lady leaning at her window watched me for a long time
Go away singing"

almost as he breathes, he can gather up all the threads of the poem, and, as he had done in "La Chanson du Mal-Aimé," knit them together. He evokes again all that he has sacrificed to the new flame, the misery of the nightmare autumn, "les dragues les ballots les sirènes mi-mortes," and even further back the springtime of his love under the sign of the Virgin. Cleverly now he is returning again to complete the structure of the poem with the same setting with which he began, love in spring; and he is also again using lines that he had written in 1902, traditional alexandrines, like those of the first section.

It is this same classical metre that he chooses in order to make the last addition to his new *art poétique*, and this again appears as one of the notable features of "L'Esprit nouveau." The supreme task of the poet will be that of prophecy. He sees himself as equal to the Grand Master of the Knights Templar prophesying in the flames:

> Templiers flamboyants je brûle parmi vous
> Prophétisons ensemble ô grand maître je suis
> Le désirable feu qui pour vous se dévoue[29]

He then goes on to raise the hair on our heads by actually fulfilling his claims:

> Liens déliés par une libre flamme Ardeur
> Que mon souffle éteindra O Morts à quarantaine
> Je mire de ma mort la gloire et le malheur[30]

Death at forty, glory and misfortune; "povre Guillaume";[31]

[29] "Blazing Knights Templar I burn amongst you
Let us prophesy together O Grand Master I am
The desirable fire which sacrifices itself for you"

[30] "Bonds unloosed by a free flame Ardour
That my breath will quench } you forty who died / you who died at forty
I mirror by my death glory and misfortune"

[31] There might in fact be another, or an added interpretation of this phrase, "O Morts a quarantaine": not those who have died at forty or in their forties, but those who have died in bands of forty, and the reference may well be back to the image in "La Chanson du Mal-Aimé,"—"Les quarante de Sébaste," the forty martyrs of Sebastapol who died frozen into the ice. This would continue the theme of martyrdom which had been struck with the sacrifice in the fire, and enrich it with the typically Apollinairian conception of inevitable, ubiquitous dichotomy. He is the fire; at the same time his breath is icy and will put out the fire. In short, as he says in the final biting phrase, "Je mire de ma mort la gloire et le malheur."

he has really, as he claims, hit the target, "l'oiseau de la quintaine."

It is with the most deceptive ingenuousness that he returns
at last to the initial setting, the sunny village and the dancing
lovers. For this strange image, "l'oiseau de la quintaine" also
has erotic undertones. The *quintaine*, an iron ring suspended
in the air as target for the lance was a term used in medieval
Italian for sexual intercourse. Thus Apollinaire characterises
his own doubt, feigned even as it was shot down, for he is not
really this kind of bird, but truly the Phœnix arisen with love
and the sun from his own heroic nest of ashes.

> Incertitude oiseau feint peint quand vous tombiez
> Le soleil et l'amour dansaient dans le village
> Et tes enfants galants bien ou mal habillés
> Ont bâti ce bucher le nid de mon courage[32]

His courage at this moment was in fact radiant. Each time
he opened his mouth it was to issue a clarion call: this
was really the time when he felt that he, and his friends, and
those who enlisted under his banner, could change the face
of the world. In June he wrote a Preface to the Catalogue
of an exhibition of modern art in Le Havre entitled "Les Trois
Vertus plastiques" in which this Messianic note is again deep-
throated. One can hardly call this piece of prose art-criticism: rather is it a manifesto, emotional, lyrical; yet another
chapter of the new *art poétique*, and remarkable for exactly
the same qualities that are evident in his poetry of the same
period, preaching the same doctrine that nature is now
trampled underfoot, that the time has come for the artist to
be the master, that he must give himself the spectacle of his own
divinity, and that the pictures which he proffers for the admiration of men must also bestow on them the honour of exercising
momentarily their own divinity. Workmen or gardeners
have shown less respect for nature than artists. Each divinity
creates in its own image; so must painters, and leave to photo-
graphers the mere reproduction of nature. "Before everything

[32] "Uncertainty feigned painted bird when you fell
Sun and love danced in the village
And your gallant children richly or poorly dressed
Have built this pyre the nest of my courage"

else, artists are men who want to become inhuman." This seems an apparent paradox from a poet who has just declared that he is in search of a new humanism. In fact the conviction of extending the bounds of human possibilities is consistent, even if the terms used are not so.

They are hardly meant to be. What does one make logically of a passage like this?

> In vain the seasons shudder, whole peoples are rushing unanimously towards the same death, science destroys and remakes that which exists, universes are flying away for ever out of our conception, our mobile images repeat themselves and are reborn heedlessly, and colours, scents, sounds astonish us, then disappear from nature.
>
> This monster of beauty is not eternal.
>
> We know that our life has had no beginning and will have no end, but our main concern is with creation and the end of the world.

It can only be regarded as a poet's vision akin to those in "Le Brasier" and "Les Fiançailles," of the eternal mobility of the cosmos, even a surprising intuition of an expanding universe, of infinity matched against the finite limits of man, and man's frenetic, unnatural aspiration to put a stop to time. His favourite symbol is similarly used:

> The flame is the symbol of painting and the three plastic virtues burn in their own radiance.
>
> The flame has the purity which suffers no foreign body and cruelly transforms everything it touches into itself.
>
> It has that magic unity which enables it to suffer division and yet remain unique.
>
> It has finally the sublime truth of its light which nobody can deny.[33]

These reiterated symbols of fire and light may tell us little about the nature of painting, but they held a very particular importance for Apollinaire. Here and in the two poems they lie curled at the centre of his new creed, containing all its mystery and inherent contradictions, symbols from now on of the divine nature of poetry.

[33] Re-published in *Chroniques d'Art*, 1960, p. 56.

There is no doubt that in this he had been influenced by his desultory reading of the Cabbala, and Illuminist and hermetic writings in general. It would not have taken a profound study for him to have noticed that the symbol of light is the most important in occult literature. According to the Cabbala man can have knowledge of the Ancient of Ancients only by means of light which comes from on high. Swedenborg stated that God could be symbolised only by the sun which gives life to all natural things. Now Apollinaire at this time makes a specific reference to the first of the alchemists who gave his name to hermetic philosophy: Hermes Trismegistes. As an introduction to the series of limpid, little poems forming *Le Bestiaire ou le cortège d'Orphée*, which also appeared in 1908, he thus admonishes the reader to admire Derain's wood-cuts:

> Admirez le pouvoir insigne
> Et la noblesse de la ligne
> Elle est la voix que la lumière fit entendre
> Et dont parle Hermès Trismégiste en son Pimandre[34]

In fact this is a very cavalier interpretation of the passage in *The Pimander* where Hermes Trismegistes describes his vision of all nature being converted into light and of a voice coming out of the light, the voice of light which is "God, a thought more ancient than nature, and the shining Word of that thought is the son of God";[35] in short, "In the beginning was the Word and the Word was with God and God said Let there be Light." And fire is the active, speedy part of the light which flies upwards. Ballanche, the mystic philosopher of Lyons, also describes a similar vision. "I had nevertheless a real but obscure and indefinable sense of the essence and the unity of everything that exists. Then I heard a sound, but an intellectual sound and this sound appeared to me to be the voice of light."[36]

It is also at this time that it is no longer Merlin the magician

---

[34] "Admire the distinguished power
And the nobility of the line
It is the voice which came forth from light
And which Hermes Trismegistus speaks of in his Pimander"
[35] Hermes Trismegistus, *Le Pimandre*, 1579, Ch. I, Sect. IV, p. 5.
[36] Ballanche, *Orphée*, II, Geneva 1830, p. 149.

with his private, circumscribed magic, or an amalgam of ineffectual, dead kings who symbolise the poet, but a much more positive, active figure with mystic powers—Orpheus. In the work of Ballanche, Orpheus is the poet-prophet whose function it is to unite the world through poetry: "You trust in the inspiration of the word: this beautiful and inconceivable doctrine which has come to you like the breath of life, like the light by which your eyes see, because in fact your origin is celestial";[37] the last phrase of which is couched in precisely the same terms as Apollinaire's description of his Enchanter.

It is not difficult further to substantiate Apollinaire's conception of light being the prime mover, the divine principle, of the word being its manifestation, of the poet thence being the great visionary, the receptacle of the light, consumed by the active part of it, the fire, which is also poetry: "Ce feu oblong dont l'intensité ira s'augmentant/Au point qu'il deviendra un jour l'unique lumière."[38] Later in 1912 and 1913 when he felt that he had really discovered a new kind of poetry that could also be linked with a new kind of painting, as Cubism pure and simple could never be, faithful to his own way of thinking he christened it Orphism, and invented as its battle-cry: "J'aime l'art d'aujourd'hui parce que j'aime avant tout la lumière et tous les hommes aiment avant tout la lumière, ils ont inventé le feu."[39] In "Collines" and in "La Jolie Rousse," both of which are again declarations of the poet's mission, his vision is equally characterised by fire, "la grâce ardente," "la raison ardente": the marvels of the future are "des feux nouveaux": in "Collines" he makes the same rapprochement as did the alchemists between gold, the sovereign secret of life and the purefying action of fire which would reveal it:

> Des bras d'or supportent la vie
> Pénétrez le secret doré
> Tout n'est qu'une flamme rapide[40]

---

[37] Ballanche, *Orphée*, II, Geneva 1830, p. 149.

[38] "Cortège," *Alcools, Oeuvres poétiques*, 1956, p. 74.

[39] *Chroniques d'Art*, 1960, p. 282.

[40] "Golden arms support life
Penetrate the golden secret
All is but a rapid flame"

The comparison with Rimbaud again imposes itself. "Et je vecus étincelle d'or dans la lumière nature."[41] There had also been "le petit bouquet flottant à l'aventure" of "L'Emigrant de Landor Road." Jeanine Moulin[42] makes out a convincing case for a definite influence from 1908 onwards. Their conceptions of the role of the poet certainly seem to have much in common, but this may well have been because they had culled them from the same sources. Apollinaire was already fascinated by hermetic writings at a very early age when it seems unlikely that he would have known much about Rimbaud. What does seem likely is that he would eventually recognise Rimbaud as a kindred spirit in this respect, after the same ends.[43] There is a definite possibility that it was *L'Alchimie du verbe* which was responsible for the revelation of 1908. Nevertheless this revelation did not open up virgin territory. Whether it was due to Rimbaud or to Marie Laurencin, to Picasso, Mallarmé, or Nerval, to Jarry or Max Jacob, or to all of them combined with the spirit of the time, or whether it was all Apollinaire's own doing, it merely confirmed him in the direction in which his own temperament and his own ambitions had already set him.

[41] Arthur Rimbaud, "Délires II," "Alchimie du Verbe," *Sasison en enfer.*
[42] Moulin, p. 98.
[43] Since this went to press, I have become aware of Francis Carmody's *Evolution of Apollinaire's Poetics 1901-1914*, 1963. Mr Carmody goes further than any other critic in defining Rimbaud's influence on these 1908 poems, and produces very convincing confrontations.

VIII

Pourquoi faut-il être si moderne . . . ?

IF Apollinaire felt like the Grand Master of the Templars he certainly did not always behave like one, but rather at times like the court jester: and this did him no good in the eyes of the public, who are rarely to be persuaded that high seriousness can be borne aloft on the geyser of laughter, or that one man has the right to more than one *persona*. Indeed there is a certain dramatic irony about Apollinaire at this time of his life, rather as if his vaticinations were taking place on the edge of a volcano. Out of his vitality and his confidence he really thought that every way of embracing life was permitted —"je voudrais éprouver une ardeur infinie"—and of course for society this is *hybris*, and unwittingly he was piling up the black marks against himself.

These appear innocuous enough now, but they were all going to count against him when, by an improbable linking of circumstances, he came up against society's most rigid manifestation, the law. Again ironically—and Apollinaire's life as well as his work is always backed with irony—some of the activities which helped to establish his reputation as a joker, a "mystificateur," now emerge as a vindication of the sureness of his intuitive judgment. One of these apparent bad jokes, for instance, was the championing of the Douanier Rousseau. To take a poor old man and to set him up as one of the great painters of the time was really to invite the reaction, "il se fout du monde."

Not that this was Apollinaire's doing alone, but as he had constituted himself a spokesman, it was he who received most of the opprobrium. Remy de Gourmont and Jarry had both patronised Rousseau much earlier: Picasso and all the Montmartre band had adopted him and Apollinaire was merely toeing the party line. Undoubtedly the other artists saw more of the Douanier's real qualities as a painter. Rumour had it that Apollinaire was not at first very pleased with his portrait, *Le Poète et sa muse*, and that Rousseau had difficulty in being paid. As late as May 1908 Apollinaire was still using measured terms about him.

> Monsieur Rousseau's Exhibition is both touching and agreeable. This autodidact has undeniable natural qualities and it appears that Gauguin admired his blacks. But on the other hand, the Douanier is too lacking in general culture. One cannot abandon oneself to his ingenuousness. Its chancy, even ridiculous nature is too evident. . . . And one is irritated by Rousseau's tranquillity. He feels no disquiet, he is self-satisfied but without false pride. Rousseau ought to have remained a mere artisan.[1]

Words that are very different in tone from the panegyric that he wrote in 1911, the year after the Douanier's death, about "that poor old angelic creature Henri Rousseau." It is amusing to see how Apollinaire goes back to his same terms of reference, but takes care to modify them:

> This serenity was of course only pride. The Douanier was aware of his strength. Once or twice he let fall the opinion that he was the greatest painter of his time. And on many points it is possible that he was not mistaken. For if in his youth he had no artistic education (and that is obvious), it appears that later when he wanted to paint, he looked at the masters with passion, and that, almost alone among the moderns, he divined their secrets.[2]

By now Apollinaire had decided that Rousseau was a banner to wave on the side of the angels against the Philistines. He was always aware that it was important to cheer for a side as well as to encourage individual players: but even if he did not at first fully appreciate Rousseau's pictorial achievements, he certainly prized him for representing in painting those naïve, primitive qualities that he himself found in folk-songs and nursery rhymes. Appropriately in the poem "Souvenir

[1] *Chroniques d'Art*, 1960, p. 54.
[2] *Op. cit.*, p. 162.

du Douanier" he uses just one of these charming jingles as his recurring refrain.

> Je tourne vire
> Phare affolé
> Mon beau navire
> S'est en allé[3]

This healthy naïvety he regarded as a basic strength in any art, and he ends his article in *L'Intransigeant* on a real Michelin guide note.

> There are little restaurants where the dishes that have been simmered by the *patronne's* own hands, where the wines cared for with love by the *patron*, are more delectable than those of certain fashionable establishments where everything is superior to what is served. In this way the Douanier's painting is of excellent quality in its unluxuriant surroundings. No, it is not hygienic art but healthy art purely and simply.

"La bonne cuisine bourgeoise" in short, and he really does go on to add the "worth the detour" accolade: "Et il vaut qu'on s'y arrête."

Very much more personal and also a much more serious black mark against him in the public eye was his continued activity in the field of pornography and erotic literature generally. From his earliest days he had always turned to pornography as an easy means of making money; and this need was still very pressing. He had now given up his job in the bank and was still casting around in order to live entirely by his pen. The collaboration with *La Phalange* had helped—as well as the poems and articles published there, he had also done a regular job of novel reviewing—but in April 1909 this came to an end. Apollinaire at all times, hated to be tied down to one group or school. He was too variable, too much an individual, and also had too big a conception of his own role to enlist for long behind a Royère. One of the tasks that he now took on in order to earn his living was the editorship of a whole

---

[3] "I turn about
Crazy lighthouse
My lovely ship
Has sailed away"

series of libertine authors entitled *Les Maîtres de l'amour*, which in fact he continued to bring out at regular intervals right until his death. This, although done for the same reason, was rather a different matter from the enormities and adolescent high spirits of *Les Onze mille verges*: there had to be an appearance of research and scholarship, a Preface and notes, some attempt to assess the importance of this whole aspect of literature. Apollinaire was to spend much of his time in the next few years working to this end in the Bibliothèque Nationale, and in all was to produce fourteen works in the series ranging from the Italians, Aretino and Baffo, to the Englishman John Cleland, and including Sade, Mirabeau, Crébillon, Grécourt, Nerciat, and even a volume of anonymous German storytellers. Seven of these titles were to appear in the year 1910 alone, which must have represented a considerable amount of prolonged and concentrated work. But by all accounts he did not appear to find it too much of a burden. André Salmon[4] claims that he never spent the whole space of one day at the Bibliothèque Nationale; Fernand Fleuret described his peregrinations amongst the tables in search of his friends and depicted him sitting staring absently into space, singing a little refrain of his own composition: "Foutre, foutre, foutre."[5]

Nevertheless the work was done thoroughly and most conscientiously, possibly, one suspects, even too thoroughly on occasion, because if he could not find the appropriate documents, he was quite capable of inventing them. Who, for instance, is the Ugo Capucci from whom he quotes in his edition of *Le Théâtre italien*? But generally his erudition and scholarship were reliable and with his friend Fernand Fleuret he was given the job of cataloguing the books in the *enfer* of the Bibliothèque Nationale.

The first work that appeared in this series was *L'Œuvre du Marquis de Sade*, and a surprisingly impressive piece of scholarship it is. Apollinaire was a man of many parts and he always seems to be capable of being both more serious and more flippant than one normally expects. In fact the short Preface is a model in its *genre*, although Sade was obviously not as much

---

[4] André Salmon, *Souvenirs sans fin*, VOL. III, 1961, p. 134.
[5] Fernand Fleuret, *De Gilles de Rais à Guillaume Apollinaire*, 1933, p. 285.

a personal favourite as Aretino who was his next subject. It offers a succinct biography: it gives proof of an extensive documentation with reference to rare manuscript copies of the works and to much previously unpublished material, in particular Sade's letters from the archives of the Comédie Française: it also spotlights yet again Apollinaire's uncanny insight and intuition. "It seems," he writes, "that the hour has come for these ideas which have matured in the ignominious atmosphere of the *enfers* of Libraries, and this man who seemed to count for nothing during the nineteenth century may well come to dominate the twentieth." Yet another prophecy which, whether we like it or not, seems to have been fulfilled.

Apollinaire himself generally follows the line of common sense about Sade, without in any way being bowled over by him. He calls him "one of the most astonishing men who have ever existed," "one of the most liberated of spirits," and admires the fine courage of a German scholar, Dr Eugen Duehren, who had recently written about him:

> There is yet another point of view which for the historian who is concerned with civilisation, for the doctor, the jurisconsult, the economist and the moralist, makes the works of the Marquis de Sade into a veritable well of science and new ideas. These works are instructive chiefly because they reveal everything that is closely bound up with the sexual instinct, which as the Marquis de Sade recognised, influences practically all human relationships in some way. Every investigator who wishes to determine the sociological importance of love will have to read the principal works of the Marquis de Sade. Not at the level of mere appetite, but on a higher plane, it is love which presides over the movement of the universe.

To which Apollinaire cries a fervent "Bravo" as he quotes Dante: "L'amor che muove'l Sole et le altre stelle." He also agrees with Duehren that by his new theories Sade created sexual psychopathy a hundred years before Krafft-Ebbing.[6]

About the recognition of Sade's importance time has proved Apollinaire right: but at that period he was alone in his assessment, and so courageous. Characteristically, though,

[6] *L'Oeuvre du Marquis de Sade,* 1911, p. 24.

there are moments when intoxicated by his initial perceptions, he is caught up in amusing but preposterous paradoxes. "Justine," he declares, "is the traditional kind of woman, servile, miserable and less than human. Juliette on the contrary represents the new woman that Sade described, a being of whom we have no clear idea, who is emerging from humanity, who will have wings and renew the universe." Both suffragettes and space-women might have been astonished at being given such a grandmother. Similarly Apollinaire indulges in his private kind of fantasy when he suggests that it might have been the Marquis' seditious cries down the funnel that served to empty his slops through the window of his cell in the Bastille which excited the already inflamed populace to attack the fortress.

This of course was one of Apollinaire's character traits, endearing or maddening according to the eye of the beholder. It was a combination of high spirits and a peculiarly cerebral kind of fantasy, of taking an idea and following it not merely to its end but beyond. Extreme in everything, there were many moments when he was so carried away that he just did not know when to stop, and sometimes even, like Balzac in this respect, was caught up in the web of his own inventions. Once when walking with Fleuret, who actually finished his days in an asylum, he persuaded himself so convincingly that the end of the world (again the fascination of the Apocalypse) was at hand, that a latter-day Flood was upon them and that the waters of the Seine were rising about their ears, that finally he was clutching Fleuret and staring about him with the haggard eyes of a doomed man. It was probably this quality of fantasy which accounts for Salmon's recent accusation of a certain lack of humanity. When in 1910 the Seine really did flood its banks Salmon claims[7] that Apollinaire was excited by the strangeness of it and only began to think of the inconvenience and danger to river-dwellers when he actually saw the water lapping round his own home. This seems to be a small cause from which to deduce such a sweeping generalisation; fortunately there were many other occasions and particularly during the testing-time of the War when Apollinaire proved to be the most generous and sympathetic of comrades.

[7] André Salmon, *Souvenirs sans fin*, VOL. II, 1956, p. 115.

One of the biggest larks of all at this time was a literary female impersonation which managed to hoodwink everybody throughout the whole of 1909. Actually this again was not originally his idea, but that of Eugene Montfort, the editor of *Les Marges*. One of the particular phenomena of the period was the appearance of a formidable *florilège* of gifted women writers, Anna de Noailles, Renée Vivien, Colette, Gérard d'Houville, Jane Catulle, Gyp, Rachilde, Marcelle Tinayre amongst them; so much so that in many histories of the time they are all lumped together under the heading *Feminine Literature*. Montfort conceived of the idea of devoting a column exclusively to the criticism of women writers. At first he approached several of the women themselves, but they were much too wary to engage in such a perilous undertaking. It was then that he thought of the versatile Apollinaire who was always ready to turn his pen to any task in order to earn some money. Together they hatched a plot whereby Apollinaire would write under a feminine pseudonym: Louise Lalanne. There was really nothing untoward in this. Apollinaire had written under many pseudonyms on many subjects, even politics and economics and finance: this was mere child's play. But as usual he entered into it with a little too much enthusiasm. Assuming a woman's name, he also assumed a woman's cattiness, and soon the fur was flying. His articles attracted great publicity, the secret was kept, everybody was agog to know who was this unknown authoress. Louise Lalanne even began to publish airy, delicate little poems (some of which are said to have been written by Marie Laurencin). But of course she never put in an appearance. She would accept invitations and then make last minute excuses. In short it was one of the stunts of the day, like Willy's of dressing up Polaire and Colette as twins and parading as Le Papa des Claudines. The impersonation lasted a whole year, and Apollinaire the Grand Master of poetry, thoroughly enjoyed thus appearing in "travesti" and was most conscientious about sending in his copy on time. Eventually the secret had to be revealed, and at a banquet given by *Les Marges* Louise Lalanne sent a preposterous letter saying that she had just eloped with a cavalry officer: and then "took off her skirt" and revealed her true identity.[8] It was again a great joke, but the ladies whom he had scratched never forgave him, and, unwittingly, he had made more enemies.

When Apollinaire described Sade as "the most liberated spirit who had ever existed" he was obviously picking out an aspect of the man which he felt was valid also for himself. This idea of complete freedom, a life according to no logic but that of one's own fantasy, outside convention and society, in short, life as much an autonomous creation as a work of art, was what he still had the nerve to pursue at this time. Somebody described him to the publisher Stock as "a mysterious, unfathomable creature, a mixture of folly and common-sense."[9] In everything he showed himself to be a strange mixture of not completely integrated opposites, still precariously poised between them, as on a rope bridge between opposing peaks. Still trying to push forward, still wanting to live every moment to the full, still grasping at every opportunity, he made, like every opportunist, some moves which might have seemed silly, but some also which were strategically sound. Thanks to Paul Léautaud whom he had recently met, "La Chanson du Mal-Aimé" which had been lying in a drawer at the *Mercure de France* for years, was unearthed and published in May 1909. Two years later, as a result of this introduction, he began his regular collaboration with the *Mercure* in the shape of "La Vie anecdotique": it was also the *Mercure* which published *Alcools* in 1913 (although it did in fact use Apollinaire's own earnings to do so). In January 1910 he joined the daily paper *L'Intransigeant* as one of the Thirteen, a corporate body of gossip columnists. It was in this paper that shortly afterwards he was able to take over the art-criticism from André Salmon, one of the most important of all the opportunities that presented themselves at the time. For this now made him into a professional art-critic with the right to pontificate and the platform to do it from. It was a great step forward in his championing of Cubism. As opposed to friendly *exposés* in little reviews, here was a regular outlet in an important national daily and he made full use of it; although it must be added to his credit

[8] For this whole episode cp. Eugène Montfort, *Apollinaire travesti*, 1948.
[9] Adéma, p. 122.

M

that, conscientious in this as in all things, he noted with sympathy and care the works of myriads of lesser artists, and reserved his whip-lashs only for the dregs of Academicism.

In *Les Marges* in 1909, in addition to Louise Lalanne's contributions, he began in his own name a series of articles on "Les Contemporains Pittoresques," which was to include his old friends Gourmont and Jarry, Moréas, Mendès and Ernest La Jeunesse. In November 1909 he gave a lecture on "Les Poètes d'aujourd'hui" at the Université populaire in the faubourg Saint-Antoine. He was in fact beginning to be widely known and discussed. *L'Intransigeant* offered its readers this picture of him in August 1910.

> If you saw Guillaume Apollinaire sitting solidly with his Gambier No. 656 in his mouth, his vast chest confined by a waist-coat with silver buttons, you could not possibly imagine the complexity and subtlety of the soul that is hidden behind this solid Dutch burgher exterior.
>
> A scholar speaking all the Italian dialects, a poet who has also written charming erotic verse, an art critic who appreciates the efforts of the most independent of Independents, Apollinaire loves subtle beauty, solid erudition, old wine, art that is groping its way, and scholarly conversation which hovers with one foot in the air between two opposing truths. He is a wise man after the fashion of Æsop.
>
> He is suspected of having a slight penchant for practical jokes. He is so complex, so much an artist.

Later that year *Le Figaro* added its brush-strokes to the portrait:

> He talks with such precise detail about the landscape and inhabitants of so many countries that nobody knows exactly where he comes from, nor where he has been. Doubtless it is to lead people astray even more that his name situates him right back in the Middle Ages. Yet he belongs to the latest generation of writers produced by *La Revue blanche*.
>
> His face is full, and yet oblong, his eyes are gentle and yet have a strange light; his mouth appears too small for laughter, and yet opens up into great bursts of mirth then closes tightly again: his lips are so red that they give his otherwise tranquil face a suggestion of blood, the vivacious blood of a voluptuary,

but also the blood of cruelty. And as there is a world of irony in his incomparable good manners, so all the gestures of this corpulent man are quick and supple, and the clean-shaven mask of his face would be that of an ecclesiastic, if it had not also the extreme mobility of the mime.[10]

An imposing but disconcerting figure, respected and yet still in the top-heavy position of being well-known as a journalist and critic and spokesman of the *avant-garde*, while having only a very slight body of published work behind him. Of this he was very conscious, although he never let the taste of sour grapes spoil his palate for the works of his friends. He had for instance written a most glowing article in *Vers et prose* when Salmon published his volume of poetry, *Féeries*. But his own, announced ever since 1904 under different titles, still showed no signs of appearing. As usual it was equally difficult to find a publisher willing to invest in a volume of poetry, or to find the money to have it printed himself.

Short stories however were a different matter. He was always proud of his talent as a story-teller, and by now had more than enough to fill a volume. In the spring of 1910 he thankfully signed a contract with Stock for a collection of stories to be called *Phantasmes*. When it appeared in October of that year it had become *L'Hérésiarque et Cie*, with the dedication, "À Thadée Natanson" (of *La Grande France* who had been his first publisher) "ces philtres de phantase." Most of these stories date back to Monaco, to Stavelot and to Germany. There is, however, a little batch of recent date which deals with the weird adventures of a certain character whom he calls Dormesan or the Baron d'Ormesan. Despite the possible reference to Francesco d'Aspermont, the real original for the Baron was a strange Belgian, Géry Pieret, whom Apollinaire had known when he worked for the *Guide du rentier* and whom he had often befriended, and honoured (yet another one), with the title of secretary and—in these stories at least—of Baron. The trouble was that Pieret, apart from being an inveterate gambler, seemed to have no respect for the law, a trait which both fascinated and terrified Apollinaire, and transformed Pieret into a most potent distiller of "phantase."

[10] " Guillaume Apollinaire," *La Revue des lettres modernes*, 1962, p. 73.

It was not so much the actual association with Pieret but the broadcasting of his own delight in what amounted to criminal activities, which was in fact the most foolhardy action of all, and the one which finally made Apollinaire aware that he could not with impunity flout society by mixing this kind of fiction with real life. There might even be an æsthetic moral too, for not only did these stories help to put him on the wrong side of the law, but also they are much less good than his earlier ones. Here his revelling in the macabre seems gratuitous and is not counterbalanced by any flights of fancy or pithy observations. One of the stories, "Un beau film," is worthy of Sade, another, "Cox City," inspired by the Gold Rush, is an extraordinarily complacent display of butchery and anthropophagy.

"Le Toucher à distance," however, unites his life-long fascination with Hebrew lore and his science-fiction whimsy into an amusing and exciting story, as original as any of the early ones. Dormesan manages to perfect a machine which has something in common with Jarry's time machine, with Apollinaire's own in "Le Roi Lune," for a combined gratification of the senses and a desire for ubiquity in history, and with the television set. He can project his physical person into many places at the same time, and so successfully poses as the Messiah. This event provokes one of those world cataclysms which seem to have haunted Apollinaire's imagination at this time. Jews everywhere begin to flock to Palestine, naturally taking their money with them, and this awakens such consternation that all the rich Jewish bankers are put in prison (like the poets in *Le Poète assassiné*), "a fact which caused a great number of financial disasters, panics in Stock Exchanges, bankruptcies and suicides."

If Pieret had not Dormesan's power of making himself appear everywhere, he had a great facility for making objects of art disappear into his own pocket. From the Musée de Louvre for instance: "I'm off to the Louvre, Mademoiselle Marie," he would say, "is there anything you want?" Everybody must at least have suspected what he meant by this *double-entendre*, but nobody wanted to inquire further or feel personally responsible for Piéret's tricks. Such was the general permissiveness and the sense of the autonomy of their own little world, in which normal standards just did not apply, that when he brought home in his pocket two little Iberian statuettes (of no enormous value let it be said), Picasso was quite happy to buy them in order to further his researches into primitive art, and to ask no questions.

But Apollinaire and Picasso could not have been totally unaware of the true state of affairs. According to Apollinaire himself,[11] he later grew nervous about the statuettes and tried to persuade Picasso to restore them. He even says that he suggested to him an idea originally inspired by the Inspecteur des Beaux Arts, although this in itself sounds highly suspect, of making them the centre of a publicity campaign for some big newspaper, as proof of the laxity of supervision in the National Museums. But Picasso apparently preferred to do nothing. Whatever the real truth of this particular story, it is obvious that even in the early days Apollinaire suspected some of the dangers of being involved with a creature like Pieret, for this is how he describes Dormesan:

> . . . I thought of this friend who had vanished, whose imagination and habits certainly gave cause for concern but in whom nevertheless I was keenly interested. The affection which I had felt for him as a schoolfriend, when he was called simply Dormesan; the numerous encounters in which he had given me the chance to appreciate his singular character; his lack of scruples; a certain chaotic erudition, and a very agreeable cast of mind, caused me sometimes to crave for his company again.[12]

Apollinaire even goes so far as to put Dormesan in prison at the end of "Le Guide," appealing to the narrator to intervene on his behalf, and with that uncanny prophetic irony of his declares: "And I could do nothing for the Baron d'Ormesan and as I do not like having anything to do with the Law, I did not even reply." Here he really was playing with fire.

This dabbling in all kinds of experience, seemed also to be the keynote of his poetic activity at the time. After the single, incandescent flame of his visionary poems of 1908, he

---

[11] *Tendre comme le souvenir*, 1952, p. 71.
[12] *L'Hérésiarque et Cie*, 1936, p. 268.

obviously needed to branch out into different directions. In July 1909 to celebrate the marriage of Salmon he wrote "Poème lu au mariage d'André Salmon," which he claimed to have composed on the platform of a bus on the way to the wedding. As he always worked much harder at his poems than he chose to admit, this was most probably not true, but it does bear witness to the apparently casual tone of the poem and the repetitive flow of its rhythm in long, supple, variable *vers libres*, a form which was to emerge as his favourite during the latter part of his life just as the octosyllabic six-lined stanza had been his predilection in earlier days. Although Apollinaire had shown his mastery over *vers libre* as far back as 1901, it seems clear that this poem was written under the immediate influence of Whitman. In his *Dossier d'alcools* Michel Décaudin points out[13] that an article on Whitman by Montfort had appeared in *Les Marges* that same month, and as Apollinaire was at that time a regular contributor to the review, he could hardly have failed to read it. Apart from the use of *vers libre*, the whole theme of those who are "fondés en poésie" being alone able to renew the world is Whitmanesque, and there is even a direct reference to *The Leaves of Grass*: "Les feuilles ô liberté végétale ô seule liberté terrestre."

But this, like the Mallarmean echoes of "Le Brasier," is only the starting point, and Apollinaire's own voice makes itself clearly heard above it. What is peculiarly his own is the juxtaposition of the naïvely confident affirmations of faith in friendship, in poetry and in love, "l'amour qui emplit ainsi que la lumière / Tout le solide espace entre les étoiles et les planètes," alongside a melancholy sense of isolation as of a person embarked on some hazardous undertaking. He is able to make this particularly moving by exteriorising himself as he had done in "Le Brasier" with the image of the lady at the window watching his troubadour self. Now he looks nostalgically backwards at the little lonely figures of the two of them, André and Guillaume, in their youth, "trompés trompés pauvres petits et ne sachant pas encore rire"; and then as if he himself were so moved by the pathos of this and the whole emotional complex of friendship, that inspiration sweeps him away, he

[13] Décaudin, p. 138.

swings out into his particular resonant music, all stops out, where rhyme and assonance intrude again almost uncalled-for:

> Nous partîmes alors pèlerins de la perdition
> A travers les rues à travers les contrées à travers la raison
> Je le revis au bord du fleuve sur lequel flottait Ophélie
> Qui blanche flotte encore entre les nénuphars
> Il s'en allait au milieu des Hamlets blafards
> Sur la flûte jouant les airs de la folie[14]

The backward look at his own past, in nostalgia, regret, self-pity, and its corollary, an anguish at the passing of time, seem to have become an obsessive theme with him at this time. They are indeed often listed among the main subjects of his poetry, but it is only at this particular period—1908 to 1912—that they crop up so frequently and so insistently. "Le Bestiaire" had introduced the regret:

> Belles journées souris du temps
> Vous rongez peu à peu ma vie
> Dieu! Je vais avoir vingt-huit ans
> Et mal vécus, à mon envie[15]

In "Le Voyageur," a poem published in 1912 but probably written earlier, it is his whole past that he surveys, flicking over the images from it as he would the pages of an old photograph album ("Qui donc reconnais-tu sur ces vieilles photographies"): Albert and himself in their sailor suits, the submarine splendour of Mediterranean swimming ("Vagues poissons arqués fleurs soumarines"), the cypresses of the Rhineland, the "orphaned steamer" of his separation from Annie, the bridges of his peregrinations through Paris. This same kaleidoscope figures again in the whole central part of "Zone," and in both poems it is accompanied by the same sense

[14] "Then we set off pilgrims of perdition
Across streets across countries across reason
I saw him again by the river where Ophelia floated
Who still floats white among the waterlilies
He went away amongst wan Hamlets
Playing the tunes of madness on the flute"

[15] "Beautiful days mice of time
Bit by bit you gnaw away my life
God! I shall soon be twenty-eight
Wasted years to my regret"

of desolation as rings through the "trompés trompés pauvres petits" of 1909. "Ouvrez-moi cette porte où je frappe en pleurant" is the entreaty that in "Le Voyageur" unleashes his particular remembrance of things past. It is as if the stepping over the threshold of maturity was particularly prolonged and anguishing for him. In 1911 and 1912 he had good reason for disquiet, but in the years just before, his life seemed rosy enough, and the age of thirty is not normally a crisis point in a man's life.

It is possible that this particular complex about time and the past, is once again linked with the same obsessive problem which he imagined that he had solved triumphantly in 1908. How to be modern, how to create poetry anew? It was for this reason that the poor young men, he and Salmon, had been deceived: because they were "épris, épris des mêmes paroles dont il faudra changer le sens," intoxicated with poetry, when poetry as they knew it had to suffer sea-change. And as time went on the problem was becoming more acute, his responsibility greater. By thirty he should be at the height of his powers and master of his craft. If he did not find some solution now, there could no longer be any excuse of youth or immaturity, but only fundamental incapacity. In "Le Brasier" and "Les Fiançailles" he had thought that he had found the solution, but in fact it was so only for those particular poems at that particular moment and not enough, as he had imagined, to inaugurate a whole new æsthetic. To build up a poem like a *mille-feuilles* of images was a valid premise, but even within those two poems the images, effective though they are, are limited and often repeated, and depend on a white-hot pitch of intensity which could not always be guaranteed. It was probably again more a question of subject matter than method, this always, unless he was driven by a strong emotion, proving his stumbling-block.

In the course of 1909 another solution, and another possibility of being modern, appeared to present itself. While he had been working for *La Phalange* he had met there Jules Romains, who, about the middle of 1908, broke away to found with Duhamel and Charles Vildrac the group called "Le Groupe de l'abbaye" and the doctrine of "Unanimisme." Now it was entirely characteristic of Apollinaire to batten on to the germ of a new idea wherever he found it, knowing full well that he would never be a doctrinaire slave but could always integrate it into his own way of thought and make it his own. Surely too much importance can be attached to the sheer originality of an idea, as opposed to what is built up from it, which must be the final criterion. In any case the whole doctrine of Unanimism, of the individual being at one with the whole of life, uniting in himself the past as well as all present living forms was very much in line with a sentiment that Apollinaire had always been struggling to express, even from the days of "Merlin et la vieille femme" and *L'Enchanteur pourrissant*. For a while he was undoubtedly most stimulated to see it spelt-out and formulated as the corner-stone of a new æsthetic. It was one way of turning the sense of "Je voudrais éprouver une ardeur infinie" into poetry. During 1909, under this influence, he conceived the idea of writing a "revolutionary calendar in verse," and in a lecture given at the Salon d'Automne of 1909 Romains cited a fragment of his entitled "Brumaire," which Michel Décaudin has identified[16] as the "Cortège" of *Alcools*. Apollinaire repaid the compliment by quoting Romains in November in his lecture at the Université populaire. The only other poem that remains from this project is "Vendémiaire," and this is the one unadulterated example of Apollinaire trumpeting out in a fine flush of enthusiasm the Unanimist theme, and at the same time of his dove-tailing it perfectly into his own desire to celebrate life dionysically. The idea of Paris wanting to slake her thirst on the wine distilled from out of the whole world is introduced by the poet in his role of Grand Master proclaiming to posterity "Hommes de l'avenir souvenez-vous de moi," and is rounded off by his declaring that it is he who is the throat of Paris and who has drunk the heady liquor of the universe until he is in a state of cosmic intoxication.

> Actions belles journées sommeils terribles
> Végétation Accouplements musiques éternelles
> Mouvements Adorations douleur divine
> Mondes qui vous ressemblez et qui nous ressemblez

---

[16] Décaudin, p. 128.

Je vous ai bus et ne fus pas désaltéré
Mais je connus dès lors quelle saveur a l'univers
Je suis ivre d'avoir bu tout l'univers[17]

He had already used this image of men fermenting like grapes in the wine-press in "Onirocritique": in fact "Vendémiaire" is closely linked with the 1908 poems both in imagery, (kings, fire, stars, sirens and the young swimmer occur yet again), and in its Messianic mood. Here, though it is exceptionally, he manages to sustain the one uninterrupted note of triumph and megalomania throughout: the sweeping rhythm of the initial rhyming alexandrine seems to carry him along triumphantly, even through the occasional *vers libres*, at a breathless, slightly frenzied pace. There are none of the sudden shifts of mood, the doubts and ironical sidelong glances at himself, only a huge desire to gourmandise after experience. It could be that his confidence was bolstered up to and kept at this pitch by the feeling that at this moment he was not entirely alone in his aims for poetry. This sort of professional solidarity was always of the utmost importance to Apollinaire, an extension of his emotional craving for love and affection. He was always ready to join associations of writers, to sit on committees and help the younger generation as much as he backed up his own.

In fact the manuscript of "Vendémiaire,"[18] not unexpectedly, does reveal traces of the old nagging doubts, the loneliness, the groping in the dark:

Et parmi tout le peuple habile des machines
La poésie errait, plaintive et si divine!
Je la pris dans mes bras, moi, poète inconnu
Et le seul de mon temps qui m'en sois souvenu[19]

---

[17] "Actions beautiful days terrible slumbers
Vegetation Couplings eternal music
Movements Adorations divine sorrow
Worlds which are like each other and like us
I have drunk you and not slaked my thirst
But I knew after that the flavour of the universe
I am intoxicated because I have drunk the whole universe"

[18] Décaudin, p. 225.

[19] "And amongst all the clever crowd of machines
Poetry was wandering, plaintive and so divine!
I took her in my arms, I, unknown poet
And alone of my time to have remembered her"

There is even a reference to his obsession with his own climacteric, and time that has died on him, in the familiar schizoid image. In the street a man calls his attention to a corpse. It is himself:

> L'homme reprit en m'entraînant: Aie bon courage
> Te voici parvenu au milieu de ton âge[20]

But in the finished version he chose, and it is the choice which is significant, to omit these, and to leave intact his hymn to joy.

"Cortège"—almost certainly the original "Brumaire"— which also owes a certain superficial debt to Unanimism, follows a very different course. It seems feasible to see it as a mirror of his progress through his various, recent allegiances. Like "Les Fiançailles" it is yet another version of an *art poétique*: it cannot be coincidental that he ends it with a faithful echo of Boileau.

It begins in exactly the same vein as "Le Brasier" and "Les Fiançailles," using the same method of packing abstruse images tightly together—the bird which flies upside down and rests in the air and has two eyelids (this latter fact he had already noted in one of the Druids' songs in *L'Enchanteur pourrissant*), space, light, the earth seen from the sky—to express the same complex of his religious faith in poetry and the chiaroscuro of his own glory.

In a completely different tone of voice he then switches to the ironical note that had informed the humble but limpid stanzas of "Le Bestiaire."

> Un jour
> Un jour je m'attendais moi-même
> Je me disais Guillaume il est temps que tu viennes
> Pour que je sache enfin celui-là que je suis[21]

and then through the transition of his own powers of divination, "Moi qui connais les autres," he is launched into the

[20] "The man said as he dragged me away. Have courage
Here you are half-way through your life"

[21] "One day
One day I was waiting for myself
I said to myself Guillaume it is time that you came
So that you can know what sort of person I am"

Unanimist theme of surveying the cortège of past and present
figures who have contributed to form him, Guillaume.

This contemplation of the past, which for so long had been
his great poetic stimulus, is then sufficient to awaken the old
Janus in him. Tempted by the comfort and security of it, he
now gives way to a temporary denial of his self-imposed
burden, lets himself run along the sleepers of impeccably
traditional alexandrines, petrified unusually for him in the
past historic, towards a confession of his vertigo before the
empty, formless chasms of the future.

> Temps passés trépassés les dieux qui me formâtes
> Je ne vis que passant ainsi que vous passâtes
> Et détournant mes yeux de ce vide avenir
> En moi-même je vois tout le Passé grandir
> Rien n'est mort que ce qui n'existe pas encore
> Près du passé luisant demain est incolore.
> Il est informe aussi près de ce qui parfait
> Présente tout ensemble et l'effort et l'effet[22]

And out of all the past, in complete revulsion from his
recent, dizzy contemplation of the cosmic future, he chooses
to go right back in that last couplet to the confined womb
of seventeenth-century classical form.

Inevitably a deleted part of the manuscript of the poem
is more explicit, and the whole complex is out of the bag.
After one of the repetitions of his playful little refrain, "Un
jour je m'attendais moi-même," comes the tell-tale cry from
the heart. "Pourquoi faut-il être si moderne?"[23] Why must
one be so modern? But it is not, as some critics imply, any sort
of recanting or changing of horses in mid-stream, only a moment
of lassitude under the self-imposed and at times almost overwhelming burden.

[22] "Past time dead the gods who formed me
I live only passing by as you passed by
And turning my eyes away from this empty future
In myself I see the whole Past wax big
Nothing is dead but that which does not yet exist
Next to the gleaming past tomorrow is colourless
It is unformed also next to that which perfect
Presents at the same time both effort and effect"

[23] Décaudin, p. 126.

IX

La Santé

Poor Guillaume Apollinaire! In 1911 a very different kind of burden was to be loaded on to his shoulders. His imprisonment on the charge of receiving the stolen Iberian statuettes and possibly of even stealing the Mona Lisa is a famous and many-times garbled story, and the moral that seems to emerge from it is as he himself put it—"If somebody were to accuse me of stealing the bells of Notre Dame, I'd take to my heels at once," or in the words of the Good Soldier Schweik, "I'm innocent, that's why I'm arrested." If you are not only innocent, but stateless, illegitimate, mid-European (therefore obviously Jewish), a leader of the artistic *avant-garde* (therefore not to be taken seriously), and a purveyor of pornography (therefore a corrupter of youth), you are asking for punishment. It is a rather sinister cautionary tale, and although it was to end more or less happily, it might well—without the writers' solidarity which Apollinaire was so right to prize—have had disastrous consequences for him.

Actually Apollinaire's behaviour about the whole affair, if not suspect, still seemed to belong to the realms of his own fantasy, and so was bound to appear indiscreet. In December 1910 *L'Hérésiarque et Cie*, which broadcast the adventures and the crimes of the Baron d'Ormesan, was in the running for the Prix Goncourt, and although finally unsuccessful, it attracted more publicity thereby than it might otherwise have done. The stories being highly original, more than one critic underlines the family likeness between creator and literary offspring: "Guillaume Apollinaire's book *L'Hérésiarque et Cie*," pronounced the reviewer for *Le Figaro*, "resembles him as a son does his father"; and it did not need particular perspicacity to see the outlaw vein of violence which ran through it. Moreover Dormesan and Pieret could be and were easily identified, Apollinaire and his picturesque acquaintance being well known to a large number of people in artistic circles.

In the spring of 1911 Pieret had arrived back from America with money. (Had this anything to do with the Gold Rush of "Cox City"?) All this he promptly lost at the races and so had to be sheltered once again under Apollinaire's elastic roof. There were apparently some occasions on which it also had housed tramps from under the bridges of the Seine. In May he abandoned himself to his favourite temptation once more and stole yet a third statuette which he hid in Apollinaire's flat in Auteuil. Now it is not certain whether Apollinaire knew about this from the beginning or discovered it only later. But, by the most extraordinary of coincidences, it was at just this time, August 1911, that the Mona Lisa was stolen from the Louvre by somebody quite unconnected with Pieret. Nevertheless the coincidence was too great for Apollinaire not to suspect, as indeed everybody else did whatever Pieret said, that he was the culprit for that theft also. And naturally enough, this, the Mona Lisa being of even greater moment than the bells of Notre Dame, had enormous consequences. Apollinaire was terrified. He saw himself trapped into complicity. He did not want to give away his *protégé*, nor did he want to reveal his own part or Picasso's in condoning the 1907 affair: and Picasso still had those two statuettes. Frantically, like the hunted man that he was, he cast around for some way out. Eventually with characteristic lack of realism, he fell back on the earlier solution of counter-attack, of offering the statues to some newspaper who could restore them to the Louvre and thereby make a big publicity stunt out of the lack of care that was taken to guard the nation's art treasures. Everybody's honour—and incidentally their skin— would be saved. And a valid point would be proved. In fact he could almost persuade himself that he was rendering a great service both to the nation and to art. As he himself was by this time the art-critic of *L'Intransigeant* he took the opportunity of writing an article on 24 Aug., after the theft of the Mona Lisa, accusing the Musée du Louvre of laxity in its security system. "It is real laziness, indifference, utter carelessness," he declared sententiously in a supreme moment of dramatic irony.

From now on the plot thickens, and accounts of it begin to vary. Apollinaire himself says[1] that immediately he knew about the Mona Lisa he turned Pieret and his statue out of his flat, and Pieret then sold the statue to *Paris-Journal*. Another version is that it was he himself who was responsible for handing it over. Even if Pieret did so it was probably either on Apollinaire's advice, or because he had overheard him suggest it. At any event *Paris-Journal* handed the statue back to the Louvre with great fanfares of publicity.

There remained the two statuettes in Picasso's possession. These obviously presented a greater problem, a complicity of longer standing. Again Apollinaire worked himself up into a state of frantic anxiety. How to get rid of the objects? They were almost as bad as a corpse. Fernande Olivier gives a fantastic account[2] of the behaviour of Apollinaire and Picasso on the night that they decided to dispose of the incriminating evidence. Not for nothing had they been imbibing all these years the exploits of their ganster hero Fantômas. Now they obviously began to see themselves in a similar light. They who never so much as looked at a playing card, promptly set to in true Apache manner, and, smoking in utter silence, played cards until it was dark enough for them to steal out into the streets with their loot in a suitcase. She claims that at first they intended to drop it in the Seine, but that their professional artistic consciences at last won the day, and in the early hours of the morning they too ended up in the offices of *Paris-Journal*. The scandal this second, preposterous time was even greater, so much so that even Pieret was terrified and came to Apollinaire begging him to save him (just as Dormesan had done in the story written a year earlier). Apollinaire gave him money and packed him off for the Gare de Lyon.

Of course somebody talked. It was an example of Apollinaire's naïvety to imagine that the secret could be absolute, or that he had no enemies who would be delighted to stab him in the back. An anonymous letter was written to *Le Parquet*, the police arrived on Apollinaire's doorstep and he was immediately arrested on the certain charge of receiving

[1] *Tendre comme le souvenir*, 1952, p. 72.
[2] Olivier, p. 184.

stolen goods and under suspicion of collusion in the theft of the Mona Lisa. He was treated exactly like a common criminal, handcuffed, taken off to La Santé in a police van and put into solitary confinement in a cell where the first thing that he noticed was the spine-chilling inscription scratched on the wall "Dédé of Menilmontant for murder." He was then interrogated at length, his flat was ransacked, and his *concierge* was questioned about his personal habits, particularly whether he used to receive little girls or boys. The effect of this summary treatment, the solitude in the condemned cell, the shock to his touchy pride, his poet's sensibility, his personal fastidiousness, and above all the nightmare fear of future consequences all combined to overwhelm him. There was only one consolation in his suffering. He employed his time writing poetry.

The police kept up their interrogations. They threatened that if he did not reveal all he knew, they would search the homes of his mother and his brother and Marie Laurencin. This sense of bringing shame to his family seemed to affect him very deeply. In the manuscript of the *A la Santé* poems[3] there are three verses childish in the repetition of this litany of distress:

Pauvre maman   Et vous Marie
Mon pauvre frère   O mon amie
Pardonnez-moi   Pardonnez-moi
Pardonnez-moi   Pardonnez-moi

Vous qui m'aimez
O mes amis
Pardonnez-moi
Pardonnez-moi[4]

---

[3] Décaudin, p. 211.

[4] "Poor mother   And you Marie
My poor brother   O my love
Forgive me   Forgive me
Forgive me   Forgive me

You who love me
O my friends
Forgive me
Forgive me"

It was this finally which wore him down into admitting Picasso's part in the affair. There was really in fact very little else to admit because he did not even know Pieret's whereabouts by now. Picasso was summoned and questioned along with Apollinaire.

Here is Apollinaire's version of that confrontation before the examining magistrate. As nobody else is in a position to give one, except Picasso who has not chosen to do so, this will have to serve, although it may not be gospel truth.

> The next day confrontation with my friend who denies knowing anything about the affair. I thought I was done for but the examining magistrate, seeing that I had done nothing, but that I was simply a victim of the police because I hadn't wanted to betray the fugitive, authorised me to interrogate the witness, and using Socrates' favourite *maieutic*, I quickly forced X to admit that what I had said was true.[5]

In the meantime, however, relief forces were being massed in Apollinaire's defence. The most relevant was a strange letter on 9 Sep. from Pieret, who was obviously not without his kind of honour, and who signed himself as the Baron d'Ormesan. It was written from Marseilles and declared that his patron was innocent, and that he alone was to blame.

Amongst well-known writers and journalists and artists a petition was arranged, and *Paris-Journal* published a manifesto on Apollinaire's behalf. Toussaint-Luca, his childhood friend and now a barrister, gathered together his particular legal batteries, and on 13 Sep. helped at the final interrogation with the examining magistrate, after which Apollinaire was provisionally set free.

There had naturally enough been enormous publicity about this extraordinary story. A leading art-critic and poet suspected of stealing the Mona Lisa! It was the big news story of the day, and a pitiful photograph of Apollinaire in handcuffs, looking like a whipped dog, had been in all the papers. Although many people had rushed to his defence, quite a number had been only too glad to have the chance of attacking him. In particular, the deplorable anti-Semites got to work,

[5] *Tendre comme le souvenir*, 1952, p. 73.

N

and with their usual excess of zeal accused the "foreigner" Apollinaire of being Jewish. Moreover, the body of drearily academic painters whom he had been busy ridiculing found here a means of having their revenge. Even three months later the attacks and sly references were still continuing, always directed at Apollinaire's weak spot, the fact that he was a foreigner of doubtful origins and that if was not careful he could be extradited. The paper *L'Oeuvre* managed to rake up his activities for the Bibliothèque des Curieux. "Try to find out how I can get myself naturalised," he wrote despairingly to Toussaint-Luca, "for what on earth will become of me if I'm expelled from France?"[6] He was in fact put on probation and the charge was not finally annulled until June 1912. One cannot exaggerate the effect that the whole affair had on him.

Purely practically, such an incident could do him no good in the public eye: even after an acquittal some mud always sticks. It definitely increased a sort of dubious, outsider reputation which he had always tended to have. Gide for instance, although attracted by him, had been a little mistrustful of this "Bohemian" side to him. The doors of some papers, for example *Le Matin* and *Le Passant*, to which he had been contributing, were henceforth closed. In defiance then, his own attitude towards the *avant-garde* was hardened and strengthened and he began to feel even more sharply the need to experiment and to break with the past. Emotionally it very much increased his sense of insecurity, which the warm camaraderie of the last years had been helping to dissipate. Some of the people whom he had thought of as friends had passed by on the other side: and in his low moments for some time now he would indulge in a sense of martyrdom, even of crucifixion. But he had also been able to pick out those who were his real friends, and it so happened that some of these were of recent date and also amongst the most progressive of all the artists. This again confirmed him on the road to experiment.

Naturally his poetry was greatly influenced. The experience directly provided subject matter, and later, indirectly, newer experimental modes of expression.

[6] Toussaint-Luca, p. 90.

In prison he had turned, as always when he was in distress,
to poetry. And to express this strong emotion, made even more
intense by solitary confinement, he chose, inevitably, the strict
discipline of traditional form, pouring out his woes spon-
taneously into the carefully turned music of the *A la Santé*
stanzas: and here the manuscripts reveal comparatively
little alteration or patchwork, but only deletion. One feels
that if Guillaume Apollinaire ever talked in his sleep it must
have been in verse. "What a difficult thing prose is!" Even
vers libre seemed at times rather too much of a strain, and
rhyme creeps inexorably back.

Characteristically too, in these poems written at a genuinely
critical moment of nightmare terror, there is again no small
measure of self-dramatisation. "Et quelle voix sinistre ulule /
Guillaume qu'es-tu devenu." The role of Verlaine was an
obvious one to watch himself playing: whether he thought
first of the poet and followed in his steps towards religion, or
whether an instinctive recourse to prayer reminded him of
Verlaine's attitude in "Sagesse," there are definite echoes,
quotations almost, of this poet, which if one did not know
Apollinaire's supple, adaptable, highly impressionable nature
might make his whole reaction seem like play-acting:

> Que deviendrai-je ô Dieu qui connais ma douleur
> Toi qui me l'as donnée[7]

and

> J'écoute les bruits de la ville
> Et prisonnier sans horizon
> Je ne vois rien qu'un ciel hostile
> Et les murs nus de ma prison[8]

But the really basic attitude to religion, Apollinaire's
own original twist, comes out in a manuscript poem, of
which he eventually used only one stanza (that beginning

[7] "What will become of me o God who knowest my suffering
Thou who hast given it to me"

[8] "I listen to the noises of the town
And prisoner without horizon
I see nothing but a hostile sky
And the naked walls of my prison"

"Que lentement passent les heures"). First there is the global self-pity of the introduction:

> Je suis Guillaume Apollinaire
> Dit d'un nom slave pour vrai nom
> Ma vie est triste tout entière
> Un écho répond toujours non
> Lorsque je dis une prière[9]

(That octosyllabic line, "Je suis Guillaume Apollinaire" had an invincible fascination for this man who had in early years been so worried to know who he was. He uses it in the extremes of self-assertion, as well as here in the extremes of abasement, but never in half-measures.) Then comes the hint of an identification with somebody quite other than Verlaine:

> Je viens de recevoir des lettres
> Vous ne m'abandonnez donc pas
> Jésus que l'on emprisonna
> Et que les douze abandonnèrent[10]

From now on, for the next year or so, he makes even more explicit this sense of his own crucifixion. It was to become the more developed version of the theme of "La Chanson du Mal-Aimé" and *L'Enchanteur pourrissant* and the burning martyrdom of "Le Brasier." For, at about the same time as the unfortunate episode of La Santé—and this may not have been entirely fortuitous—it was borne in upon him that Marie was growing away from him. In October 1909, perhaps even then sensing this, he had moved from Montmartre to be near her in Auteuil. She by now had really found her own feet in the world; she had become well known as a painter (largely thanks to Apollinaire's publicity), she had learned how to use her particular ugliness as a kind of charm; in short his Galatea had come to life. And now when he was at his most defenceless

---

[9] "I am Guillaume Apollinaire
My real name is Slav
My life is utter sadness
An echo always answers no
Whenever I say a prayer"

[10] "I have just received some letters
And so you are not abandoning me
Jesus who was put in prison
And abandoned by the twelve disciples"

and really needed her, she was wanting to lead her own life and not to devote herself wholeheartedly to his exigent, possessive demands. As yet she made no complete break: he could only sense that she was no longer under his dominion as she had been, but their love was in its death throes. And it was at this stage only that it proved a direct source of inspiration in his poetry. Marie, who earlier had barely figured, now becomes the poignant subject of a series of some of Apollinaire's most popular poems. In the year following his imprisonment, from the end of 1911 onwards, he wrote "Le pont Mirabeau," perhaps the best known and most musical of all, "Per te præsentit aruspex," in which he himself gives voice, now ironically, to the Pygmalion idea, "Cors de chasse," "Marie," which mirror progressively the growing realisation of this dying of love, and at last "Zone," one of the finest of all his achievements, which gives way to the anguish that mourns its passing.

"Le pont Mirabeau" is closely linked with the *A la Santé* poems. The manuscript version of "Dans une fosse comme un ours"[11] continues thus right into the famous refrain of "Le pont Mirabeau":

> Quand donc finira la semaine
> Quand donc finiront les amours
> Vienne la nuit sonne l'heure
> Les jours s'en vont et je demeure[12]

which with its echo of Villon, "Allé s'en est et je demeure," shows that Apollinaire had cast his mind back to yet another illustrious criminal who had preceded him into prison, and which proves that even in this autumn of 1911 he had sensed the change in his emotional life, and felt the need to withstand it by an assertion of his own identity. The whole experience seems to bring to a head this haunting sense of time passing and with it his youth, his liberty, his love, his life. "Le pont Mirabeau" with its most plangent, incantatory rhythm seems to be intended as a sort of charm, to conjure up the wished-for

[11] Décaudin, p. 212.

[12] "Whenever will the week end
Whenever will love end
Night may come the hour strike
The days pass by and I remain"

state of solidity "à deux" against the fluidity of a world of change, their arms steady and joined like a bridge over the continual flow of life:

> Vienne la nuit sonne l'heure
> Les jours s'en vont je demeure[13]

It is a far cry from the confident Zaroastro claims of 1908: nevertheless the refrain "je demeure" springs from the same source even if now it smacks only of wishful thinking.

"Marie" is similar to "Le pont Mirabeau" in its pronounced musical quality and in containing a line from the same manuscript of *A la Santé*, "Quand donc finira la semaine." Similarly Apollinaire here uses the flow of water as an image. This time however it is not merely of life, but of his own inexhaustible suffering. In "Marie" the pain seems to have grown more acute: the music is the staccato, stabbing rhythm of the Stavelot jig, not the gentle flow of the Seine: the pictures of the past are more vivid and therefore more heart-searching, and although the first verse conjures up Stavelot, it is the young Marie of the skipping-rope who is in his mind, the "gamine de Paris," Tristouse Ballerinette; the whole idea of youth and gaiety being backed up by the reference to Apollinaire's own youth and a possible similarity of colouring between Marie and Mareye. In the same way, the second verse stretches back into the past through an evocation of Marie's paintings, to the inclusion of the Stavelot notebook line: "Oui je veux aimer mais vous aimer à peine." Similarly Annie and Germany are integrated into the idea of Marie in the third verse: "les brebis s'en vont dans la neige." Thus all his loves are condensed into one, and this is made the more heartbreaking because it is only "un coeur changeant," fickle and not belonging to him. He is the "mal-aimé" for ever. But he has matured considerably since the days of that "chanson." Instead of the violent outpourings, this is a dense, allusive evocation, made poignant not by rage and sobs but by delicate shafts of irony, "Et puis encore, que sais-je."

Three years later he was to write to another woman "I

[13] "Night may come the hour strike
The days pass by and I remain"

do not mind if love makes me suffer at times. It is an inexhaustible source of poetry. It's true though that the suffering
must not last too long."[14] It would seem in "Marie" that that
saturation point had nearly been reached: "Quand donc
finira la semaine!"

"Passons, passons, puisque tout passe" in "Cors de chasse."
In *A la Santé*:

> Que lentement passent les heures
> Comme passe un enterrement
> Tu pleureras l'heure où tu pleures
> Qui passera trop vitement
> Guillaume avant que tu ne meures
> Comme passent toutes les heures
>
> Années passées, lointaine ronde
> Les ans passaient comme une ronde
> Où sont les printemps[15]

He seems to have been veritably haunted at this time by the
snows of yesteryear. In "Cors de chasse," which is a masterpiece of condensation, twelve octosyllables of very limited
rhyme scheme containing a whole love story, he now strikes a
different pose in an attempt to master his grief. He takes up
again his kingly stance, his "Moi qui sais des lais pour les
reines" attitude. "Notre histoire est noble et tragique." Not
for him to sink into common pathos or self-pity. If the past is
congealed by art, worn "like the Greek actor's mask," external-
ised in a strict form, it will no longer hurt, but only ennoble.
But the poet is in fact no king: he finds his pose too difficult
to sustain. With the fluctuation of mood, to which he is
notably addicted, it is instead the opium-scattered wits of

[14] Rouveyre, p. 216.

[15] "How slowly the hours pass by
Pass like a funeral
You will weep for the hour when you are weeping
Which will pass too quickly
Guillaume before you die
As all hours pass by

Past years distant dance
The years passed like a dance
Where has Spring gone"

Thomas de Quincey that he calls to mind, a besotted dream, and after all the noble composure he is swept away in flux and regret for time past:

> Passons passons puisque tout passe
> Je me retournerai souvent[16]

And that past is reduced to nothing, only echoes spent upon the dying wind like the sound of hunting horns:

> Les souvenirs sont cors de chasse
> Dont meurt le bruit parmi le vent[17]

He had let Matisse portray the artist's progress as a journey from "study" to "conscience." From the showing of "Cors de chasse" he could well have described the crystallisation of his own poetry as the change from gushing geyser to one shining raindrop.

Not for many years had Apollinaire written such a collection of poems—there were other less successful ones like "Per te præsentit aruspex" and "L'Enfer"—in strictly traditional metre, with so many obvious echoes of the past ringing through them. In "Cors de chasse," for instance, are heard strains of Verlaine, Villon, Moréas, and Vigny. And yet it would seem that here he was really playing tricks with this bogey time that he felt was cheating him so. For it was at precisely the same period when he chose to cast his own poems into completely classical mould, that his attitude was becoming more outspoken about the *avant-garde* generally; that as opposed to merely taking the opportunity of speaking up on their side whenever he could, he now systematically tried to formulate the credo of modern art in his own words, and really took the banner into his own hands. This more militant attitude, it is interesting to note, can be traced back directly to the period of his imprisonment. One of the factors was undoubtedly the sympathy that he had met with in certain new friends, the Delaunays and the Picabias who were the most forward-looking

[16] "Let us pass pass by since everything passes
I shall often look back"

[17] "Memories are hunting horns
Whose cry dies on the wind"

of all the *avant-garde*; so much so that they were even regarded by the Cubists as heretics.

"Friends without whom I cannot live" he had written in "Le Bestiare" in 1908. Fortunately there were many of the old faithfuls too who had stood by him: and they also, although unwittingly, helped to foster his championing of novelty.

Another group, headed by André Billy and Salmon and Dalize, seeing him so dogged by persecution mania after La Santé and so saddened by Marie, hit on just the right idea to cheer him up and restore him to his former self. Once again they would found a review and once again Apollinaire would play his favourite role of editor. This was the most excellent of medicines, but it worked even more radically than his friends had realised: for Apollinaire saw the new review not merely, like the old *Festin d'Esope*, as yet another "revue des belles lettres," but as the much-needed platform from which to trumpet the virtues of Cubism, the "new painting." Immediately after his release from prison he had been lifting his voice again even more fervently in praise of Cubism in his column in *L'Intransigeant*, "the most elevated, the most sublime form of art," he called it, but there he was limited by space and his duty to record the qualities of other artists as well. He had no opportunity in a daily paper, nor would such partiality have been tolerated, to attempt any analysis or theorising, and still grouped the Cubists *en bloc*, although already by 1912 after the great period of analytical Cubism when Braque's and Picasso's painting were indistinguishable, individual tendencies had confused the general picture and there was even now a strong band of dissidents within the group. In his enthusiastic way he immediately seized the new review for these purposes, but his friends were by no means so zealous. "You and your bloody Cubists," said Dalize, "you'll frighten everybody off." However, once launched, Apollinaire steamed on regardless and in the first number of *Les Soirées de Paris*, which appeared in February 1912, he published alongside two of the most traditional of his recent poems, "Per te præsentit aruspex" and "Le pont Mirabeau," an article entitled "Du Sujet dans la peinture nouvelle," in which with his usual percipience he announces the beginnings of non-figurative art.

> These painters, even if they still observe nature, no longer imitate it and they carefully avoid the representation of natural scenes observed and reconstituted after study. . . . Thus we are approaching an entirely new kind of art which will stand in the same relation to the art that we have previously known as music does to literature. It will be pure painting in the same way as music is pure literature. . . . The young artists of the extreme schools follow the secret aim of creating pure painting. It is an entirely new plastic art. It is only at its beginning and is still not as abstract as it would wish to be. The majority of the new painters are doing mathematics without knowing it, or them, but they have not yet abandoned nature which they study patiently in order that she shall show them the path of life.

This was the first of a whole series of very conscious strategical moves. In February in *Les Marches de Provence* he writes an article on Picasso in which he claims that all the qualities that Michelangelo had stipulated as necessary for good painting are present in Picasso. In February, both in *L'Intransigeant* and in *Le Petit bleu* where he had also begun an art column, he criticises the Italian Futurists strongly. They had declared that their aim was to portray "the simultaneity of states of soul." Apollinaire approves the idea of simultaneity, that is, movement, but is repelled by their "states of soul." They just do not approach the quality of a Picasso or a Derain. They are still interested in the subject rather than plastic preoccupations, and it is these plastic preoccupations which are going to lead to the new art. What is more, they are loud-voiced and insolent and swollen-headed, and above all they are not French. For he had also become more pro-French than ever since La Santé.

In March in *Les Soirées de Paris* he publishes four letters of Cézanne, thus crowning the great ancestor of the movement. In his review of Le Salon des Indépendants of the same month, he seems now to be recognising the need to distinguish between at least two tendencies within Cubism: Picasso on the one hand, and what he calls the "Imagistes," Dufy and Lhote on the other. Also, and this is the most interesting point of this review, he singles out Delaunay as an isolated figure with a monumental vision of the universe and extols the great canvas *La Ville de Paris*: "This picture marks the arrival of a conception of art that has perhaps been lost ever since the great Italian painters."

In April and May in *Les Soirées de Paris* he continues his task of explaining globally to the public some of the aims of the new painting. Courageously, under the title "La Peinture nouvelle," he embarks on a definition of the fourth dimension, a term which had been floating through the studios and cafés of Montmartre for several years, and which boomerang-like had been used against the young painters by those scoffers, whose creed it is that anything new is a joke in the worst possible taste, directed personally against them. Apollinaire's attempt to define the fourth dimension has been similarly used against him. Given the existence of something like a fourth dimension, call it time, space or the infinite, and given the fact that man's understanding hitherto has been largely three-dimensional, it would seem that Apollinaire does quite well in evoking, if not in actually defining in exact terms, the painters' conception of it:

> As it offers itself to the human understanding in plastic terms the fourth dimension claims to be composed of the three known measures: it figures the immensity of space stretching out into eternity in all directions at one specific moment. It is space itself, the dimensions of the infinite: it is this which endows objects with their plasticity. It gives them the proportions that they merit in the work, whilst in Greek art for example, a partially mechanical rhythm ceaselessly destroys proportions.

Later he goes on to say that this is merely a "Utopian expression: an aspiration towards the sublime which needed to be noted historically." As such, his definition is unexceptionable. From it, he then leads on to the very pertinent point that the new art now takes the whole universe and not merely man himself as its ideal, that it aims to express the grandeur of metaphysical forms: and once again he clings to his eternal lifebuoy of a belief that it is poets and artists who change the face of the earth. Without them would be chaos.

Unfortunately he chooses to accompany these declarations with one of his own poems, "L'Enfer," which with the triteness of its subject and the platitude of its versification, would provide scant assistance to a world that had fallen into such a state. The publication of a poem like this does in fact make one wonder if at this particular moment he was not putting his best energies into his art propaganda.

Throughout the summer however, there was to be a complete stop to all his activities. After giving a lecture on "Le Sublime moderne" to inaugurate an exhibition of the art of Normandy in Rouen, he is silent until October. And for the best of reasons. It was in June that the inevitable break with Marie came and although at heart he expected it, when it actually happened he refused to believe it. It was simply unthinkable that Marie, whom he had created, should deny him! Serge Férat tells[18] of how one evening he went to dinner and Marie was not there. Guillaume left to fetch her but she refused to come. "You've got too bad a temper," she kept saying. Now Apollinaire sank again into one of his great troughs of despair. With him love was always a symbol for the whole of life. When love failed him it was as if everything, all the springs of being, had dried up, energy, hope, religion, sunshine, and even for a while that last resource of poetry. He could not bear now to stay in his own flat in Auteuil near Marie, where he had been happy with her and known his moments of megalomania, but gratefully accepted Férat's offer of his own house while he was on holiday. There he sequestrated himself and refused to do anything, to work or even go out for a whole month, so totally had his self-confidence deserted him. One of his devoted friends, Marc Brésil, writes of him, and it is already some time after the rupture, as if he were a very sick man to be nursed night and day. It must have represented a complete nervous breakdown, as, so he had implied, the separation from Annie had done, only this time exaggerated by his experience of La Santé:

> I have been with him all the time, or if I left him for a few hours I was still working on his behalf. Saturday morning when I

---

[18] Durry, p. 51.

went back to him after a whole day away, I found him just as miserable and downcast and prostrated as in the first days. Above all don't talk about it, pretend to believe in his energy, in his mind and inflexible will because he is never weaker than when one pities him. . . . We shall certainly win through if we let the crisis take its normal course. Paul Reboux asked him for two stories for *Le Journal*. He hasn't done one yet despite all my efforts and I can't be cross with him because I know he is so miserable, so low, so good-natured with such a sad kind of good nature, and weary, so weary, wearied by everything. . . . He must feel that he is surrounded by affection.[19]

Fortunately he was. The Picabias for instance did their best to cheer him up. They took him with them on a day trip to England and later to Mme Picabia's home in the Jura for a holiday. The Delaunays also more or less adopted him. In fact later on in the autumn, when he had decided to leave the now hateful Auteuil and to move to a new apartment in the boulevard Saint-Germain, which, however, was not yet ready for him, he actually lived with them for two or three months. And eventually friendship and affection, combined with the old fervent faith in art, helped his normally exuberant nature to reassert itself. For even in the darkness of his despair poetry and art still managed to shine, if at first only thinly. Responding obviously to his friend's own idealism he writes to Delaunay:

I think of only one thing, my good friend, and that is that I am sadness itself, but not a miserable, impoverished kind of sadness which deadens everything. Mine shines like a star, it illumines the path of art through the terrifying night of life.[20]

Nothing could be common or mean for Apollinaire. Just as in "Cors de chasse" he had declared: "no indifferent detail renders our love pathetic," so his particular sadness must be a different thing from ordinary sadness, global, transcendental, and out of it finally must spring poetry.

And he was justified. Out of the miserably pathetic details of his mental sickness, when he was nothing but a lost child, alone and rudderless, needing to be comforted at every moment, there emerged the very fine long poem "Zone" which really does illumine the path of modern art.

[19] Adéma, p. 152.   [20] *Op. cit.*, p. 153.

One of those literary controversies, which tend to blind one
to a work's intrinsic merits, has grown up around "Zone."
It is a question of whether Apollinaire was influenced by the
poem "Pâques à New York" by the younger poet Blaise Cendrars, and has been debated so fully mainly because "Zone"
has appeared as something of a milestone in modern poetry:
the implication being that if Apollinaire "copies" from Cendrars
much of the merit of "Zone" would melt away, priority being
all. The most complete and sensible treatment of the whole
vexed problem, as well as the best analysis of "Zone," is that
of Marie-Jeanne Durry in her *Alcools*,[21] and she rightly points
out that even if Apollinaire was influenced by Cendrars' poem
it was only superficially, that "Zone" is an entirely different
poem and that its real modernity lies in specifically Apollinarian characteristics which are not present in "Pâques à
New York." I would even go so far as to agree with Michel
Décaudin when he states[22] that finally what strikes one about
the two poems is their dissimilarity and not their resemblance.

Cendrars presumably wrote his poem in April 1912 in
New York. The subject is the onset of a religious crisis in the
midst of loneliness and poverty and extreme hunger and cold
in a strange land: the scene is a night of peregrination through
the streets and particularly the poor districts of New York,
which at the same time evokes memories of past travels. The
poem is couched in rhyming couplets of irregular length with a
marked tendency to the repetitiveness of the litany:

> Où sont les longs offices et où les beaux cantiques
> Où sont les liturgies et les musiques . . .
>
> Je pense, Seigneur à mes heures malheureuses
> Je pense, Seigneur à mes heures en-allées . . .
> Je ne pense plus à Vous, je ne pense plus à Vous.[23]

---

[21] Durry, pp. 235-301.
[22] Décaudin, p. 83.

[23] "Where are the long services and where the beautiful canticles
Where are the liturgies and the music
I am thinking, O Lord, of my unhappy hours
I am thinking, O Lord, of my hours gone by
I no longer think of You, I no longer think of You"

Now it is quite obvious that it did not need Cendrars to teach Apollinaire how to write in this kind of metre, which he had already mastered when the younger man was only a child, and about which, in any case, there is nothing particularly modern (for example, Maeterlinck, Gourmont, Francis Jammes, Whitman). Nor did Apollinaire need Cendrars to be persuaded to turn round and take a backward look at his own past; for this had been one of his favourite subjects in the last few years, (for example, "Poème lu au mariage d'André Salmon" and "Le Voyageur"). The particular kaleidoscopic effect could well have been inspired by the faceting of Cubist painters, but the mobility of it again was very Apollinarian. As for wandering round Paris, "J'erre à travers mon beau Paris," and "Soirs de Paris ivres du gin," Apollinaire had written in 1904. It had always been one of his favourite pastimes. Possibly the religious theme might have been suggested by "Pâques à New York," although even then Apollinaire's thoughts had recently been turned in that direction: and the interest in the Jewish quarter and the "pauvres émigrants" again is in no way alien to Apollinaire, whose stories, at least, had often been set in similarly sordid and picturesque *milieux*. It is of course the combination of all these similar themes which is suspect, and which makes a statement of the known facts imperative, although any certain deduction about priority is still not possible.

The pro-Cendrars case is as follows. Cendrars himself claims that on his return from New York he went to see Apollinaire whom he had known slightly before, and gave him a manuscript copy of the poem, but he does not specify the date. In any case the poem was published privately in October and Apollinaire had an inscribed copy of it in November. Robert Goffin, and it was he who first brought the controversy to light, then adds[24] an anecdote about Cendrars reading this poem aloud at the Delaunays. Apollinaire is said to have turned white and to have muttered, "Beside that what is my volume of poems worth?" This was the long-awaited volume (entitled first *Eau de Vie* and then *Alcools*) which he had been preparing of his collected poems. On 31 Oct. Apollinaire received the proof-copy of *Eau de Vie* and at this stage there was no sign

[24] Goffin, p. 145.

of "Zone." "La Chanson du Mal-Aimé" was the first poem. During November while he was correcting the proofs he obviously decided to insert "Zone" because he then added the proofs of this poem (which was then called "Cri") that he had just received from *Les Soirées de Paris* for the December issue. He also did a rather strange thing. He stuck on to the end of the poem a cut-out strip bearing his own name in block capitals. M. Tristan Tzara who possesses this interesting proof copy believes[25] that this addition of his signature to "Zone," the first poem in the book, is a defiant gesture, a manifesto of his own modernity and priority; M. Décaudin that the poet thus merely means "Zone" to serve as prologue, in order to announce the themes of the book. It is obviously impossible to be certain exactly what was intended here.

Despite the apparent haste of sticking in "Zone" at the last moment, this again is no positive proof that it was actually written in November, or that he was in a hurry for it to be published before "Pâques à New York. It could have been merely that he was proud of it and wanted it included in the volume. On the other hand the Apollinaire partisans bring up the fact that when he was with the Picabias in Etival in late September he read them a poem without a title, which Gabrielle Buffet—Madame Picabia—claims[26] was ostensibly this poem. After the reading he declared to them that he would call it "Zone" in honour of that part of the Jura which was called "la Zone." Why then was it still called "Cri" in the proof?

Jean Mollet has stated[27] that when Apollinaire received his copy of "Pâques à New York," he called his attention to the unexpected resemblance with his own poem. There is even an anecdote from the pen of Sylvain Bonmariage[28] that Apollinaire had told him that the passage about the birds in "Zone" had first been written in rhymed alexandrines and that he had sent it in for a competition held by *Le Matin* in 1910. But no trace of that competition can be found!

[25] In conversation with the author.
[26] Gabrielle Buffet in *Le Point*, Sep. 1938.
[27] Jean Mollet, *Les Lettres Françaises*, 11 Nov. 1948.
[28] Décaudin, p. 87.

There remains the second possibility, remoter, that Cendrars wrote "Pâques à New York" after seeing "Zone": for instance the detail of the Prague clock. "Les aiguilles de l'horloge du quartier juif vont à rebours" occurs in both poems, and Apollinaire had already noted this in 1902. And yet a third possibility is that, after much discussion about poetry, during which Cendrars was in the habit of talking about the need to destroy poetry entirely—"You won't get anywhere until you've mastered her"—the two poets influenced each other mutually so much that they then separately produced poems on similar themes.

It is Michel Décaudin who so far has the last word, producing[29] the trump-card of the manuscript copy of "Zone" from the notebook entitled *L'Année republicaine*. The conclusion that he draws is that this is much more like "Pâques à New York" than the finished copy and that one of Apollinaire's aims in correcting it was to cut out the similarities. Even so, and this is fairly convincing, it is obvious that Apollinaire merely used "Pâques à New York" as a starting-point, something to set himself into gear, much as a medieval poet would compose around a given line, or Shakespeare around a Life from Plutarch, or Flaubert around a newspaper story. Even a poet has to have a subject. What is fascinating in this muddled story, which has to remain inconclusive, is that it would seem to show the adaptable, mobile Apollinaire taking his good wherever he may find it—in the spoken or the written word, always careful to husband whatever may spark off his own inspiration, but eventually succeeding in transforming alien material into something quintessentially his own.

There is even an additional footnote which proves that a poet can be influenced by everything he sees and hears and that one can spend a lifetime tracking this down and still he remains irreducible. Mme Durry mentions[30] in this respect Nicholas Beaudouin, a poet who at that time was trying to evolve something called "la poésie polyplane," different levels of experience being represented simultaneously. He claims that Apollinaire once said to him "You work by plans, I work

[29] Décaudin, p. 77.
[30] Durry, p. 259.

O

by zones," zones of feeling and experience and memory welling up and being explored in turn. Soon Apollinaire also took upon himself the additional problem of portraying them simultaneously.

It is this welling up of zones of feeling which is both particularly Apollinairian and particularly modern. Mme Durry calls it "errance,"[31] the lack of any fixed centre, the American critic Roger Shattuck "plasticity."[32] It was already Apollinaire's method in "La Chanson du Mal-Aimé," but not so obviously there because the traditional form had contained each switch of mood within a strict stanza, and so had masked the abrupt transitions. Here, in "Zone," the spacing of the lines follows exactly the pattern of the emotion, one line for one flash of emotion, or one idea, a whole passage for a complex wave of recollection or meditation. Indeed it is a method in poetry which seems to be reminiscent of Proust's in the novel, what he called "la psychologie en espace," not 'la psychologie plane." Possibly it could even be Apollinaire's own answer to the problem of the fourth dimension, his own life appearing to him as a picture hanging in a sombre museum which occasionally he goes to visit.

"A la fin tu es las de ce monde ancien" is the *envoi* to "Zone," not the cry of a desperate anarchist, but of somebody who is weary of exploring the well-beaten tracks and going through the same motions, of living in the past, "l'antiquité grecque et romaine." In the manuscript the word he used was "écœuré," he is nauseated by this over-chewed cud. But the ironical fact is that it is not so much his conscious, initial stance of adopting a colourful, noisy, urban, futuristic modernity, which in any case he soon drops, nor even the then new and fashionable themes of Unanimism or of travel and movement (which Valéry Larbaud and Cendrars were also busy celebrating), which mark him out as being not merely of but ahead of his time. Instead his real modernism lies in the recording of his lack of a central essence of faith, of the belief forced on him that his existence is only the sum of the moments to which he himself has given meaning, and of the *angst* (he

[31] Durry, p. 267.
[32] Roger Shattuck, *The Banquet Years*, 1960, p. 232.

actually mentions "l'angoisse de l'amour") which results in the shape of his old bogey, dissociation of personality, that split which here he strikingly marks by changing even within one line from "je" to "tu."

In short the real subject of "Zone" is the insecurity of modern man, his disarmed solitude, his disponibility to mere circumstance and his nostalgia for the values which have already broken up. "C'était et je voudrais ne pas m'en souvenir c'était au déclin de la beauté." And in the midst of this, his search for an identity of his own to set up against the ceaseless wearing away of time.

Inevitably the manuscript is explicit and digs right into the whole complex originally set up by Apollinaire's illegitimacy and statelessness:

Je me sens abandonné sur terre depuis mon plus jeune âge
Je n'ose pas me confier à l'étoile comme les rois mages[33]

a complex which has erupted critically in these recent months:

J'ai vécu en Auteuil pendant près de trois mois
Entre les deux larrons comme Jésus mourut en croix

Et l'un, le criminel ce fut le bon larron
Il sera malheureux, et mourra en prison

L'autre le mauvais larron c'était une femme
Elle m'a pris ma vie ce fut un vol infâme

Et pour avoir vécu entre ces deux voleurs
On m'arrêta un jour, l'an dernier comme receleur[34]

---

[33] "I have felt abandoned upon earth since my earliest days
I dare not put my trust in the star like the Three Wise Kings"

[34] "I lived in Auteuil for nearly three months
Between the two thieves as Jesus did upon the cross

And one, the criminal was the good thief
He will be unhappy and die in prison

The other the bad thief was a woman
She has taken my life an infamous theft

And because I lived between these two thieves
I was arrested one day last year for receiving stolen goods"

Naturally it is this, his crucifixion with the two thieves, Pieret the good one and Marie the bad, who have taken his life which is the key to "Zone," and it disappears in the final version: one is left only with the composition that he has woven around it.

It is interesting that he begins, because at heart he is also optimistic and yes-saying and courageous, with the persona that he wants to present to the world, that of the poet, who has chosen a renewed, modern form of art as a religion. The scene is morning, the street is the trumpet of the sun, all is movement and noise, and he is in accord with his surroundings. The bridges are like a peaceful herd of sheep, religion is simple. "J'aime la grâce de cette rue industrielle." But because he cannot stay long on a fixed centre, the noise becomes gradually more strident, and with the swiftness of a cinema-camera fade-out, he has switched back in time to his own personal morning, and his young, eloquent, mystic fervour: "Vous priez toute la nuit dans la chapelle du collège."

After this effusion, out rings the Apollinairian laugh in one of his typically irreverent, bathetic images, this time of Christ as a sort of super spaceman, "il détient le record du monde pour la hauteur." As he contemplates such a feat his own imagination likewise mounts in the air, carrying the whole century with it, summoning up at the same time all those weird creatures of the past that had haunted his grandiose, adolescent day-dreams ("Jadis les morts sont revenus m'adorer"). In a marvellous space rendezvous, he gathers the familiar characters of *L'Enchanteur pourrissant* around him; Simon Mage, Enoch, Elias, Apollonius of Tyana, and then the birds he has always favoured, the "pihis" and the lyrebird, even the phœnix, and the sirens of more recent years. As they all wing towards him—for in some way he, the poet, is identified with Christ "the flying machine"—this is a review of the past, winged flights of his imagination, the universe of his own that he has created.

From this contemplation of the immensity of space as happily and busily filled as the city street by the flapping wings of his own creation, comes the sickening fall into the "angoisse" of actuality, the sight of his own tiny figure walking alone through the crowds. Now they are no longer peaceful herds of sheep but thundering mastodons, and he is overwhelmed by a desire to retreat into dark, silent claustration:

Si tu vivais dans l'ancien temps tu entrerais dans un monastère[35]

Further and further he descends into the self-defence of blasphemy and so into the confines of Hell: "Comme le feu de l'Enfer ton rire pétille," until finally he reaches the same stage as in "La Chanson du Mal-Aimé." He is driven to push his own life right outside himself, seeing it now not just as his shadow, but even further removed as a picture in a "sombre museum." The fall from out of the cosmos of his confident creation has been vertiginous, mirroring his own drop from love and faith in himself into the abyss of doubt and despair which its absence has left.

And now his defensive disgust with love and with women expresses itself in the old nausea, ("les femmes sont ensanglantées") and in the manuscript the image was much more precise and in its revulsion shows more clearly the extent of his own hurt pride. That image of women and of blood he now links with the sacred heart of the Virgin, substitute mother, object of his adolescent yearning, and prototype of a feminine ideal. It is an unbroken, emotional chain which unites the two for him: the religious and the profane are only one love and that has become a shameful one, to be precise a venereal disease, "une maladie honteuse," which is eating him away.

Again he tries to pan back into the past, now flicking through the images quickly in flashing *divertissement*, but all his memories are shot through with fears and doubts, "Nous regardons avec effroi les poulpes des profoundeurs." The rose in Prague had a canker in its heart (Annie was as faithless as Marie, and it is inevitable that he dwells on this particular spring); he sees his own face in the portrait of Lazarus, his own life seems to go backwards pointlessly like the clock in the Jewish quarter. But wherever he starts unrolling this film of his life, even going as far back as Rome, it always stops at the present moment of combined suffering, as a criminal and betrayed lover, which brings about a paroxysm of tears and the

[35] "If you lived in times gone by you would enter a monastery"

utter disaggregation of personality in the confusion of "tu" and "je":

> Tu as fait de douloureux et de joyeux voyages
> Avant de t'apercevoir du mensonge et de l'âge
> Tu as souffert de l'amour à vingt et à trente ans
> J'ai vécu comme un fou et j'ai perdu mon temps
> Tu n'oses plus regarder tes mains et à tous moments
>   je voudrais sangloter
> Sur toi sur celle que j'aime sur tout ce qui t'a épouvanté[36]

With his innate craftsman's care of balancing the construction of his poem, Apollinaire now paints a city scene in complete contrast to the introductory picture of sunshine and the morning street, filled with busy workers who are at one with the life of Paris, and so with the whole world, and with whom he too in his confidence had felt integrated. Now he follows disconsolately the course of his own aimless wanderings through a city that has become alien to him. He seeks company with other outcasts and outsiders, the Jews, the down-and-outs, the prostitutes, the "pauvres émigrants," whose only home is the red eiderdown that they carry about with them. "Ils transportent un édredon rouge comme vous transportez votre cœur." He identifies himself with the riff-raff of Paris, and for the fastidious young man, who hated the smell of "stinking plebs" in the publicity office, to have this feeling is a measure of how far he thinks that he has sunk. He "humiliates his mouth" to a poor whore. But he is even more of an outcast than all of these because they at least have some hope, some religion. "Ils ont foi dans leur étoile comme les rois-mages." And even the most abject of the women has made her lover suffer, and is therefore stronger than he.

The night ends as it had begun, in solitude:

> Tu es seul le matin va venir[37]

---

[36] "You have gone on sad and joyous journeys
Before you were aware of lies and growing old
You have suffered from love at twenty and at thirty
I have lived like a madman and I have wasted my time
You no longer dare look at your hands and at every moment
    I want to burst into tears
Over you over the one I love over all that has frightened me"

[37] "You are alone morning is about to break"

and the busy sounds of day are taking over again: "Les laitiers font tinter leurs bidons dans les rues." But he will have nothing to do with them. He has drunk the nightmare-night as if it were alcohol and it has burned and wasted him, as all his life he has been wasted. His only desire now is for claustration and retreat, a mute return to the primitive womb of his own flat, with its negro fetishes, which figure a descent through the ages into some obscure comfort at the lowest level, life merely continuing in sleep and the mists of superstition. Gradually his voice has been diminishing, the rhythm becoming less and less emphatic: from the childish desire just to go to sleep and forget: "Tu marches vers Auteuil tu veux aller chez toi à pied," it descends to a mere whispered repetition in which the only words that stand out are "autre," "inférieurs," and "obscures."

> Tu marches vers Auteuil tu veux aller chez toi à pied
> Dormir parmi tes fetiches d'Océanie et de Guinée
> Ils sont des Christ d'une autre forme et d'une autre croyance
> Ce sont les Christ inférieurs des obscures espérances[38]

And then comes the brilliantly conceived, ultimate image, sudden, final, dazzling, and terrifying.

> Adieu Adieu
> Soleil cou coupé[39]

The implacable rhythm, the repetition of the hard consonant and booming vowel in "cou coupé" and the manifold implications of the image itself, are from a masterly hand. Mme Durry underlines the identification here with Christ and religion. I think it is even more global: after stretching from Christianity through mere superstitious beliefs, the sun god is surely the most basic and primitive of all, the only thing left that he could possibly believe in, the source of life itself: and its assassination is a most potent expression of the death wish.

[38] "You are walking towards Auteuil you want to go home on foot
You sleep amongst your fetiches from the South Sea Islands and New Guinea
They are Christs of another form and of another creed
They are the inferior Christs of obscure hopes"

[39] "Farewell farewell
Sun cleft neck"

X

Orphism

ONE night in the lovely house of Louise Faure-Favier that dominates the Seine at the prow of the Ile St Louis, Apollinaire and André Billy decided not to waste the mid-summer hours by sleeping. Eventually after hours of talk they grew weary: but at dawn Apollinaire jumped up, beamed on everybody in true Apollinairian style and declared "I am reborn with the sun."[1] Happily so. Without the implication of day following night, of constant change and movement and rebirth, "Zone" would be a tragic poem. As it is, it is a record of a cycle, its end is no conclusion. All will start again and be reborn with that same sun that has seemed to have been blotted out with such finality. The Enchanter is immortal. In fact the descent into night and the assassination of the sun in "Zone" is a kind of exorcism: as is the grotesque, Apocalyptic vision of Croniamental's martyrdom in *Le Poète assassiné*. He, the poet, who can claim that he is "the greatest of living poets. I have often seen God face to face. I have borne the divine radiance that my human eyes tempered. I have lived through eternity,"[2] is persecuted and done to death through the offices of a German scientist (Marie later married a German, and science was always in Apollinaire's eyes the great and apparently successful rival to art). This little parable, his private fears being expressed in terms of the utmost irony, is further borne out when a man who has been cured of baldness by the scientist puts out one of his eyes, then Tristouse sticks her umbrella through the other. And even the poet's best friend, the artist l'Oiseau du Benin, can only invent for sole memorial "une profonde statue en rien comme la poése et comme la gloire"—yet another of Apollinaire's strangely accurate prophecies. No statue, but "la gloire."

[1] Faure-Favier, p. 118.
[2] *Le Poète assassiné*, 1959, p. 112.

PLATE 5

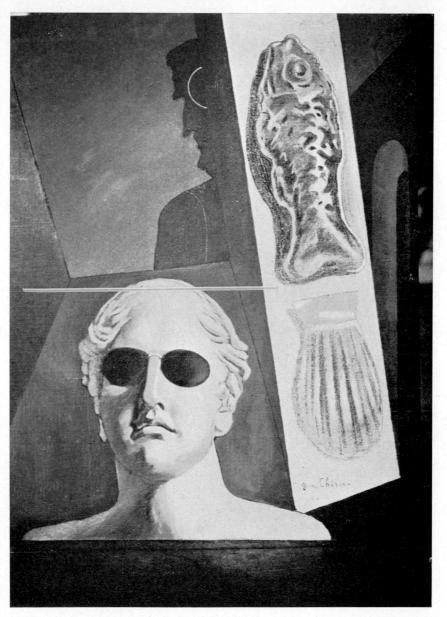

GUILLAUME APOLLINAIRE

Portrait by Chirico. By courtesy of A. Harlingue

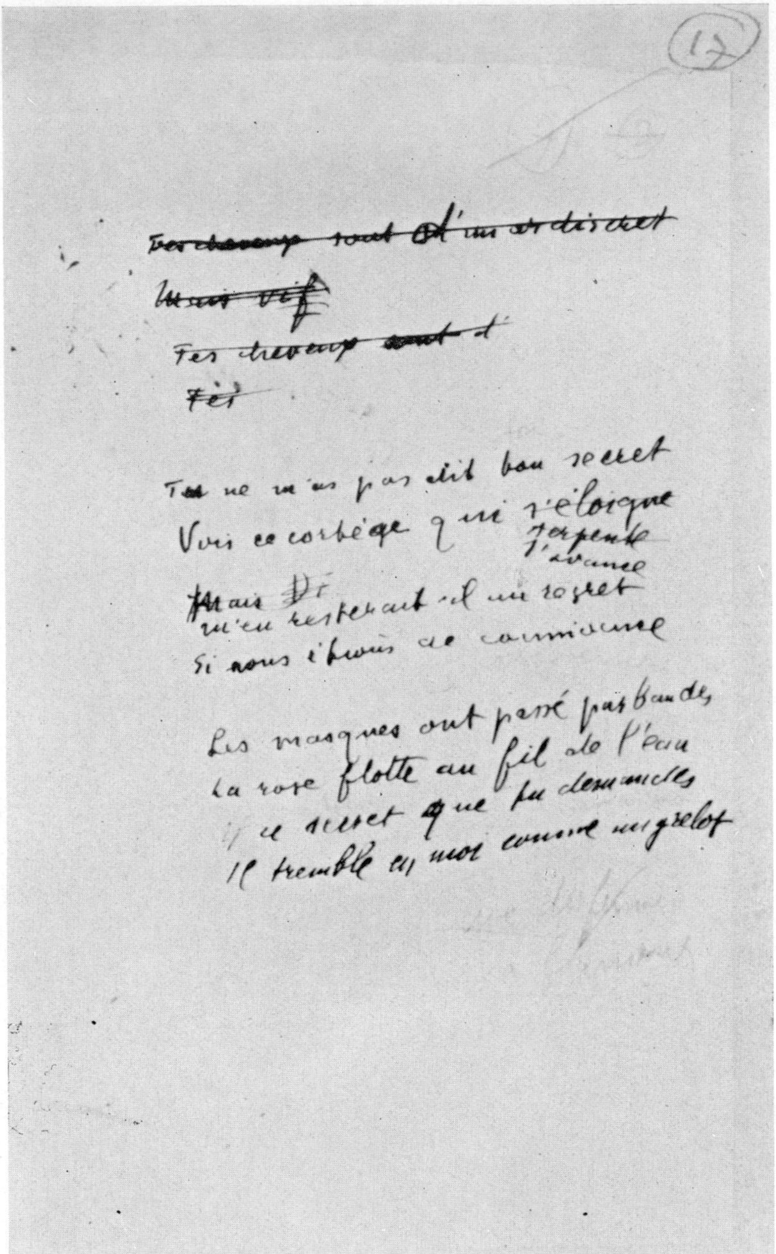

PLATE 6

MANUSCRIPT PAGE FROM *Vitam impendere amori*

By courtesy of Mme Apollinaire

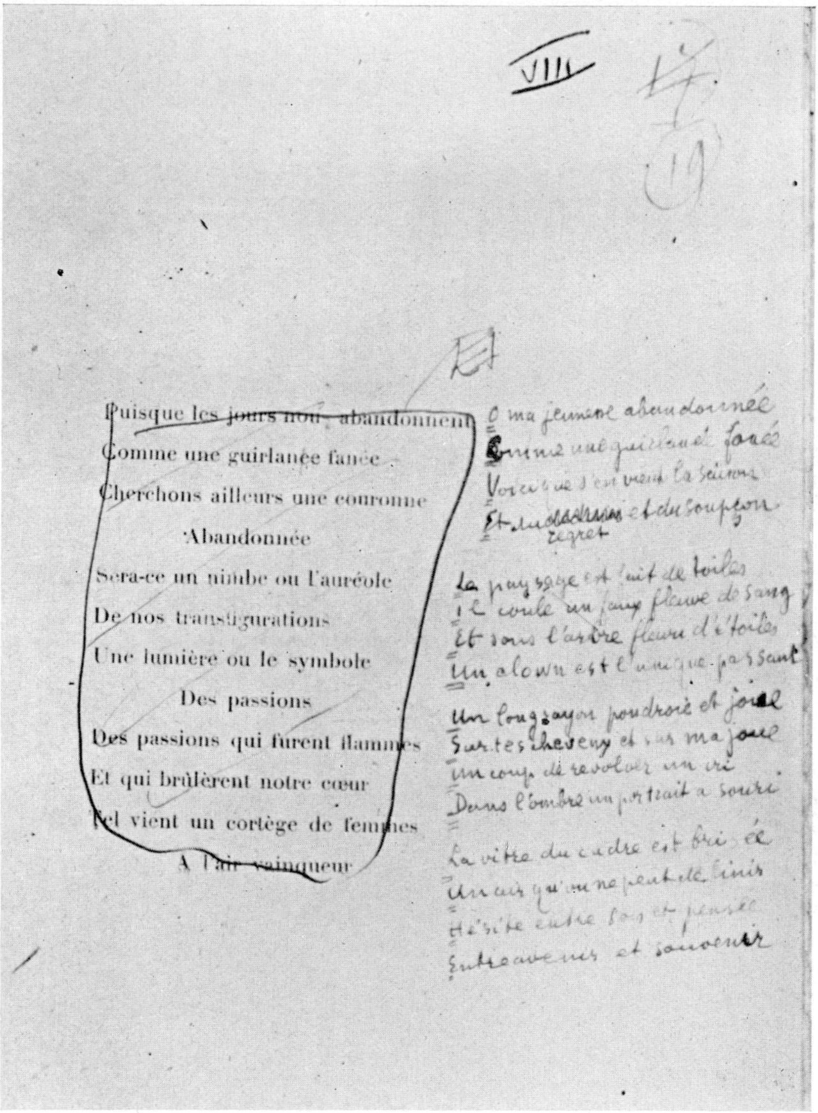

PLATE 7

VIII

Puisque les ~~jours nous abandonnent~~
Comme une guirlande fanée
Cherchons ailleurs une couronne
        Abandonnée
Sera-ce un nimbe ou l'auréole
De nos transfigurations
Une lumière ou le symbole
        Des passions
Des passions qui furent flammes
Et qui brûlèrent notre cœur
Tel vient un cortège de femmes
        À l'air vainqueur

O ma jeunesse abandonnée
Comme une guirlande fanée
Voici que s'en vient la saison
Et du dédain et du soupçon
        regret

Le paysage est fait de toiles
il coule un faux fleuve de sang
Et sous l'astre fleuri d'étoiles
Un clown est l'unique passant

Un long rayon poudroie et joue
Sur tes cheveux et sur ma joue
Un coup de revolver un cri
Dans l'ombre un portrait a souri

La vitre du cadre est brisée
Un air qu'on ne peut définir
Hésite entre son et pensée
Entre avenir et souvenir

MANUSCRIPT PAGE FROM *Vitam impendere amori*
By courtesy of Mme Apollinaire

PLATE 8

GUILLAUME APOLLINAIRE

In 1917. By courtesy of A. Harlingue

Apollinaire soldat

Having thus in "Zone" and in the figure of Croniamental lived through his own and the sun's assassination. Apollinaire was once more fit to carry on with the daylight business of living. Fortunately there was much afoot.

While he was staying with the Delaunays he became deeply involved with Delaunay's completely new approach to painting, and took it upon himself to formulate these revolutionary theories into words, and eventually to embody them in poetry.

At the beginning however he manfully tried to keep the dissidents together with the main group. For some time, and particularly during the summer of 1912, the Delaunays, the Picabias, and Marcel Duchamp had been reacting against the rigidity of "the Cubist formula which is already classified."[3] Marcel Duchamp with his famous *Nu descendant l'escalier* had been refused at the Salon des Indépendants. Picabia with his passion for advertisements, and his love of paradoxes was regarded with suspicion. And after long discussions, particularly during that autumn holiday in the Jura, it was agreed that they should hold their own exhibition, which they promptly did on their return to Paris in October under the promising title "Le Salon de la Section d'Or." As was only fitting, Apollinaire gave the inaugural lecture and celebrated the opening with a notice in *L'Intransigeant*.

It is this lecture which formed the text of his "L'Ecartèlement du cubisme,"[4] an analysis of Cubism which has often been criticised for inaccuracy by purists. It is in fact an ingenious if not heroic attempt at a virtually impossible task: that of impressing some sort of pattern on the by now highly mobile mass of experiment, always with the strategic desire of presenting a united front against the *arrière-garde* of an obstinate, reactionary public. This was Apollinaire's constant wish even against the desires of individual painters whom he was thus classifying. He saw the new movement as a real revolution with himself as general. He knew only too well from his own experience how important it was to maintain solidarity and not offer one's flanks to attack unnecessarily. Therefore in this proselytising spirit he uses all his sophistry and powers

---

[3] Gabrielle Buffet, "La Section d'Or," *Art d'aujourd'hui*, May-June 1953.
[4] *Les Peintres cubistes*, 1950, p. 24.

of persuasion to stretch the label "Cubism" out to cover many disparate tendencies, some of which had in fact nothing to do with it.

His general definition is the same that he had been formulating since at least 1908, that Cubism is no longer "an art of imitation but an art of conception which tries to elevate itself to pure creation," and he emphasises again the purely plastic problem which had so exercised Picasso of representing the three dimensions without recourse to the old tricks of perspective and *trompe l'oeil*.

Under this general heading he then ranges four tendencies; two are in the main line, (*a*) scientific Cubism which is "the art of painting new 'ensembles' with elements borrowed not from the reality of things seen, but the reality of things known," and to which belong Picasso, Braque, Metzinger, Gleizes, Gris, and, inevitably, Marie Laurencin; and (*b*) physical Cubism which is "the art of painting new ensembles borrowed from the reality of vision," and here he can find only Le Fauconnier to cite. Then there is another whole important tendency in modern painting including what he calls Orphic Cubism and instinctive Cubism. Orphic Cubism, which was to become his particular protégé and develop into "Orphism" on its own, is "the art of painting new ensembles with elements borrowed not from visual reality but created entirely by the artist and endowed by him with a powerful reality of their own." In a cunningly worded sentence he gives precedence where it is due, for his new enthusiasms did not drive out old allegiances: "The luminous works of Picasso contain this art which Robert Delaunay is busy inventing, and towards which Fernand Léger, Francis Picabia and Marcel Duchamp are also striving." After this he makes a final large gesture to include all the *proxime accesserunt*, the other artists of different tendencies and nationalities, who use elements suggested to them by their intuition, and do not rise to the heights of Orphic Cubism. This last heading of "instinctive Cubism" is really Orphic Cubism *manqué*, and is just as vague as its title suggests.

He then notes the successors of Cubism, and it is now no longer Cézanne who is the father of Cubism, but Courbet; and Derain who is his eldest son, and the Fauves who had made a sort of preamble for Cubism. Here it is obvious that Apollinaire is beginning to diverge from the original tenets of the faith; and when he goes on to make the rather curious generalisation "The new artists have need of an ideal beauty which is no longer the proud expression of the species but the expression of the universe in the measure in which it became manifestly human in light," it is evident that a new element altogether has entered into his theories. Light, which had been for long his own favourite symbol for the ideal, is now going to become his Montjoie: "I like the art of to-day because I like light above all things and all men like light above all things, because they invented fire."

Now this was the battlecry which Apollinaire had formulated in company with Delaunay, who was working on quite different and individual lines from the general run of Cubist painters. It is interesting to learn from a letter of Delaunay to Kandinsky that although Apollinaire had always admired Delaunay's works, he had not at first been convinced by his heretical theories. "I shall speak to you later about the subject in painting, about our exciting conversations with Apollinaire who is beginning to believe in our researches."[5] This must have been sometime in the summer or early autumn of 1912. The letter is dated merely 1912, but Delaunay uses the expression "chez Apollinaire," so this must have been while Apollinaire still had a home to go to. By November he had given up his flat in Auteuil and was installed with the Delaunays, delighted to feel wanted, indulging in his usual culinary orgies and of course talking till all hours, although he was bound to confess that Delaunay's fervour beat even his. "You start talking about art the moment you wake up " he grumbled. Nevertheless Delaunay's fiery idealism was a great stimulus to him and eventually he became so convinced, that for a few months, as far as painting was concerned, he more or less put himself into Delaunay's skin. In fact in their notes and writings on art of this period both men quote each other abundantly. Needless to say his adhesion to the cause was quite a scoop for Delaunay; with his single-minded enthusiasm, his possibilities of influencing the public by his

[5] Robert Delaunay, *Du cubisme à l'art abstrait*, 1957, p. 179.

journalistic activities, he could serve as mouthpiece and propagandist, for Delaunay did not express himself on paper very effectively, and it became Apollinaire's task to translate him into words.

Delaunay had set out from the same starting-point as the Cubists: how—as Apollinaire had rightly recorded—to create form, volume, movement, and depth without the old tricks of perspective and chiaroscuro. But he had decided that it was the Impressionists (they in their turn inspired by El Greco, Delacroix and "some English painters") who had after all been on the right lines in their obsession with light: but they had not gone far enough. It was the understanding of the function of light in modifying shape, colour and movement that was the main problem for modern painting. He even goes back to Leonardo to find support for this statement and quotes him as saying that the eye is the window of the soul, and therefore the source of all sensibility and movement. Of the Impressionists it was Seurat who was the first theoretician of light, his the invention of the contrast of complementary colours, the use of dots being a mere technique to bring this about. But again he had not gone far enough. The Cubists on the contrary, according to Delaunay, "carry out purely linear researches," and they reserve a secondary and non-constructive role to colour. Now Delaunay begins to attack the whole problem of colours, their particular laws and composition, their transparency and opacity, the intervals between them, their contrasts and how this creates movement, their simultaneity; in fact their qualities in terms of musical notes, with light as the general principle governing them:

> The simultaneity of colours brought about by simultaneous contrasts and by all the measures which issue from colours according to the way they express themselves in representative movement, this is the only reality with which to construct in painting.[6]

This he later summed up as "le contraste simultané," a

[6] Apollinaire's interpretation of Delaunay's theories in *Chronique d'art*, 1960, p. 268, and also Delaunay's notes in *Du cubisme à l'art abstrait*, 1957, pp. 114, 126, 132, 146.

particular method in painting, a "métier" with which to express his general conception of harmony, and eternal movement, "symbolic movement which is the representation of the Universal Drama."

Delaunay felt very much alone in France with this new conception of painting. The Italian Futurists seemed to be after the same ends of simultaneity and movement, but they were not using any new method, and Delaunay was above all things concerned with his "contraste simultané" as a "métier," that is, a whole new technique. It is significant that the artists to whom he turned, and whom he felt were capable of understanding him were the German group, Kandinsky, Klee, Marc, and Macke, and that his big one-man show at the beginning of 1913 was in the Sturm gallery in Berlin. He was in correspondence already in 1912, as we have seen, with Kandinsky. Kandinsky had sent him his *Uber das Geistige in der Kunst* and Delaunay attempts to explain[7] to him these "things which I believe and which are not known by anybody else." Nevertheless as a Frenchman he seems to feel superior, a feeling not at all uncommon at that epoch and definitely shared by Apollinaire. He boasts of "clarity which is the quality of the French race," criticises his friend for being too scholastic and of confusing everything by words, abstractions:

> You speak to me of geometry, and I don't even see geometry. . . . Your fixed idea is to start from form—that's very Cubist—but you have no right to say that I do not represent objects. Undoubtedly I use the means, the gifts provided by my sensibility, and I assure you that I don't borrow them from geometry, for my belief is something quite different. . . . It isn't up to me to speak about my belief, since I represent it.

Delaunay's the task of representing his belief, of grappling with his problem in terms of pure paint, and making "his choice of the impressions that light in the universe furnishes to his artisan's conscience," and Guillaume Apollinaire's, the duty of speaking about it. Delaunay would write down snippets,

---

[7] Delaunay's notes in *Du cubisme à l'art abstrait*, 1957, p. 178.

glimpses of his ideas and gropings, and leave Apollinaire to arrange and formulate these notes in more palatable terms and make them public. In December he published both in *Les Soirées de Paris* and in *Der Sturm*, an article entitled "Réalité peinture pure" which is a statement, actually in quotation marks, of Delaunay's "æsthetic declaration," explaining the role of Impressionists, Seurat's "contrasts of complementary colours," the importance of "simultaneous contrast" which assures the dynamism of colours and their construction in the picture, and is the strongest expression of reality; and the guiding role of light perceived by the sensibility of the artist and ordered by him into harmony. Apollinaire adds authoritatively in his own words: "Such a statement has no need of a commentary. It cries out to be understood directly and it incites to simultaneity which alone is creation. The rest is merely notation, contemplation, study. Simultaneity is life itself." In short he had been completely won over; yet again showing his intuitive awareness of the course the future would take, for it was in fact this line from Delaunay, Kandinsky, and Klee which has had more influence on the development of modern art, than the other stemming from the original Cubists.

It is not difficult to see the attraction that Delaunay's theories had for him. Purely visually he liked the bright colours and the general air of joyous explosion, and animation, in his friend's pictures. For whilst approving of the principles of Cubism, he, with his dionysiac termperament, had alway found its sombre, monochrome colours rebarbative. Of all Picasso's works he had instinctively gravitated towards the Blue and the Rose periods, and one of his favourite artists had always been Matisse. "This artist is voluptuous"[8] he had said in admiration, although he was objective enough to realise his lesser influence. But, even more important, were the possibilities of applying these theories to poetry, for this was going to be the real challenge to himself. And in fact it seemed, and this must have been the most exciting of revelations, that they would fit very nicely. For colours read images, and the "contraste simultané" could easily be translated into

[8] Notes for Le Salon d'Automne in *Les Soirées de Paris*, Nov. 1913.

poetry; and this was really what he had been tending to do since 1908; to place together disparate, contrasting images in order to build up his picture of the whole. And this idea of simultaneity, what was it in fact but an answer to his old obsession with time, a means of conquering the flux by representing everything as happening all at once, at the same time, all over the universe? From there to his pretensions to ubiquity and even to the aims of Unanimism was only a short step. Even his own temperamental mixture of conflicting, simultaneous emotions welling up and constantly swinging him from one extreme to another, his sense of the ironical kaleidoscope of his own life, could be encompassed by an art which arrived at this precious, all-governing principle of simultaneity. This surely, at last, would be the answer to the need to escape from description and imitation and representation which he had acknowledged very early in his life.

Thus although it is not exactly unjust to talk of Delaunay's influence, it was not so much a question of seed falling on fertile ground, but of the sun and the rain of friendship with a kindred spirit bringing to fruition a seed which had already been sown.

It was while Apollinaire was still at the Delaunays that he met the challenge and showed how it was possible to write a "simultaneous" poem. This product of a sunny winter's day was "Les Fenêtres," which Delaunay christened "the first simultaneous poem," and which was used at the head of the catalogue for his exhibition in Berlin in January.

There is an anecdote which has it[9] that one evening while he was sitting with other friends in a café, Apollinaire suddenly remembered that he had a poem to do for Delaunay and after he had announced the first line inspired by Delaunay's painting, the others added a line each, for example, "Nous l'enverrons en message téléphonique," "Quand on le temps on a la liberté" (a reference to two big daily papers), until the poem was completed. In any case, this would still be a proof of Apollinaire's gifts, for what a marvellous first line it is! "Du rouge au vert tout le jaune se meurt." All Cendrars could produce on the same theme was "Et voici des affiches, du rouge du vert

---

[9] The originator of this was André Billy. Both the Delaunays have emphatically denied it.

multicolores comme mon passé bref du jaune."[10]   But both the
Delaunays and Cendrars claim that he did actually compose
the poem in their flat.   And it would be very like Apollinaire, the debonair joker, to appear to take round the hat,
when in fact his method of composition was a laborious toil
of piecing together his moments of inspiration, even if that
inspiration included the raw elements of reality, in this case his
friends' conversation.   He always liked to discount the
necessary hard work, making himself out to be the pure flame
of genius.

Delaunay claimed that "Les Fenêtres" was the first poem
without punctuation.   It was at this same time, during the
month of November, that Apollinaire apparently on a sudden
whim, crossed all the punctuation out of the proofs of *Alcools*
although "Zone" appeared in December in the *Soirées de Paris*
conventionally studded with the usual dots and commas.
Apollinaire himself later made a larger claim: "I have
done all I possibly can to simplify syntax in poetry and in
certain cases I have succeeded, notably in the poem 'Les
Fenêtres.' "

Here possibly another influence was also at work.   For
the Futurists had already declared in one of their 1912 mani-
festos that punctuation must be suppressed, and although
Apollinaire had not at first had a high opinion of them,
Delaunay for his part believed that they would be the most
successful of all the *avant-garde* groups because they were the
best organised.   Soon after this Apollinaire himself did
temporarily join forces with them.   In any case it would have
been quite in character for him to seize on one of their novel
suggestions without fully approving of all their aims.

Again it was a case of this particular technique (and Apollinaire only simplifies, does not go so far as to suppress, syntax)
fitting in well with his own previous aim of escaping from
description, narrative, and conventional logic.   It also happened to be an appropriate technique for introducing his
simultaneous images; to paint in the single brush-stroke of a noun
was the quickest and brightest way of placing the image,
and of bringing out the sharpest contrast with its neighbour,

[10] Blaise Cendrars, *La Prose du Trassibérien et de la Petite Jehanne de France.*

without the modifying shadows of more intermediate parts of speech:

> Bigorneaux Lotte multiples Soleils et l'Oursin du couchant
>   Une vieille paire de chaussures jaunes devant la fenêtre
> Tours
> Les Tours ce sont les rues
> Puits
> Puits ce sont les places
> Puits
> Arbres creux qui abritent les Câpresses vagabondes[11]

"Les Fenêtres" is sometimes called the first "poème conversation." This is not strictly true: there are in it the snatches of speech picked up in the café, but there is also much more. The poet is at the window of the world, the curtain goes up on a whirling mass of incongruous, simultaneous, sense-impressions, which flash out through his images. The towers, for instance, turn upside down and become streets. And now these images are no longer symbols; they do not represent private emotions, the poet is entirely extraverted and these are the flashing, colourful impressions of the whole turning world printed on his sensibility by light:

> Tu soulèveras le rideau
> Et maintenant voilà que s'ouvre la fenêtre
> Araignées quand les mains tissaient la lumière
> Beauté pâleur insondables violets
>
> . . . Etincelant diamant
> Vancouver
> Où le train blanc de neige et de feux nocturnes fuit l'hiver
> O Paris

---

[11] "Winkles Burbot multiple Suns and the sea urchin of the sunset
    An old pair of yellow slippers in front of the window
    Towers
    The Towers are roads
    Wells
    Wells are squares
    Wells
    Hollow trees which shelter the vagabond Câpresses"

P

Du rouge au vert tout le jaune se meurt
Paris Vancouver Hyères Maintenon New York et les Antilles
La fenêtre s'ouvre comme une orange
Le beau fruit de la lumière[12]

Delaunay was right to see in this poem the poetic crowning of his theories. His Eiffel Tower, his discs of light, his yellows and reds, even Cendrars' "transsibérien" figure in it, but rendered sonorous by Apollinaire's particular tone of voice, "Où le train blanc de neige et de feux nocturnes fuit l'hiver," and signed with a characteristic gourmandising flourish, "Le beau fruit de la lumière." Virtuoso as always, he has managed to achieve authoritatively in verse that sense of speed and movement, of space and air and light and simultaneity which this little group was aiming for.

In January the two Orphists set off for Delaunay's exhibition in Berlin, and, as was his custom, Apollinaire gave the inaugural lecture on "La Peinture moderne," which was a restatement of the various points he had been making in recent articles—particularly in "L'Ecartèlement du cubisme," of October, and the Delaunay article of December, and also in an historical summary of Cubism that he had written for *Le Temps* in October. Majestically he announces to his assembled German audience that France is as supreme a mistress of the arts as was Italy in the Renaissance; and he tells them that their particular branch of painting falls into line more with Delaunay's Orphism than with Cubism proper. He then ends on his battlecry: "J'aime l'art des jeunes peintres parce que j'aime avant tout la lumière."

What is new, however, and therefore probably just recently

---

[12] "You will lift up the curtain
 And now here is the window opening
 Spiders when hands wove light
 Beauty paleness unfathomable violets

 . . . Sparkling diamond
 Vancouver
 Where the train white with snow and nocturnal lights flees from winter
 O Paris
 From red to green all the yellow fades away
 Paris Vancouver Hyeres Maintenou New York and the Antilles
 The window opens like an orange
 The beautiful fruit of light"

elaborated, is an aside about his own position as a poet. And here he produces one of his typical surprises, for the literary version that he announces is no longer Orphism, but something again quite novel: "Dramatism," and its disciples are Barzun, Mercereau, Georges Polti and himself. In fact it would seem from now on that the term Orphism shifts from being the nomenclature of a school, to defining the real vital essence of life itself as it manifests itself in art.

Now Apollinaire's gesture of thus throwing in his lot with Jacques Barzun and the already formulated Dramatism is interesting. In January "Les Fenêtres," which had already appeared in *Der Sturm* catalogue, is published in Barzun's review *Poème et drame*: again it is an evidence of this pungent desire of Apollinaire's for solidarity and co-operation, his repugnance for the role of lone voice crying in the wilderness, his enthusiastic rallying to the ranks of those who seem to be after similar ends. And Barzun's own at least sound at this time very much the same: an eschewing of description, an attempt to create a concrete, direct lyricism, an obsession with reproducing simultaneity. He had indeed gone further into experiment than Apollinaire with his researches into the possibilities of using music, and polyphony, through recording and radio. Inevitably, as always after a while, the individualist in Apollinaire asserted himself, hating to be bound by anybody else's shackles, and by October of the following year he and Barzun were involved in a quarrel about the use of the term "simultanism" and who had invented it, Apollinaire claiming eventually that because of his analogy with music, Barzun could never be more than successive.

It seems appropriate that one of Apollinaire's images used at this time and only at this time was Ariadne ("the mole Ariadne"). One certainly feels the need of some magic thread to discover a clear path through the dark labyrinth of all the "isms" in this immediate pre-war period. After Cubism and Unanimism there had been Paroxysm, Futurism, Simultanism, Orphism, Dramatism, Beaudouin's "Synoptisme polyplan" (which tried to incorporate the technique of the cinema as well as musical construction), Dynamism, Modernism, and in England Vorticism and Imagism, in Russia Rayonnism.

Looking back from a height, and not attempting to work through the maze, it would seem that they were all after much the same thing, but that they favoured varying methods of attaining it. After the narcissism of the late nineteenth century they were looking outwards now on to a changed world, and aiming to reproduce a widened sense of the cosmos, which included speed, change, energy, time, the whole mobile intensity of the life force, after the old static, centralised conception of man enclosed within the world. It would also seem that at moments of crisis, poetry, fearful of being left behind, turns to her sister arts for help. Barzun and Beaudouin were seeking analogies of method in music, even in the cinema. Apollinaire had always been led by painters, and was to end his own mad novelty-chase at the eve of the War with his attempt actually to make poems into pictures. These were two years of febrile, intensive activity with one bubble of a theory effervescing after another. In the end the group who made the most impact as a group were those who were best organised and knew how to make the most noise, the Italian nationalistic Futurists, who had as their leader that ball of fire, Marinetti. Inevitably there were moments when everything degenerated into stupid quarrels about precedence or nomenclature. For example the term "simultanism" caused much trouble. Delaunay had used it to describe his own painting, but the Futurists had already declared it as one of their aims. This not only caused an open quarrel between the Futurists and Delaunay, but served as a weapon for the susceptible Apollinaire to use against Delaunay, after his painter friend had declared that Apollinaire had been influenced by Cendrars and that of the two Cendrars was the more modern. It was this little coldness which eventually marked Apollinaire's divorce from Delaunay.

By April 1914 even Apollinaire had given up trying to classify all the "isms" and was forced to declare:

> The modern age appears, at first sight, to be governed not by the influence of one preponderant characteristic, but rather by a multitude of different characteristics, disparate, opposed, but all exuberant.

A graph of his own progress in these two hectic years is as good a cross-section as any one is likely to have. He was prepared to look at each one for a while, take what it had to offer, exploit it, then when he saw himself being tied down to reject it and go on to another. Cendrars described this shuttling to and fro: "Apollinaire goes forward, hangs back, and occasionally stops altogether."[13] Like Picasso at this period he was obsessed by the idea of constant renewal in art. "Art," he said, "is a succession of risks and the life of a poet must be in every domain an uninterrupted succession of lyrical adventures. The *Coup de Dés* is an example"; a reference which is to serve as a pointer to the direction in which his own experimentation eventually was to lead him in 1914.

Ardengo Soffici is probably most right when he said[14] that of all the "isms" that influenced Apollinaire it was Idealism that he was really in love with. It was an idealism which took the shape of a lifelong faith in art and a belief that it must constantly be renewed by being infused with the spirit of life itself. In fact this dionysiac, cosmic embrace, this infatuation with life and with art as its supreme manifestation is his greatest quality.

Infatuations are obviously deemed at times to appear silly: and one of Apollinaire's silliest, which even he himself later repudiated, was his temporary joining forces with the Futurists. This was a good example of his following an idea beyond its logical conclusion and of letting his intoxication of the moment sway his better judgment: for the Futurists were not at all liked in France and his publication of his own Futurist Manifesto from Milan in June 1913 under the celebrated headings of "Merda a" and "Rosa a," did him much harm in the eyes of the public. Destroy everything, down with the past, even its geniuses, burn the libraries, and start from scratch—this was the Futurist motto. And it had never been Apollinaire's, who had always loved and revered the great masters. He obviously had reasons for linking himself with his Italian counterparts. Possibly it was their publicity which

---

[13] Goffin, p. 143.
[14] P. A. Jannini, *La Fortuna di Apollinaire in Italia*, 1959 (henceforth cited as Jannini), p. 43

attracted him and which he wanted to exploit. It might even have been that he was still bearing Italy in mind as a second line of defence if ever he really were forced to leave France. Or genuinely he might have been visited by one of those bursts of exaggerated enthusiasm to which he was prone, and have imagined that their aims did really coincide with his.

Perhaps, though, the main factor which propelled him into the bravado of *L'Antitradition futuriste*, was the curious phenomenon which seemed to keep dogging him and vitiating his progressive stand—the time-lag between his theory and his practice. His one and only volume of poems to date was *Alcools* which was not actually published until April 1913, and despite its brave new start with "Zone," despite constant revision in proof, despite the large gesture of suppressing all punctuation, which was most probably Futurist inspired, it was chiefly made up of much older material, even of poems dating back to Stavelot and before, and the most distinctive single group was definitely "Les Rhénanes," many of which still rang with the plangent echoes of Symbolism. Naturally enough, because his recent, Apocalyptic attitude as high priest of Orphism—his collection of critical articles *Les Peintres cubistes* had appeared in March 1913—had led everybody to expect something as a whole bolder and more world-shaking, it was not particularly well received. What seemed to worry critics most of all— inevitably so because it always makes their task difficult—was the variety of tones and styles and the overall mobility. A friend such as Louis de Gonzague Frick could turn this into a compliment:

> The lyrical personality of M. Guillaume Apollinaire is presented to us here in its multiple aspects. Nobody better than he knows the art of metamorphosis, the whole game of versification, nobody better than he knows how to endow words with star-studded meanings.[15]

But others could not accept so easily this mobile, changing quality in him which escaped them, which made it impossible to pin one label on to him, which made them suspect that he

[15] Décaudin, p. 45.

was merely a gifted imitator, or even, because of the constant play of his irony, that he might be laughing up his sleeve at them. And his past reputation as a "mystificateur" the journalistic stunts, the pornography, the affair of the statuettes, even his so-called erudition, did not help. Could such a man be sincere and spontaneous as a poet? Henri Ghéon for instance manages to admit all this and to give Apollinaire the benefit of the doubt:

> To say that he is influenced is to say that he searches his pretexts outside himself: but he contrives, once he is embarked, to make his poem quite different from the one which inspired it. Let him manipulate turn by turn the "verset" of "Les Nourritures" or "Les Cinq Grandes odes," *vers libre*, the medieval epic strophe, the alexandrine, or the little quatrains of the Parnasse and of the Pléiade, what does it matter? These influences soon mingle in a sort of composite charm, where culture with all its whims plays one part, and a direct, authentic emotion another, at least in the better pieces.[16]

Others were frankly irritated and said so. The most cavalier attack, because it came from an old colleague, Georges Duhamel, and was published on 16 June in Apollinaire's own review which had actually published the volume *Le Mercure de France*, begins by describing *Alcools* as an old junk shop with its collection of bizarre, heteroclite objects, and then nastily and unpardonably presents the shopkeeper "as a mixture of the Levantine Jew, the South American, the Polish gentleman and the *facchino*." This personal attack was enough to set the tone of the whole article and to nullify any literary judgments that might emerge, but Duhamel then went on to hit really below the belt and to declare that Apollinaire was merely dragging along in the wake of his contemporaries, Max Jacob, André Salmon, Henri Hertz. Apollinaire, "the Polish gentleman," was justifiably outraged. In his anger he even invented a new word for Duhamel. Only the intervention of his friends prevented him from punishing "this *critiqueur*" with the sword. This was the second and not the last time that he reacted in this atavistic way to an insult. To save him from the charge

[16] Décaudin, p. 47.

of plagiarism Max Jacob even devoted himself to the extent of writing to the *Mercure de France*, misrepresenting the dates of his own poems.

But for want of a better label, this one stuck. Even the milder Henri Martineau was using it next month in *Le Divan*. "I cannot draw up an inventory of the richnesses of this fascinating junk shop dealer." Poor Guillaume Apollinaire! To him, fired as he was with the most sublime conception of poetry, this charge of being in his own achievement a mere charming plagiarist, an erudite imitator with a taste for the bizarre and a love of hoaxing, must really have appeared to be the martyrdom of "le poète assassiné." A lone voice like Cendrars saying "You are the only master, the master of us all"[17] was scant palliative. It is to his credit that he replied to Martineau in rather sad, but most measured terms which seem to show a real humility.

> Thank you, thank you for your article, thank you for liking my poems. However it is not the bizarre that attracts me, but life itself, and when one knows how to observe, one sees the most curious, the most moving things. Whatever people say I am not a great reader, I scarcely read at all and then only the same things from my childhood on. . . . I have never indulged in hoaxing or mystification about my work or that of others. I do not believe that I have imitated, for each of my poems is the commemoration of an event in my life and most frequently it is a sad one, but I have also moments of joy which I celebrate. I am like those sailors who pass their time in port on the seafront where so many unexpected things are washed up, where the spectacle is always renewed, and is never wearisome: but junk-shop dealer seems to me a very unjust description of a poet who has written such a small number of pieces in the long space of fifteen years.[18]

There was the rub; his old "tourment de silence," the smallness of his poetic output, which always ran the risk of being swamped by his other activities. To represent himself at the age of thirty-two he had had to go right back even to adolescence, and it was this review of all the phases through

[17] Décaudin, p. 43.
[18] André Rouveyre, "La poésie d'Apollinaire protégée par lui-même," in *Le Divan*, Mar. 1938.

which he had passed that had given the impression of instability and susceptibility to influence.   The defiant gesture of *L'Antritradition futuriste* which was published on 29 June could well have been a direct reply to the cool reception of *Alcools*, that had given him no credit for innovation or originality but at best had placed him in the school of the "fantaisistes" poets.   It was probably meant in the spirit of "I'll show them just how modern and authoritative and original I can be."

Certainly from now on, although he soon denied this allegiance to the Futurists, he was to be well embarked on what Tristan Tzara has called his "heroic period,"[19] the outward and forward march towards experimentation and renewal. Not however without a sense of tearing out a whole part of himself.   It is the tension that this idea of self-sacrifice engenders which distinguishes the poems of this period.   "Liens" which appeared in April in *Montjoie* makes this perfectly clear.   The manuscript is even adorned with a little drawing in his hand of the Pietà, Marie and crucifixion being still present in his mind; and after a brave building up of images in real "simultanist" mood:

> Violente pluie qui peigne les fumées
> Cordes
> Cordes tisseés
> Câbles sous-marins
> Tours de Babel changées en ponts
> Araignées—Pontifes
> Tous les amoureux qu'un seul lien a liés[20]

he falls back into nostalgia:

> J'écris seulement pour vous exalter
> O sens ô sens chéris
> Ennemis du souvenir
> Ennemis du désir

---

[19] In conversation with the author.

[20] "Violent rain that depicts smoke
  Ropes
  Woven ropes
  Submarine cables
  Towers of Babel changed into bridges
  Spiders Pontiffs
  All the lovers whom one link has joined together"

Ennemis du regret
Ennemis des larmes
Ennemis de tout ce que j'aime encore[21]

(This exaltation of the five senses was also one of the Futurist claims, but Apollinaire had already tried to come to terms with it in "Les Fiançailles.")

"Arbre," which appeared in another small review *Le Gay Scavoir*, launches out in the same way with that gay, bold outlook on the world that he adopted when he was stimulated and in company: "Tu chantes avec les autres tandis que les phonographes galopent." But his catching after the images of the external world seems rather strained. He even uses those taken directly from his painter friends. "Un veau dépouillé pendu à l'étal" is definitely out of Chagall: the Douanier (beloved also by Delaunay) makes his appearance:

Un douanier se tenait là comme un ange
A la porte d'un misérable paradis[22]

and Cendrars and his famous "transsibérien":

Nous avions loué deux coupés dans le transsibérien
Tour à tour nous dormions le voyageur en bijouterie et moi[23]

But, as in "Zone," once he is left to his own devices the attitude shifts. In vain does he propel himself upwards: "Et l'ascenseur s'arrêtait à chaque étage," everywhere he is haunted by the old sentimental sadness, the tenderness of melancholy. For everywhere "il y a ton image." Within the kaleidoscope of the present in Rouen, in Finland—behind the brave new robot of a brave new world, "Ce beau nègre en

[21] "I write only to exalt you
O senses o beloved senses
Enemies of memory
Enemies of regret
Enemies of tears
Enemies of all I still love"

[22] "A customs officer stood there like an angel
At the gates of a miserable Paradise"

[23] "We had booked two carriages in the Transsiberian
We took turns in sleeping the traveller in jewellery and I"

acier," is the sadness of the lost love of the past. And he even goes right back to his old adolescent complaint:

> Tout est plus triste qu'autrefois
> Tous les dieux terrestres vieillissent
> L'univers se plaint par ta voix[24]

However, change is ineluctable even if there are moments when he cannot conjure up his usual enthusiasm to salute it, but is merely forced to note that in the end the future is master.

> Et des êtres nouveaux surgissent
> Trois par trois[25]

In "Cortège" it was only the beings of the past that were alive to him; the future was horrifyingly empty. In "Le Musicien de Saint-Merry" (which was not actually published until February 1914 but which includes a line containing the date "Le 21 du mois de mai 1913") he claims at last his share of the future, his right to salute these new beings who pass beyond him even if he does not yet know their features:

> J'ai enfin le droit de saluer des êtres que je ne connais pas
> Ils passent devant moi et s'accumulent au loin[26]

This would seem at last to be the fulfilment that he had looked forward to in "Les Fiançailles," "Mais si le temps venait où l'ombre enfin solide se multipliait en réalisant la diversité formelle de mon amour j'admirerais mon ouvrage." The old confidence in his apocryphal, creative powers is restored:

> Je ne chante pas ce monde ni les autres astres
> Je chante toutes les possibilités de moi-même hors de ce monde
> et des astres[27]

This is accompanied in the manuscript by a drawing of either Christ or an Apostle declaiming with outstretched hand.

[24] "Everything is sadder than before
All the earthly gods are growing old
The universe moans through your voice"

[25] "And new beings arise
Three by three"

[26] "At last I have the right to salute beings whom I do not know
They pass before me and pile up far away"

[27] "I do not sing of this world nor of the other stars
I sing of all the possibilities of myself outside this world and the stars"

But as he follows the thread of his story, for this is a narrative poem as was "La Maison des morts," of the fantastic musician who leads away a troop of women to their perdition in true Pied Piper style, he goes through all the familiar modulations, the crab-like progress, the wistful look over his shoulder, the sudden leap forward and then the complete halts by the way-side to allow his tears to dry. It is as obvious a piece of wishful thinking as a dream, yet another attempt at exorcising Marie. The musician, without eyes, nose, and ears is another of his Doppelgängers and the air that he plays on his flute is the little ditty on which Apollinaire composed his own poems. And instead of being betrayed and abandoned by one woman, it is he, terrible and indifferent, who leads a whole troop of them astray. At first, bravely again, he flashes through novelty, the kaleidoscope of voyage, the use of advertisements, "Rivalise donc poète avec les étiquettes des parfumeurs," the sense of ascending through the future, "Nous allons plus haut maintenant et ne touchons plus le sol." But the sentimental memories pull him back like the women's clutching hands.

"Tu pleurais assise près de moi au fond du fiacre," until he is turned quite round into the past watching his cortège of women trailing into the distance of history. "C'est quand jadis le roi s'en allait à Vincennes." Darkness falls and with it his courage to look into and create the future. As in "Zone," he abandons himself to the womb of night, and of the past and of sorrow.

And with this abandonment to night, wells up again the old spontaneous, traditional use of cadence and rhyme:

> O nuit
> Troupeau de regards langoureux des femmes
> O nuit
> Toi ma douleur et mon attente vaine
> J'entends mourir le son d'une flûte lointaine[28]

Only at his morning boldest is Apollinaire yet able to stifle his natural lyricism.

[28] "O night
Flock of women's langorous eyes
O night
You my sorrow and my vain expectation
I hear the dying fall of a distant flute"

XI

The Labyrinth of Experiment

OUTWARDLY, Apollinaire seemed to have recovered from his crisis about Marie. In fact they were still seen about together and she even helped to sew the curtains for his new flat in the boulevard Saint-Germain. Louise Faure-Favier gives a charming series of vignettes of Apollinaire at this period. There is Apollinaire admiring his own eyebrows, Apollinaire delighted at discovering that he looked like Racine, Apollinaire swamped by appointments which he always forgot and work which he always accepted, his pockets constantly stuffed with reviews. Apollinaire holding forth from his amazing fund of anecdotes, Apollinaire going to the theatre and then being sucked up into the crowd and seen no more for days, Apollinaire being forced to ask a friend to paint a black tie on to his shirt because his own had stuck in a bottle, and Apollinaire finally struck by guilt at the small amount of real creative work that he and his friends achieved: "We are the generation of little bits of paper," he declared. To remedy this he and André Billy shut themselves up one day, determined not to move until they had produced the requisite number of pages. The result for Apollinaire was the story of "Arthur roi passé, roi futur," yet another of his games with time, which describes the resuscitation of King Arthur in the year 2105, and his occupation of Buckingham Palace. This April-fool story ends amusingly like this:

> The following days were employed by King Arthur in listening to the historians of the kingdom who gave a succinct account of what had happened since his death, and life took up its ordinary course again this selfsame year of 1914 on April 1st, the day that I am writing this chronicle, with George V reigning in England and M. Raymond Poincaré presiding over the Third French Republic, whilst Paul Fort prince of poets is visiting his people in the remotest districts of Scythia and

stretched out on the divan of the sitting room where I am, my friend André Billy is snoring with artistry.[1]

In the summer of 1913 Louise Faure-Favier tried to patch things up between Apollinaire and Marie and invited them both to spend a few days' holiday in Villequier in Normandy with Billy and Dalize and herself. It all sounds very amusing and full of the old high spirits and inconsequential fantasy, with its literary larks and improvisations, and the expedition to the tomb of Victor Hugo's daughter. One night at dinner in order to "épater" a rich Normandy *bourgeois*, Apollinaire launched himself into a lurid account of their Bohemian way of life which unfortunately also reached the ears of the *patronne*. The good lady, fearing that her fate would be like that of the Constants of Stavelot, immediately presented her bill. "With the amount of food you manage to tuck away," she said in answer to Apollinaire's indignant remonstrances, "one can't be too careful."

But despite all this, there remained a definite strain between the two lovers. Guillaume would fall suddenly silent or sombre; or disappear on his own. Marie was intractable. But, because his mind was anything but one-track there was also another preoccupation which helped to make him restless. For some time now his review *Les Soirées de Paris* had been in financial difficulties. There had always been a certain delay in printing and distribution, but since the April number, which had published Apollinaire's poem of homage to the Douanier, nothing more had appeared, and it was obvious that without radical revision and new funds it would, like its predecessors, die a natural death. There was also internal strife with Apollinaire tugging one way and Dalize and Billy digging in their heels and trying to hang on to the rope. All their contributors, they said, had defected because Apollinaire had frightened them off with his new hairbrained theories.

But Apollinaire was not to be brow-beaten. He already had a plan. His friend Serge Férat, the Russian painter who had been so good to him when he was at his low ebb in 1912 and his sister, the Baronne d'Oettingen, who wrote under the

---

[1] *Le Poète assassiné*, 1959, p. 224.

pseudonym Roch Grey, had private means and seemed to be willing to come to his aid, and share with him the directorship of the review. From Villequier he was thinking of going to meet them in La Baule in order to discuss the whole project. So some of his moods and silences may well have been caused by concern about the outcome of this meeting.

He need not have worried. Everything went as he had wanted and when they all came back to Paris in September *Les Soirées de Paris* had assumed a new look, with its offices in Férat's apartment in the boulevard Raspail, and freedom to devote itself as much as it liked to experiment without worring too much about money matters.

This was of course the breath of life to Apollinaire. He even abandoned his friends in his enthusiasm for *Les Soirées de Paris*, and spent all his days in the offices, and his nights in the cafés of Montparnasse. For the immediate pre-war years were the beginning of the heyday of Montparnasse which had now completely taken over from Montmartre. Most of the old Bateau Lavoir faithfuls were now to be seen at La Rotonde and La Coupole and their ranks had been swelled by notable numbers of foreigners. One of the best accounts of this rackety, motley crew is from Apollinaire's own pen in the hotch-potch of different articles and stories that he churned together in *La Femme assise*, and it well conveys the hectic sense of chasing after life, of stretching the limits of experience and pulling it to pieces, which seemed to characterise the mænad dance on the edge of the volcano that went on in 1913 and early 1914.

Apollinaire in particular welcomed the young Italians and they, when they came to Paris, flocked to see him as their acknowledged master. For them he did the honours of Paris most proudly, taking them out on his nightly wanderings, showing them things, which it seemed that only he could have discovered, and indeed, which seemed to exist only for him. "When one knows how to observe, one sees the most curious, the most touching things." One of these, according to Alberto Magnelli,[2] was an orange market, where at a little table sat an orange merchant busily writing. Instead of his bills for his oranges he was writing poems: another was the

[2] Jannini, p. 55.

brothel quarter of Paris: another the exotic restaurants: another a man who, every night, would cross the whole of Paris on foot to visit the tomb of Baudelaire in the Cimetière Montparnasse "to talk to" the poet, who apparently rewarded him by telling him many interesting things, and by reciting his poems. "Only a being like Apollinaire," writes Magnelli, "could make such discoveries, his company was an enormous pleasure." "One must know everything," was one of Apollinaire's favourite dicta, suck "the orange, beautiful fruit of light" to its pith.

The Russian Rayonnist painters Larionow and Goncharova[3] had similar experiences to relate when they visited him. He was charm himself. Even for complete strangers he seemed to be able to create an atmosphere of enchantment and magic, to invest the world with his own fantasy. It was a rare gift and undoubtedly a great part of his fascination. Certainly at this stage he was already taking on the figure of a leader not merely in his own country, but of the whole international younger generation. And at the same time with his endearing naïvety and intrinsic lack of worldly wisdom he imagined that he was heading straight for the Académie française.

It was hardly the most direct path that he chose towards such hallowed precincts. In the first number of the new *Les Soirées de Paris*—November 1913—he was still championing "this intoxication with simultaneous colour," and demanding further that there should be simultaneous sculpture and polychrome architecture. In the second number he produces another of his own surprises: "Lundi rue Christine," the first real "conversation poem." One can imagine the look on the face of the Immortals of that time if he had gone to pay his courtesy visit with this as his most recent testimonial:

> La mère de la concierge et la concierge laisseront tout passer
> Si tu es un homme tu m'accompagneras ce soir
> Il suffirait qu'un type maintînt la porte cochère
> Pendant que l'autre monterait
> . . . Ça a l'air de rimer

---

[3] *La Table ronde*, Sep. 1952, p. 86.

Des piles de soucoupes des fleurs un calendrier
Pim pam pim
Je dois fiche près de 300 francs à ma probloque
Je préférais me couper le parfaitement que de les lui donner[4]

It is important that "Lundi rue Christine" should be considered, like the later calligrams, as an experiment and not
as a definitive work, not as something accomplished but as
something attempted. Also it must be looked at in the particular light shed by that moment in literary history, a time
when any ambitious writer or artist knew that he must try
to discover something new or renounce his ambitions. Experimentation, theorising, revolution were the order of the day,
and the gesture of publishing or exhibiting one's experiments
as opposed to keeping them in note form was as important
as that of the scientist. It was essential to make known any
discovery of new lyrical possibilities, to share one's own personal
progress, and even those steps that led up blind alleys. Not
without good reason did Guillaume Apollinaire talk much
from now on of art as "L'Aventure," nor André Breton describe
him as "a singular man, the one whom with my own eyes I
have seen incarnate to the highest degree the whole lyrical
adventure."[5] Whatever guiding trend was in the air, Apollinaire with his acutely susceptible intuition, would be at the
centre of it. He was always stimulated by competition and used
other people's enthusiasm like a pair of stilts in order to achieve
greater heights of his own. It would have been inconceivable
for a man of his temperament and natural talents and sense of
leadership not to have felt at that time that is was his bounden
duty to explore the unknown. "En attendant, demandons

[4] "The *concierge's* mother and the *concierge* will let anything by
If you are a man you will come with me tonight
We'd only have to have one chap holding the outside door
. . . It looks as though its rhyming
Piles of saucers flowers a calendar
Pim pam pim
I owe a bill of 300 francs to my governor
I'd rather cut off my you know what than give it to him"

[5] Quoted by Marie-Jeanne Durry in *Omaggio ad Apollinaire*, Rome (Ed. dell'
Ente Premi) 1960.

Q

au poète du nouveau—idées et formes," Rimbaud had declared,[6] and nobody yet seemed to have met that challenge.

But in fact Apollinaire's governing principle was neither new nor unknown. This quality which he himself had christened "Orphism," and which later he re-baptised as "surnaturalisme" and then eventually "surréalisme," was what he had always aimed at capturing, life at its most intense pulsation, the life-force naked, bereft of the cluttering trammels of everyday existence. It was this mysterious quality which came to him at moments either through the weaving patterns of his own fantasy or through an ecstatic, visionary enthusiasm by which he felt united with all other manifestations of life in the cosmos. There were even times when if he simply looked at the world around him with enough loving intensity "the most curious and moving things" would be washed up by the sea of life at his feet. And finally, after his years of intense self-absorption, it was these last that, by a simple opening of the windows of the world, he was eager to explore. Pick up the flotsam of life, the snatches of spoken words, the black cat crossing the restaurant, the sawdust on the floor, and piles of saucers on the tables, strand them together like pearls on a necklace, and perhaps the miracle will happen, a poem will be born. "Ça a l'air de rimer." Perhaps this after all will be the new and best method for achieving simultaneity. "Lundi rue Christine" is only one logical step forward from "Les Fenêtres," and from "Les Femmes" of 1902. There the poet was still imposing a pattern, fitting it into the framework of rhyme in "Les Femmes," illuminating the scene with the big spotlights of his own images in "Les Fenêtres." Here he emulates his painter friends who have been busy finding in art "a method of becoming inhuman," by eliminating himself and all his subjective emotions. He has become merely the all-seeing eye, the all-hearing ear. It also has another point in common with Cubist paintings: it builds up its new *ensemble* by using real fragments of speech, just as the Cubists had built their pictures out of pieces of real material rearranged into a new harmony. It could even be likened to the omnipresent, recording eye of the cine camera;

[6] Letter to Paul Demeny, 15 May 1871, *Oeuvres complètes*, Paris (Pléïade), p. 256.

or, in its concentration on objects rather than on the subject, to the method of the *nouveau roman*.

Nevertheless the poem-conversation as such was only an isolated experiment. In the same number of *Les Soirées de Paris* in his notes on the Salon d'Automne, Apollinaire was still acknowledging that, "in painting everything is represented at the same time, the eye can wander over the picture, come back to a certain colour, look first from top to bottom or do the opposite: in literature, in music, everything is successive and one cannot return to this or that word or sound just as one wants." It was the old problem of how to let the successive represent simultaneity; and here he is content to resign himself still merely to giving the impression of simultaneity. In this same article he also makes a remark which underscores his own attitude to experimentation. "There have been errors, and they were inevitable, but the effort that they have cost will serve the future developments in art."

Apollinaire has often, and not only on the appearance of *Alcools*, been accused of inconsistency. On the contrary, as one follows him step by step each month in *Les Soirées de Paris*, at a time when he was capping one apparent novelty by yet another, one is amazed by his dogged tenacity of purpose. In February (the January number being wholly consecrated to the Douanier), he is still worrying at the idea of simultaneity and how best to achieve it. The Futurists, he says, have not made much progress with their "mots en liberté," their telegraphic style and simplified syntax—which in any case was not original but had sprung from Rimbaud and Mallarmé and the Symbolists—because this is still only a technique for description, and for "direct expression" there is as yet nothing to beat "the sentence, nor above all the poetic line; rhymed or rhythmical, regular or irregular." But for the really new impressions there will be new methods. "Soon poets will be able, by means of gramophone records, to launch throughout the whole world, veritable symphonies of poems. Added to horizontal poetry which will not of course be abandoned, there will be a vertical or polyphonic poetry from which we can expect important, unexpected works." This was still the line of Barzun and Beaudouin. Nevertheless, despite the apparently extravagant idea of disc poetry he still comes back to the importance of using life and nature as the only sources for art, and describes Orphism as "external truth," a vague definition which, indeed, had to remain vague in order to cover all the different tendencies which he thought valid.

In his own poetic offerings at this time he seemed to be still working along certain old veins of fantasy: although in fact "Un Fantôme de nuées," (published in December in *Les Ecrits français*), and "Le Musicien de Saint-Merry," (February in *Les Soirées de Paris*), had undoubtedly been composed during the course of 1913 and so again lagged behind his theories. Nevertheless, "Un Fantôme de nuées" is a very successful example of the way in which through fantasy he manages to communicate a sense of the "Orphic" quality in life, that delectable shock of realising the extent of its mystery and multiplicity: "Doigts roulant une cigarette amère et délicieuse comme la vie."

It begins in the most ordinary, habit-coated way in lines, which like those of "La Maison des morts" he had first cast as a prose-story:

Comme c'était la veille du quatorze juillet
Je descendis dans la rue pour aller voir les saltimbanques[7]

and then suddenly the prose is peeled off reality. Like Rimbaud again—"je voyais très franchement une mosquée à la place d'une usine"—he persuades himself into a sort of hallucination. Portents arise, images balloon up, the strong man's weights are

Poids formidables
Villes de Belgique soulevées à bras tendu par un ouvrier russe
de Longwy[8]

---

[7] "As it was the eve of the fourteenth of July
I went down into the street to see the mountebanks"

[8] "Formidable weights
Towns of Belgium lifted up in the outstretched arms
of a Russian workman from Longwy"

The life force past and future trickles out through the face of the thin man:

> Vois-tu le personnage maigre et sauvage
> La cendre de ses pères lui sortait en barbe grisonnants
> Il portait aussi toute son hérédité au visage
> Il semblait rêver à l'avenir[9]

Good and evil intermingle in the "apache," another mountebank wears only his shadow, and finally all the grace and artistry and harmony of the world is summed up in the movements of the little boy walking on a ball:

> Le petit saltimbanque fit la roue
> Avec tant d'harmonie
> Que l'orgue cessa de jouer
> Et que l'organiste se cacha le visage dans les mains
> Aux doigts semblables aux descendants de son destin
> Foetus minuscules qui lui sortaient de la barbe
> Nouveaux cris de Peau-Rouge
> Musique angélique des arbres
> Disparition de l'enfant[10]

Symbolically this miraculous child represents the hidden "Orphic" spirit which alone can illuminate the cloudy confusion of the century:

> Mais chaque spectateur cherchait en soi l'enfant miraculeux
> Siècle ô siècle de nuages[11]

---

[9] "Do you see this wild-looking man
The ashes of his forefathers were coming out of his greying beard
He carried also all his inheritance on his face
He seemed to be dreaming of the future"

[10] "The little mountebank did a cartwheel
With such harmony
That the organ stopped playing
And the organist hid his face in his hands
Hands with fingers like the descendants of his destiny
Minute fœtuses which came out of his beard
New Red Indian war-cries
Angelic music of the trees
Disappearance of the child"

[11] "But each spectator searched within himself for the miraculous child
Century o century of clouds"

It is the supposed outlook of the child, the wonderment of seeing the world for the first time in all the clarity of strangeness, which here conveys most admirably the poet's conception of "Orphism," and to which he was giving a kind of double accolade, for already Picasso had consecrated that "enfant miraculeux" for all time in art.

The shock of surprise is naturally enough one of the elements which reinforce or even open up the awareness of this whole Orphic mystery. Logically, then, Apollinaire goes on to advocate it as another procedure in the technique of the modern artist. Apropos of Chirico he declared in March in *Les Soirées de Paris*, "This painter has recourse to that most modern of incentives, surprise, in order to depict the inevitable character of modern things." And many years later he is still being true to himself in claiming this as one of the tenets of his famous "Esprit nouveau." And the young Surrealists were being true to him when they took it up as their own "most modern incentive in depicting the inevitable character of modern things." Now revelation had so often come to Apollinaire through the medium of painting, that it is not unusual to see him fired yet again by an artist's trick of technique. Just before he died, he was planning to collect all the poems inspired by his painter friends into one volume. This would have shown most clearly how fertile a point of departure he found in a particular work of art, how in fact he was always glad to use a painting as subject matter for a poem. In emotional crises, in solitude and the well of narcissism, poetry dropped from him as profusely and as naturally as beads of sweat: it was then as difficult for him to keep quiet, and not to express himself melodically, as it might have been for another less gifted writer to achieve such lyricism. But, because the pattern of his life swooped up and down in such spectacular curves, there were periods between the emotional upsurges when he seemed to lead exactly the opposite kind of life, a frenzied, extravert, activity. Then after all the wallowing in private emotion he seemed to have reached the other pole of intense, over-stimulated celebration, during which he was impelled to force his muse and consciously seek out subjects. Any complete survey of his work reveals this fascinating oscillation between the periods of emotional plenitude and inspiration which inevitably express themselves in richly regular verse, and those of self-conscious, almost competitive poetry-making when more than all else he is concerned with experiment.

The search for subjects is a common enough problem. Even the most fertile of geniuses have not always enough subject matter within them to fill out the hours when their addiction glues them to their desks. As a newspaper column acted as the fertiliser for Flaubert or Stendhal, so a painting could often be guaranteed to set the machinery of creation going for Apollinaire. And it is hardly surprising that he who was so easily influenced that his friends could often tell whom he had been with merely by his manner of speaking, he who had come back from his year in Germany looking like a Prussian *Junker*, should in a poem about a painter adopt some of that painter's own particular tricks of technique.

Delaunay and his spinning, contrasting colours had had their day for Apollinaire, at least as a seminal influence. And indeed when Apollinaire embarked yet again on a polemic which threatened to end in a duel, Delaunay was prepared to act as one of the seconds for his opponent, the painter Henri Ottmann who had taken exception to a critical article of Apollinaire's in *L'Intransigeant*.

On his forward march Apollinaire knew many other enthusiasms. In March he had written in glowing terms of Chirico. In April in *Les Soirées de Paris* appeared a poem entitled first "Rotsoge" and then "A travers l'Europe," and dedicated to Chagall. Here again he uses surprise as his open sesame and manages to produce a series of images in true surrealist vein:

Un jour fait de morceaux mauves jaunes bleus verts et rouges
Où je m'en allais à la campagne avec une charmante
   cheminée tenant sa chienne en laisse
Il n'y en a plus tu n'as plus ton petit mirliton
La cheminée fume loin de moi des cigarettes russes[12]

---

[12] "A day made out of mauve yellow blue green and red pieces
   When I went off to the country with a charming chimney holding
      her dog on a lead
   There aren't any more you haven't got your little reed-pipe any more
   The chimney is smoking far away from me Russian cigarettes"

Nothing exemplifies better Cendrars' dictum, "Guillaume Apollinaire advances, retreats, and sometimes stops altogether" than his hop-scotch progress through 1914. In May, under the pseudonym Jean Cérusse, he is defending himself against being classed as a "fantaisiste" by using the term "surnaturalisme" and declaring: "The fantasy of Guillaume Apollinaire has never been anything but a great concern for truth, a minute concern for truth." And with one of his battlecry endings, he ranges himself once again by the side of Boileau: "Rien n'est beau que le vrai."

The very next month this upholder of order and tradition made another of his apparently disconcerting leaps forward. He published, as usual in *Les Soirées de Paris*, "Lettre océan" which is commonly regarded as the first of his calligrams, and an article "Simultanisme—librettisme"[13] justifying the theory that it embodied. The poem is spread out lengthwise over the space of four sides of paper: on the first page are reproduced the Mexican and U.S. postmarks, and the wireless waves across the ocean: on the second, the poet on the pont d'Iéna: on the third the Eiffel Tower in the centre of a circle of sound impressions—first the factory sirens, "Hou, hou, hou, ou, ou," then the buses, "ting, ting, changement de section," then the gramophones "666, ou, ou, ou," and the new, squeaking shoes of the poet, "cré, cré, cré": and finally, fanning out on the circumference of the circle, overheard snippets of conversation, "priétaire de 5 ou 6 im." But in fact, as the article makes clear, for all its apparent novelty, "Lettre Océan" is again only a logical development from "Lundi rue Christine," as that poem had been from "Les Fenêtres." He is merely going one more step forward in attempting to reproduce simultaneity, this time actually placing the words on the page so that the impression is no longer successive but as simultaneous as that given by a picture. The reader has to take it in all at once, not each line successively in turn. "Here," Apollinaire writes in explanation, "we have given poems where this simultaneity exists not only figuratively but literally, since it is impossible to read them without immediately conceiving the simultaneity that they express, conversation-poems where the

[13] "Simultanisme—librettisme," *Soirées de Paris*, Jun. 1914.

poet placed at the centre of life registers in some measure all its ambient lyricism." It is the old problem of trying to hold all life in the palm of one's hand, but seen in the new light of finding a different kind of typography to present this simultaneity literally. With his usual sense of fairness, and his constant desire to clarify the present state of affairs he maintains justifiably that his own works, *L'Enchanteur pourrissant*, "Vendémiaire," "Les Fenêtres," have always attempted "to accustom the reader to thinking of a poem simultaneously as a slice of life." But this was still only "in the spirit." It was, he acknowledges, Cendrars and Sonia Delaunay who first made

> an attempt at written simultaneity in which the contrasting colours accustomed the eye to take in at one glance the whole of a poem as a conductor reads the superimposed notes of a score all at once, or as one sees all the plastic and printed elements of an advertisement.

Here he is referring to Blaise Cendrars' famous "Prose du transsibérien" painted in different colours by Sonia Delaunay. He discounts Barzun's chorus and gramophones because they still remain successive. Sébastien Voirol with his "Sacre du printemps" written in different-coloured inks was nearer to representative simultaneity. Of the painters, ever since 1907 Picasso and Braque and Léger had been wrestling with this problem when they represented several sides of an object at once. Duchamp and Picabia had tried to come to terms with it, but Delaunay was its champion, making it his actual technique. In poetry "typographic simultaneity" was first hinted at by Villiers and by Mallarmé (it is obvious that Mallarme's influence on Apollinaire was multiple and had not ceased in 1908), and in some measure issued in by Marinetti and the Futurists. From now on it is he, Apollinaire, who will pursue these researches wherever they may lead.

It is characteristic of him, that then after thus placing himself midway in a whole path of tradition, he promptly starts up a tempting by-way. The problem of typography seduces him entirely, and in July he is producing his "ideograms" proper, which are really little pictures made up with words. "Voyage," for instance, figures several of these.

There is the bird made out of "Télégraphe oiseau qui laisse tomber ses ailes partout," the cloud, "Adieu amour nuage qui fuis et n'a pas chu pluie fécon refais le voyage de Dante," the train, "Où va donc ce train qui meurt au loin dans les vals et les beaux bois frais du tendre été si pâle," and for once Apollinaire does not despise a question mark because it serves well as a puff of smoke; finally the night sky is patterned with letters for stars "Je ne vois plus que la douce nuit lunaire pleine d'étoiles C'est ton visage."

In "Coeur couronne et miroir" these three objects are pictured by sonorous lines of poetry, "Mon coeur pareil à une flame renversée," "Les rois qui meurent tour à tour renaissent au coeur des poètes," "Dans ce miroir je suis enclos vivant et vrai comme on imagine les anges et non comme sont les reflets." All of which seems to have led him rather astray from simultaneity.

There has obviously been much discussion about these little innovations of Apollinaire's, although in themselves they constitute a very small number of his poems. Later he will use an ideogram as a *divertissement* in the course of a longer poem. He himself appears to underline their importance by entitling his second big volume *Calligrammes*. But if it is originality which is in question, the ideogram is in fact less new than the poem-conversation.[14] Carried away by his fantasy, inflamed by a glimpse of supposedly virgin territory, Apollinaire has in fact joined hands again with tradition, even if a very minor tradition, for one can trace back, as Michel Décaudin, with his usual scholarly thoroughness, has so ably and fully done in the notes in his edition of *Calligrammes*, the origins of the "poème figuré" through Mallarmé and Gabriel Martin and Victor Hugo, to Rétif de la Bretonne, to Panard and Rabelais, and eventually to Greek poets such as Simmias of Rhodes and Dosiades. As M. Décaudin points out, Apollinaire in his early notebook of 1899 was mentioning the word "idéogrammes," meaning then only the Chinese characters,

[14] In his recent *Evolution of Apollinaire's Poetics 1901-1914*, Francis Carmody points out that Martinetti had produced ideograms in the Futurist manifesto of 11 May 1914, and states categorically: "Thus far, Apollinaire's ideograms are pastiches of Martinetti's."

but obviously fascinated even at that stage by the idea of conveying the meaning of a word by its shape. It is interesting in this context to note that it was also during this immediate pre-war period that Pound and Flint were preoccupied with the Japanese translations of Chinese poems, and that in the June number of *Les Soirées de Paris* Apollinaire writes an article on the English Imagists and quotes some of their aims. The first of these is the direct exposition of the subject. "We present the object without idle commentaries, we make an image of it and the emotion is in this way released." He also reviews six of Pound's poems, four of which are inspired by the Chinese. This seems to be not a question of a direct influence but yet another concrete example of how certain ideas drift together from different sources at certain prescribed periods.

Apollinaire did his best to present his ideograms as a revolution in poetry. Under the pseudonym of Gabriel Arbouin, in July he writes "Devant l'idéogramme d'Apollinaire" and spells out his intention. "It is a revolution in the full strength of the word . . . because it will be necessary for our intelligence to accustom itself to understand synethetico-ideographically instead of analytico-discursively." There is no longer any link of logic or grammar. And that had been tenuous enough even in "La Chanson du Mal-Aimé." The ideogram represents naked ideas in visual order. He recognises that this may not be popular, and may even appear to be a regression because "rhythm has always seemed more appropriate for the communication of emotion than a naked idea."

The whole irony of Apollinaire's position at this moment is blatant. In "Lettre-Océan" he may with great effort have managed to hew out of himself "naked ideas," ("cré cré cré hou hou ou") but the next little batch of ideograms is in fact composed of his usual, musical, rhythmic lines, all with the sonorous cadence that characterises him as indelibly as does a certain melodic line its composer. The little poem "Il Pleut," for instance, arranged so prettily in vertical lines of raindrops is a perfectly sober piece, which most certainly communicates emotion through its rhythm:

Il pleut des voix de femmes comme si elles étaient mortes même
    dans le souvenir

C'est vous aussi qu'il pleut merveilleuses rencontres de ma vie
  ô goutelettes
Et ces nuages cabrés se prennent à hennir tout un univers de
  villes auriculaires
Ecoute s'il pleut tandis que le regret et le dédain pleurent une
  ancienne musique
Ecoute tomber les liens qui te retiennent en haut et en bas[15]

"A pretty poem," Apollinaire justly boasted of this. He
had always loved to doodle over his manuscripts, he occasionally tried his hand at water-colours, he was as passionate
about visual art as about poetry. Therefore he must have
been delighted with this new discovery. "Anch'io son pittore"
was the naïve title with which he was toying for a whole volume
of these ideograms. It was an intoxicating thought. Only
the most carping of critics can begrudge him his new game.
It is only too easy to question the validity of these uses of typography; even though their shade still haunts us, and people are
still experimenting with the possibilities of different types, for
example of capital letters for exclamation, or a contrast of
type for past and present. But the poet himself, who is securely
"fondé en poésie," knows that poetry is no sacred cow, but a
part of life, and that there is room in it for laughter as well as
tears, for bright ideas and serious experiments, for chatty
letters to friends and for "le joli poème."

It might have been embarrassing for him if he had had to
continue to press home the ideogram as the spear-head of a
revolution. But the whole idea of such a revolution was now
to be crushed by the infinitely greater cataclysm of the War.
It was through this and not through any of the recent artistic
experiments that, as Apollinaire saw immediately, they were
all to say goodbye to a whole epoch.

[15] "It is raining women's voices as if they had died even in the remembrance
   It is you also that it is raining marvellous encounters of my life o droplets
   And these rearing clouds take to whinnying out a whole universe of
     auricular towns
   Listen to it raining whilst regret and disdain weep a bygone music
   Listen to the chains falling that bind you from head to foot"

XII

Nice and Nîmes

IN June Marie had suddenly announced that she was going to be married. In was in June too that Apollinaire had launched "Lettre océan." It would seem that one of his reactions to an emotional upset was a hardening of his attitude to artistic innovation. Similarly after the crisis of the previous summer he had plunged headlong into Delaunay's hot-bed of simultanism. Whatever tricks a woman might play with him, he must still prove that he was supreme as a king of poetry.

But as always, whether as king or as "mal-aimé" he was inevitably short of money. He was still obliged to earn his living by all manner of literary odd-jobs. In the course of this year two of his pornographic novels, *La Fin de Babylone* and *Les Trois Don Juan*, appeared. He produced a new edition of the story of *Perceval le Galloys* and he was contemplating an edition of the works of Jarry in co-operation with Dr Saltas. At the end of June he jumped at an opportunity which was offered to him by the paper *Comœdia* to go with his recently acquired friend, the artist and cartoonist André Rouveyre, to Deauville, in order to do an illustrated gossip column, akin to his regular "chronique anecdotique" for the *Mercure de France*, on the Deauville season. It seemed like an ideal chance of having a paid holiday. But in the event it turned out to be a very brief interlude. They arrived on 26 July and on 31 July at midnight the announcement of general mobilisation drove them hurriedly back to Paris. Nevertheless Rouveyre's account [1] of Apollinaire during those few days when the looming catastrophe made everything stand out in relief, gives a vivid impression of the man's presence, his personal magic. There was the endearing appetite which was not gluttony but a great relishing and savouring of the good things of life; there were the mysterious disappearances and prolonged absences which might almost

---

[1] Rouveyre, pp. 9 ff.

have been part of a plan to keep his companion mystified,
there were the jokes and the enormous laughter and the wit;
in the casino, for instance, somebody's nose was a personification
of Nietzsche's theory of the "éternel retour." And yet again
here is one more person to testify to his power of investing everything around him with his own new dimensions of fantasy.
Like a painter seeing colours and forms more clearly than other
men, Apollinaire saw ordinary objects and people wrapped in a
halo of mystery and strangeness. Take for instance a pair of
toads. Rouveyre used to carry this odd couple Do and Di
about in a cage. At first Apollinaire was repelled by them;
then gradually they came in some way to symbolise the peculiar
beauty of those few poignant summer days, when the world
as he knew it was about to end, and his own heart was crying
out for a love that had departed. The strange croaking of the
toads on the heady midsummer air is the point around which a
whole complex of yearning and desire and nostalgia crystal-
lises. A year later the toads reappear metamorphosed on the
battlefield into his private symbol of a Golden Age:

> Zénith
>   Tous ces regrets
>   Ces jardins sans limite
> Où le crapaud module un tendre cri d'azur
> La biche du silence éperdu passe vite
> Un rossignol meurtri par l'amour chante sur
> Le rosier de ton corps dont j'ai cueilli les roses . . .[2]

If one saw a negro in coloured robes and a turban bicycling
through the streets of Deauville, one might look twice, or one
might not even notice him at all. But to Apollinaire this was a
marvellous portent, something "surnaturel," a rainbow-
coloured messenger from whatever gods still survived in his
Pantheon. In the article that he wrote for *Comœdia* when the
brilliant little interlude was over, "La Fête manquée," he

---

[2] "Zenith
    All those regrets
       Those limitless gardens
  Where the toad modulates a tender azure cry
  The hind of dismayed silence passes quickly by
  A nightingale bruised by love sings upon
  The rose-tree of your body whose roses I have plucked"

writes, "On the morning of the 31st a marvellous negro dressed in a robe of changing colours, silvery blue and dawn pink, bicycled through the streets of Deauville. We saw him go down the rue Goutant-Biron towards the beach. At last he reached the sea and apparently dived in. Soon all that was left of him was a sea-green turban which was gradually engulfed by the bitter waves."

Whether that negro ever really existed, he and his fate were certainly portents. The party was over: and late that same night after the announcement of general mobilisation, Rouveyre and Apollinaire left for Paris in Rouveyre's car. As often happens at these moments of general catastrophe, nature seemed to make a parade of its own beauty. The dawn was spectacular, and Apollinaire was inspired by that whole unusual episode, the exquisite beauty lined with anguish, the long night drive opening up on to the unknown, even by his own personal suffering "the infinite emptiness of my heart" into one of his Messianic, prophetic utterances, "La Petite Auto." Characteristically he begins on a casual, factual note (although his facts are wrong and he has mistaken the month) in what could be prose.

> Le 31 du mois d'Août 1914
> Je partis de Deauville un peu avant minuit
> Dans la petite auto de Rouveyre
>
> Avec son chauffeur nous étions trois[3]

And then with the realisation that "Nous dîmes adieu à toute une époque," he swells out into one of his Apocalyptic visions of monsters rising from the deep (like the old Leviathian in the bottom of the Rhine) and of great eagles covering the sky. "Les morts tremblaient de peur dans leurs sombres demeures." It seems incredible that the man who could write this line should only a few weeks before have been advocating a purely visual rhythm. But then he had always maintained that there was room for everything. "Je chante toutes les

[3] "The 31st of August 1914
I left Deauville a little before midnight
In Rouveyre's little car
With his chauffeur that made three of us"

possibilités de moi-même," and in this same poem goes on to include a picture of the "little car" figured in words, a compromise which he often adopts from now on.

Even on this brink of a universal disaster which he forsees clearly—the armies struggling on the frontiers, the shipwrecks feeding the sea-beasts, the single combat of aeroplanes—his essential optimistic belief in progress and revolution does not desert him. In fact it is intensified. Out of chaos a new world will be born, and he feels that he will have helped to create it; a really extraordinary claim in the circumstances, for it is not as a soldier that he is thinking, but as a visionary and poet, and one which gives a fair picture of his idealism, his egocentricity, and the sheer weight of his personality. If he had lived he would most certainly, whatever he had chosen to write, have been one of the giants of the epoch:

> Je sentais en moi des êtres neufs pleins de dextérité
> Bâtir et aussi agencer un univers nouveau[4]

However it is almost axiomatic that after such a claim his own entry into the new epoch should be not a triumphant plunge, but a dallying in limbo. Not that this was his own fault. Immediately on his return to Paris he weighed his position carefully. Apart from his atavistic feeling for soldiery, his highly developed sense of honour, and his constant desire to prove his loyalty to France, it was obviously expedient for him to enlist in the army. How otherwise would he live, when most of the papers which kept him going would probably have to close down? And so he straightaway tried to join up: but because he was not of French nationality, he was refused. Now the fact that his adopted and beloved country did not seem to want this offer of his services and even perhaps his life, must have been bitter and chastening, especially when the taunts of Jew and foreigner were fresh in his memory, and it is hardly surprising that when Paris began to be bombarded at the beginning of September, he accepted an invitation to stay in Nice, nor that for the space of a few months he abandoned

---

[4] "I felt within myself new dexterous beings
Building and also organising a new universe"

himself entirely to lotus-eating. He knew and loved Nice, and he had many friends there. It was a strange, unreal episode in his life, circumscribed by his "chambre meublée" and the fact that he was existing on very little money. Its purposeless unreality was further enhanced by the habit of opium-smoking. In Paris, even in the Montmartre days, he had often dabbled with the drug: Dalize had been an inveterate addict. In 1910 one hears[5] of him indulging in great opium sessions: but until now opium seemed to have made few breaches in the vast architecture of his frame, and this is the only period where one can trace a real influence on his behaviour. "The War has become an artificial paradise"[6] he wrote, and it does not need great perspicacity to see that this was how he was seeking to drown his sense of guilt at not being directly involved.

Paradise would not have been paradise for Apollinaire without an Eve. And here in Nice he found a new and particularly seductive one. He was always more than willing to play the game of falling in love, and this moment, with Marie gone for good, his direction in life uncertain, and time heavy on his hands, was highly propitious. The very instant that he caught sight of the elegant, young, red-haired Louise de Coligny crossing the Place Masséna in a big straw hat he was charging into the amorous lists. The next day he was writing[7] to her the most gallant of letters full of tortuous compliments and precious phrases: "I imagined that by the side of a Louise like you I should only have wanted to be a Taciturnus." Five days later he is declaring that when he shuts his eyes at night he sees her breasts multiplied to infinity and that they are "worthier than the golden apples guarded by the Hesperides to be conquered by a hero." Already it seems to him "that I have always known and loved you, only you and can never love another." Now this elaborate initial wooing was always Apollinaire's way: perhaps it is traceable to his Italian blood, the florid tradition of the *cavaliere servente* kneeling at his lady's feet. But with Louise de Coligny it was

---

[5] Adéma, p. 125.
[6] *Op. cit.*, p. 189.
[7] Rouveyre, p. 129.

R

even further exaggerated, because quite apart from the fact
that she was highly attractive, she also bore one of the most
illustrious names of France. In her veins, as Apollinaire was
pleased to boast, ran the blood of St Louis. Until now he
had never had much to do with "le monde" and had never
seemed to feel the lack of such converse. But even he could not
fail to be impressed by this example of history made flesh,
and such dazzling flesh at that. There was, indeed, something
of the Proustian infatuation with the Duchesse de Guermantes
in the first stages of his approach. Louise de Coligny, moreover, though still young, behaved very much like the "grande
dame," that she felt herself to be. Essentially she took the
ways of "le monde" as her sole criterion. All of this contrived
to make Apollinaire realise that he himself was far from being
an "homme du monde," that in more ways than one he was a
true son of Bohemia, that however he intensified his courtly
manners and gallantry they did not strike quite the right note
of casual, aristocratic ease. In short he was put on the wrong
footing from the start. Nor did the opium help. It robbed
him of his usual conquering spirit and left him besotted, almost
grovelling at the feet of a spoilt girl.

For any woman this is not the best of approaches;   more
particularly so for this capricious, wilful creature. André
Rouveyre, who has analysed the whole affair with infinite
subtlety in his *Apollinaire*, gives a very clear picture of her at
this stage of her life. She had been brought up strictly, and
now that she was free she was determined to extract what she
could from life, and particularly from men, with no care for
other people's feelings. She seems to have been the sort of
woman who justifies the existence of the sex war. Attractive
and aware of it, unscrupulous, unaccountable, exigent sensually
and prepared to go to any lengths for her pleasure, cold,
worldly at heart, and yet intelligent in her way, witty, gay, with
sudden bursts of warmth and intimacy. She would lead men
on, then brusquely put obstacles in their way; and yet she
was no tease. She made a great point of telling them to expect
nothing, that she would not fall in love with them, was incapable of love, but still went on to play the game. She puts
one in mind of Balzac's description of the Princesse de Cadignan,

"a female Don Juan, but it would not have been to supper that she invited the Commendatore."

She was amused and fascinated by Apollinaire. He was obviously a rare bird in her world. But she soon corrected him if he made any social gaffes and then made no secret of her contempt. The fact that he was a poet left her quite unmoved, and there is something very touching about Apollinaire's constant need to remind her, "I am the greatest poet in the world." One can imagine her shrugged shoulders at that claim. On the other hand if he had been a member of the Jockey Club he would immediately have won her respect.

This indifference and slight disdain, coupled with moments when she too had smoked opium and seemed to respond to his adoration, the general blowing hot and cold, the momentary revelations of sensuality, were enough to inflame Apollinaire's infatuation into a real passion. What is more she refused to sleep with him. One day after she had rebuffed a specific advance, in a frenzy of frustration and anger, and an upsurge of the desire to assert his virility, he went straight to the recruiting office. This time he was accepted, and shortly afterwards at the beginning of December told that he had to leave. Naturally enough once the step was taken he then regretted his decision most bitterly. On 5 Dec. he wrote to her announcing his departure for the next day: for he had not actually told her when they had met that afternoon. He was, he said, "sad unto death."

Now the roles were reversed. As soon as he asserted himself, she capitulated. He had no sooner arrived at his barracks at Nîmes than she was on the doorstep ready to satisfy his every desire.

From later references in poems and letters it appears that the following days were spent in a great burst of violent, exacerbated eroticism, as if they knew that this was to be all of their experience together and wanted to encompass the whole range of sexuality in this one short space of time. It is common knowledge that they indulged in sodomy and flagellation and much comment has flowed under the pont Mirabeau about that. As is usual, posterity has demanded that all the poet's secrets, and in particular his erotic tastes, should be made public. If Apollinaire had lived he would obviously not have published poems containing lines like, "Te souviens-tu du jour où l'on te demanda la schlague devant une mer furiesue"[8] or the poem in honour of "les neuf portes de ton corps,"[9] all of which he has had the privilege of opening. With all the poems of the posthumously published *Poèmes à Lou*, it must be remembered that they were written only as love letters. Apollinaire always expressed himself most easily in verse. He also wrote quantities of gossipy letters to his friends in casual rhymes. Undoubtedly he would have used these letter-poems, indeed in some of the poems of *Calligrammes* he did use whole passages from them in his completed mosaics, but as they stand they cannot in any way be judged as finished, poetic achievements. Many still remain unpublished because they have been deemed even more intimate than those in *Poèmes à Lou*. So in a sense the reader is playing the role of *voyeur* and has scarcely the right to pass judgment.

Apollinaire would have been in no way ashamed. Violently passionate, as greedy for sex as he was for food and for life generally, extremist in all things, completely and unself-consciously pagan, and what is more, by now something of a professional sexologist, he was not likely to be worried at this stage of his life by what are commonly regarded as perversions. "When love is sublime," he wrote to Lou when even she began to have doubts, "one can do whatever one likes."[10] He manages with consummate ease to fuse tenderness with brutality. "Ma démone enfant," "diablesse exquise," "mon esclave enfuie"[11] he apostrophises her, revelling in the paradox: flagellated flesh becomes in a poetic image the charming "chairs fouettées de la roseraie."

He adored Lou completely, he wanted to subjugate her proud, independent spirit entirely and make it his, and it was an added intoxication for him to know that she who had looked

[8] *Poèmes à Lou, Oeuvres poétiques*, 1956, p. 434.
[9] *Op. cit.*, p. 459.
[10] *Op. cit.*, p. 396.
[11] *Op. cit.*, p. 426.

down her aristocratic nose at him could be so completely his
sexual object: at the same time he had this delicate tenderness
for her. It did not seem incompatible to him that he could
revere a woman and also want to whip her into submission.
He was certainly not the man to despise a woman for letting
him dominate her. This was merely the normal positioning
of love. She on the other hand had more devious reactions.
At the time she obviously complied and enjoyed it. Later when
she had gone back to her old life in Nice, she began to feel
ashamed and complained to him that he had debauched her
by teaching her his favourite vices. In reply he made two
points: first that they were not vices when one is in love (but
of course she was not really in love with him), and secondly,
that these tastes must have existed in her too for her to have
wanted to respond (to which, with reason, she could find no
answer). But the facts were that she had been first piqued
by his act of resistance to her, and then temporarily swept away
by the violence of his passion and unrestrained sensuality, but
that very soon after she left him she reacted against it all,
whether out of sheer indifference, or revulsion, or fear, or a
desire to be free from his excessive demands, one cannot know.
At all events, "your love is too egotistical," she complained
to him later.

But it took Apollinaire some time to realise that her love
such as it had been, had very quickly burnt itself out. He had
already decided that if he was going to be a soldier he might
as well put his heart and soul into it, and so whether Lou
was there or not he threw himself into the life of the barracks
with his usual jovial enthusiasm. He was, as always, conscientious and ambitious, and determined to become an
officer as soon as it was possible. He was in the artillery and
so had to follow an intensive course of training which included
learning to ride, not an altogether easy task for such a
corpulent man. He was thrown countless times and each
time got up laughing: eventually he decided that as he
had to do it anyway he found a definite "voluptuousness"
in the act of riding. He was proud that he had such a
good constitution, proud that he was making such good
progress, particularly as he was much older than most of his

companions. In a letter home to Serge Férat he declares[12] categorically:

> I'm very happy and it seems to me that I was always intended to be a soldier. I like it very much. My friend [Lou] says that I'm acting the part as if I were in an opera, and it's true.

Which was quite a perspicacious remark. He saw himself in this role, even sometimes—because of the riding—as a medieval knight preparing for war. "As-tu connu Guy au galop" runs the refrain of "Saisons," and in the poem addressed to Rouveyre, "C'est Lou qu'on la nommait," he sees himself as a warrior in an "image d'Epinal" setting off to war on his big charger, "sans pitié chaste et l'œil sévère."

In those early days, bolstered by Lou's apparent capitulation and his enthusiasm for his new part, he was radiantly active, joking and laughing with the young soldiers, reading them his poems aloud in bed, listening to their stories of home. And as usual he was very popular. Apparently they respected him most of all for the quantity of white wine which he managed to drink. He also mixed with the townspeople and kept an ear open for the local gossip and curious stories and, as he bumped over the stony countryside on his horse, would hold forth about art and poetry just as he was used to do in the cafés of Paris. He even managed to impress the Colonel in Chief by sending him a copy of *Alcools*: so obviously when he had to pass an examination in French he won first prize although, as he said, he had put in his essay all the nonsense he could possibly think of.

It seemed as though, after that debilitating period in Nice, he had once again reawakened into virile, honourable activity. Above all he enjoyed the feeling of comradeship and solidarity with the other men. As he wrote proudly in a poem to Lou showing her that he was no longer under her yoke, but now a real man with higher allegiances:

> Je tire ma pipe libre et fier parmi mes camarades
> Ils partiront avec moi pour les champs de bataille
> Ils dormiront la nuit sous la pluie ou les étoiles
> Ils galoperont avec moi portant en croupe des victoires

---

12 Adéma, p. 197.

Ils obéiront avec moi aux mêmes commandements
Ils écouteront attentifs les sublimes fanfares
Ils mourront près de moi et moi peut-être près d'eux
Ils souffriront du froid et du soleil avec moi
Ils sont des hommes ceux-ci qui boivent avec moi
Ils obéissent avec moi aux lois de l'homme
Ils regardent sur les routes les femmes qui passent
Ils les désirent mais moi j'ai des plus hautes amours
Qui règnent sur mon coeur mes sens et mon cerveau
Et qui sont ma patrie, ma famille et mon espérance
A moi soldat amoureux soldat de la douce France[13]

During the autumn in Nice he had written no poetry of moment. *Calligrammes* contains only "L'Oeillet la mandoline et le bambou," an ideogram of that particular vintage. "Ombre de mon amour" repeats the limited obsession with ideograms of a fig, and again a carnation and an opium pipe, a palm-tree ("Je vous salue Lou comme fait votre arbre préféré le palmier), and a brandy bottle. But now that he is in Nîmes he pulls out the organ stops again and chants out in full voice his hymns to Lou, to the soldier's life and to his motherland "la douce France." These three subjects now are to be a source of endless inspiration, so much so that the ideogram is relegated to a minor place within the poem. At this time he wrote to Mollet. "I have found new methods of poetry, more astonishing and very much more complicated":[14] but from the published poems of *Calligrammes* it is difficult to see

---

[13] "I draw on my pipe free and proud amongst my comrades
They will leave with me for the battlefields
They will sleep the whole night in the rain out in the open
They will gallop with me carrying victories before them
They will obey with me the same orders
They will listen attentively to the sublime fanfares
They will die near me and I perhaps near them
They will suffer from the cold and the sun with me
They are real men those who drink with me
They will obey with me the laws of men
They watch the women who pass by on the roads
They desire them but I have higher loves
Which reign over my heart my senses and my brain
And which are my motherland my family and my hope
I soldier in love soldier of gentle France"

[14] Adéma, p. 198.

what these new methods could be. Even "2ᵉ Canonnier conducteur" which appeared in a Swiss *avant-garde* review *Der Mistral*, and which attracted the attention of Romain Rolland as a novelty, is still relying for its effect on typography and on the inclusion of ideograms. It is true that one of the ideograms[15] figures specifically "la putain de Nancy qui a foutu la VXXXXX à toute l'artillerie," but this is only a repetition of the shock tactics of surprise. He also at this time makes some play with the popular refrain, as for example in "Veille":

> Mon cher André Rouveyre
> Troudla la Champignon Tabatière
> On ne sait quand on partira
> Ni quand on reviendra[16]

which is obviously set to the tune of "Marlbrouck s'en-va-t'en guerre." Perhaps one of the aspects of novelty was the letter form of so many of these poems. As a soldier this was a most necessary and topical innovation, leaving room for all manner of expression and mingling poetry ever more closely with life, which seemed of late to have been one of Apollinaire's most pressing concerns. But in the love poems that he wrote to Lou when once again he is inundated with emotion, traditional metre and rhyme take pride of place.

At the end of December he rushed off to Nice for two days' leave, sure after the permissiveness and the declarations of love of finding a devoted mistress. The idyll seemed to continue still, and Lou saw him off at the station on 2 January. In his compartment was a young schoolteacher on holiday from Oran. She was pretty and shy, but when he with his usual charm, and velvety look, began to talk to her about what she was reading, and then about books and poetry and finally revealed that he too was a poet, she was well on the way to falling in love with him. He told her that he would send her a copy of *Alcools*. They said good-bye. She went off in heart-thumping

---

[15] "2ᵉ canonnier conducteur," *Oeuvres poétiques*, p. 214.

[16] "My dear André Rouveyre
Troudla la Champignon Tabatière
We don't know when we'll go away
Nor when we'll come home again"

confusion, and when she arrived home told her family in great
excitement about "her poet." He took a mental note of the
encounter and stored it away for possible future reference,
but made no effort to send the promised book. He still had so
many other things on his mind.

Primarily there was the daily, common round which continued to be satisfying but exacting. And then his absence
from Lou and the vehemence of his desire for her, and also the
ironical realisation that although he poured out the treasure
of his poetry to her daily she scarcely even bothered to read his
letters and his poems and that she really set scant store by his
profession.

> Now I beg you not to make fun of my profession as a poet.
> I know that you don't mean it unkindly but it's a habit that
> you could fall into easily. First of all being a poet does not
> prove that one can do nothing else. A lot of poets have done
> other things and acquitted themselves very well. On the other
> hand the poet's profession is not useless nor mad nor frivolous.
> Poets are creators (poet comes from the Greek and actually
> means creator, and poetry means creation). Thus nothing
> appears on the earth, nothing is made manifest to men's eyes
> if it has not first been imagined by a poet: love itself is the
> natural poetry of life, the natural instinct which impells us to
> create life, to reproduce. I am telling you this to show you
> that I am not carrying on the profession of poet simply to look
> as though I'm doing something without actually doing any-
> thing at all. I know that those who give themselves up to the
> labour of poetry are doing something essential, primordial
> and divine. I am obviously not speaking of mere versifiers.
> I am speaking of those who, painfully and lovingly, put all
> their genius into the gradual revelation of some new things,
> and who on their deathbeds are still inspired by this same
> love.[17]

Her blank incomprehension at least had the merit of
impelling him to formulate his credo so precisely. And the fact
that for Lou "poet" signified "good-for-nothing" and that his
letter-poems were to her more of a joke than anything else,
drove him to write more and more poetry out of the stuff of his

[17] Rouveyre, p. 192.

daily life, and to try in his impassioned way to combine his desire, "that natural poetry of life," with the most humble events and sights around him. He must prove to her that he was a real creator. And so he wrote, thinking that she would be honoured by seeing her charms writ large on the barracks square:

> Les branches remuées ce sont tes yeux qui tremblent
> Et te je vois partout toi si belle et si tendre
> Les clous de mes souliers brillent comme tes yeux
> La vulve des juments est rose comme la tienne
> Et nos armes graissées c'est comme quand tu me veux
> O douceur de ma vie c'est comme quand tu m'aimes
>> L'hiver est doux le ciel est bleu
>> Refais-me le refais-me le
>> Toi ma chère permission
>> Ma consigne ma faction
>> Ton amour est mon uniforme
>> Tes doux baisers sont les boutons
>> Ils brillent comme l'or et l'ornent
>> Et tes bras si roses si longs
>> Sont les plus galants des galons[18]

For the poet there is licence: he is free to see a silken purse in a sow's ear, but a woman like Lou was not exactly flattered to be compared thus with a mare, nor to be so intimately associated with the coarse life of the *poilu*. As a simple soldier he had little *cachet* in her world and in her letters she now begins

[18] *Poèmes à Lou, Oeuvres poétiques*, 1956, p. 385.

> "The quivering branches are your eyes a-tremble
> And I see you everywhere you so beautiful and so tender
> The nails in my boots shine like your eyes
> The mare's vulvæ are pink like yours
> And our oiled guns are like you when you want me
> O sweetness of my life like you when you love me
> The winter is mild and the sky is blue
> Do it again do it again
> You my dear furlough
> My confinement to barracks my sentry duty
> Your love is my uniform
> Your soft kisses are the buttons
> They shine like gold and decorate it
> And your arms so pink so long
> Are the most gallant of stripes"

to grumble about his lack of *savoir-faire*. When last he had been with her in Nice, he had not raised his cap to one of her friends, and this had been frowned upon. It is really rather pathetic to see him having to excuse himself in front of this vain, spoilt woman for something so petty.

> I am a poet, Lou, and poets are often distrait like La Fontaine and Gérard de Nerval and others. Nevertheless you are right to tell me about it and please apologise to M. and all the others who were shocked by it.

Then up comes the touchy pride again.

> Anyway I am a poet and soldier too for the moment. I have no desire to be an "homme du monde," nor smart in any way, above all if it prevents me from my daydreams.

And then the counter-attack:

> It's incredible how little bits of women like M. whose language would bring a blush to the face of all the gunners in all the regiments put together can be so fussy about a cap . . . and even a Pole knows very well how to get himself killed when it's necessary, with his cap on his head, for the sake of the French and particularly the Frenchwomen.

However gallantry has the last word:

> Anyway I can't really hold it against her, because she is charming and gay.[19]

In short Lou's brief period of infatuation was over. Her old worldly life had reclaimed her, and she was now looking at Apollinaire, eccentric poet and simple soldier, with a very critical eye. When he went to see her again for a brief leave at the end of January her disapproval was obvious. He had gone full of ardour and stories of his barracks life: she was bored and indifferent. But she was loath to make a complete break; there was always room for one more admirer. So although she showed him her coldness she also allowed him to keep the illusion that she was going to come to stay in Nîmes in order to be near him. Apollinaire went back depressed

[19] Rouveyre, p. 193.

and already forseeing the future break. At Tarascon he had to change trains and while waiting he wrote a poem which he called "Guirlande de Lou." This is one of the best of *Poèmes à Lou*, and a nice example of Apollinaire's intrinsic qualities as a poet. He is not concerned now with writing for publication, but with expressing himself in the most natural, spontaneous way, visited by his particular kind of inspiration. He is far removed from theorising; not searching for subject matter, but submitting to it; swamped by such a fullness of emotion that it just has to well out of him in a sonorous litany (which may well have been indelibly imprinted on him in the days when his foster-mother haunted the churches in Rome), full of repetitions and parallelism, rich with rhyme and assonance, an irresistible Puccini-like flow of melody. It also shows with what intensity he was capable of experiencing the present. Mephistopheles would have found in him a hopeless victim because, unlike Faust, he would have found every moment too beautiful. Here is Lou, and his love for her, and all its complex extremes, beauty in obscenity, the exquisiteness of sorrow, the end suspected before the flowering; here is all life—soldiers and battlefields and women's prayers, and death too and France with its history, and flowers and light and the miracle that is himself, the poet. And all of this is one, and life will always continue:

> Hausse tes mains Hausse tes mains ces lys de ma fierté
> Dans leur corolle s'épure toute l'impureté
> O lys ô cloches des cathédrales qui s'écroulent au nord
> Carillons des Beffrois qui sonnent à la mort
> Fleurs de lys fleurs de France ô mains de mon amour
> Vous fleurissez de clarté la lumière du jour
>
> Tes pieds tes pieds d'or touffes de mimosa
> Lampes au bout du chemin fatigues des soldats
> —Allons c'est moi ouvre la porte je suis de retour enfin
> —C'est toi assieds-toi entre l'ombre et la tristesse
> —Je suis couvert de boue et tremble de détresse
> Je pensais à tes pieds d'or pâle comme à des fleurs
> —Touche-les ils sont froids comme quelqu'un qui meurt
> Les lilas de tes cheveux qui annoncent le printemps

> Ce sont les sanglots et les cris que jettent les mourants
> Le vent passe au travers doux comme nos baisers
> Le printemps reviendra nos lilas vont passer[20]

Now that love was failing him, his excitement and enthusiasm as a soldier inevitably began to wane. More and more he came to think of his own eventual fate. Soon the training would be over and he would be sent to the Front. And if he were killed, Lou his one and only love, would weep for a day and then forget him. To counteract this he indulges in a real anthropomorphic vision, where he himself alone incarnates the life force:

> Le fatal giclement de mon sang sur le monde
> Donnerait au soleil plus de vive clarté
> Aux fleurs plus de couleur plus de vitesse à l'onde
> Un amour inouï descendrait sur le monde
> L'amant serait plus fort dans ton corps écarté[21]

But he still wanted to believe that she was coming to Nîmes. André Rouveyre publishes the letters that he sent her then, describing all the little arrangements he has made;

[20] "Raise your hands raise your hands those lilies of my pride
In their corolla all impurity is made pure
O lilies o bells of the cathedrals that are being destroyed in the north
Belfry chimes that are ringing out to death
Fleurs de lys flowers of France o hands of my love
You deck with brightness the light of day

Your feet your golden feet sprays of mimosa
Lamps at the end of the road weariness of the soldiers
—Come along it is I open the door I have come back at last
—It is you sit down between the shadow and sadness
—I am covered with mud and tremble in distress
I was thinking of your pale gold feet as I would of flowers
—Touch them they are cold like somebody who is about to die
The lilacs of your hair which announce the spring
Are the sobs and the cries uttered by dying men
The wind blows through them soft like our kisses
The spring will come again our lilacs will fade"

[21] "Si je mourais là-bas," *Oeuvres poétiques*, 1956, p. 392.
"The fateful spilling of my blood over the world
Would give to the sun more and brighter light
To the flowers more colour more speed to the tide
An unheard-of love would descend upon the world
The lover would be stronger in your opened body"

he has rented a room, they can make it pleasant with rugs and books, she can cook her own lunch, hang her washing out, take her dogs for a walk while she waits for her soldier lover. Such a cosy existence was never what Lou had had in mind. In fact she had distinctly different plans. There was in her life, and Apollinaire knew and accepted this, one steady protector whom, revealingly, she called "Toutou" (the pet name for a dog). He was obviously the man who was going to stand by her in all her unstable rocketing through life. Toutou was now at the Front, and Lou had decided that it would be more exciting to visit him there than to come back to Nîmes; and so she set off north.

Apollinaire seemed to accept this: he could hardly do otherwise. But then there came no news from her at all. On 12 Feb., four days after her departure, he was writing in desperation:

> Quatre jours mon amour pas de lettre de toi
> Le jour n'existe plus le soleil s'est noyé
> La caserne est changée en maison de l'effroi
> Et je suis triste ainsi qu'un cheval convoyé[22]

It needs surely a poet born and not merely bred, to choose, when frantic with worry and despair, to write to the loved one in regular quatrains of alexandrines.

Still Lou kept silent and the next month was a period of progressive desolation for Apollinaire, another of his terrible crises when he felt near to a complete breakdown. Again out of these depths came a *cri du cœur* that is impeccably modulated, leaving no doubt that the best individual passages of his poems always emerged from a surfeit of suffering:

> O Lou ma grande peine ô Lou mon coeur brisé
> Comme un doux son de cor ta voix sonne et resonne
> Ton regard attendri dont je me suis grisé
> Je le revois lointain lointain et qui s'étonne

---

[22] "Four days my love and no letter from you
The day no longer exists the sun is drowned
The barracks have changed into a house of horror
And I am as sad as a convoy horse"

Je baise tes cheveux mon unique trésor
Et qui de ton amour furent le premier gage
Ta voix mon souvenir s'éloigne ô son du cor
Ma vie est un beau livre et l'on tourne la page
  Adieu mon Lou mes larmes tombent
  Je ne te reverrai plus jamais
  Entre nous deux ma Lou se dresse l'Ombre
  Et souviens-toi parfois du temps où tu m'aimais
    L'heure
    Pleure
    Trois
    Fois[23]

By 17 March when eventually he received a letter from her, full of reproaches for the way that he has bothered her and the demands that he has made upon her, he had gone through the whole gamut of rage and prostration: now he manages to reply with a certain dignity. "I want to be cured of you. . . . One suffers and suffers and then one learns how to stop suffering." She has absolutely drained him for the last two months, she has even turned him into a coward, because he refused to volunteer for the Front, thinking that she might come to Nîmes. He has had a real "cerebral anæmia." André Rouveyre here confronts us with a most startling revelation. There was a word in the manuscript letters which for years he failed to decipher. "Je me — le 18." Eventually

---

[23] *Poèmes à Lou, Oeuvres poétiques*, 1956, p. 411.

"O Lou my great sorrow o Lou my broken heart
  Like a soft hunting call your voice sounds and resounds
  Your tender eyes which intoxicated me
  I see them far far away looking at me in surprise

  I kiss your hair my unique treasure
  Which was the first gage of your love
  Your voice my memory fades away o hunting call
  My life is a beautiful book and the page is turned
    Farewell my Lou my tears fall
    I shall never see you again
    Between us my Lou rises the shadow
    And remember now and then the time when you loved me
    The hour
    Weeps
    Three
    Times"

he decided that this word was, "tuais," that the sentence then read: "If I had no letter from you by the 18th I was going to kill myself." Threats, of course, are one thing, actions another, but even the thought reveals the violence of this thwarted passion.

But now the man and the poet have conquered, and he can even afford to be generous:

> I bear you no grudge. You have embellished my life during these few months, you have made vows which exalted me. For a while they lifted me above ordinary men. I believed them and I was happy. So I should be and I am extremely grateful to you. I shall always be your friend, and even without it being a question of love, you can, as a woman and in the name of the memories that your name evokes count on me in everything and for everything.

This was no empty declaration. He did in fact later behave generously towards her, bore her no grudge, and was always ready to defend her.

At the end of March the two disillusioned lovers met in Marseille. She was cold, disdainful: but he, snatching at a straw, despite the fact that he had said he would "will" his love to die, made a strange proposal, to which she agreed. They would lead their independent lives, but they would tell each other all, even the most intimate, physical details of their future affairs. This would seem to be almost more of a perversion than flagellation. But something, even fornication at second-hand, is always better than nothing, and at this moment Apollinaire needed every emotional stimulus to keep aflame his sense of the intensity and importance of living even in constant view of death. The medieval knight must have some sort of lady whose favours he can wear.

Lou of course did not keep her promise, but the correspondence between them continued for many months, even alongside another new impassioned courtship of his. From the Front he was to write all his daily news and gossip, he made his will in her favour, he told her when she was in Paris after her return from the Front to use his flat, boasted that it was one of the most singular in the whole world—like himself, indicated to

her which of his pornographic novels to read, recommended
her to his dentist and to charge her bill to his account, saved
up on his own small allowance to send her money when she
was in need, even told her to leave her dogs with his mother.
But hearing of certain Bacchanalia in his flat, he cautiously
begged her not to make too much noise in case he should be
turned out. He also continued to pour out of the cornucopia
of his love of life his thoughts about poetry, and himself, and
nature, and life, which she probably scarcely bothered to
read. "To be is to know the truth." He uses, so he explains,
a small and immediate sensation to create others more vast
in a sort of ascending scale to infinity. He is highly-strung,
"nerveux," because he is a child of activity. He regards himself as one of the superior forms of creation. Nature should be
used as a servant to create even more beautiful things for man.
What man has made is of greater value than unsentient nature:

> and yet as soon as one digs deeper one sees in nature something
> superior to artifice. It is life itself, and for a work of art to
> attain this, inspiration is necessary. And inspiration is rarely
> met with in the works which are directed only to the super-
> ficial pleasure of the senses. That is why it often happens that
> inspired works are not immediately agreeable. Love is also
> a work of art, and it is more important that it should be
> animated by inspiration which is life itself rather than be, from
> the beginning, purely and simply agreeable.[24]

"Love is also a work of art." These were not idle words.
He really acted on them: and the next chapter in his emotional
life was to be one of the most astonishing examples of his need
and his power to create this kind of work of art out of the raw
stuff of life.

[24] Unpublished material communicated to the author by André Rouveyre.

S

XIII

The Trenches

O N Easter Sunday two weeks after he had thought of killing himself, Apollinaire left Nîmes for the Front. It was on this journey that he wrote:

How profound life is! This is the same journey that I used to do when I was a child with long hair and serious eyes. . . . I am transported with enthusiasm about leaving. Now a new life is beginning, where one's character will reveal just what one really is.

The fact of actually going to war had put him into a state of exaltation. In the train he poured out verses to Lou, "Je ris de bonheur en t'écrivant ces rimes." He still desired her, he knew that he had lost her, he still counted over his memories of her, but now by some alchemy of his imagination he had been able to make of this hopeless love a great source of inspiration.

> O mon amour mystique ô Lou la vie
>   Nous donnera
> La délectation inassouvie
>   On connaîtra
> Un amour qui sera l'amour unique
>   Adieu mon coeur[1]

It was really a case of eating cake that had already vanished. But if the inspiration is there, then everything becomes food for love. And his first sight of the horrible trenches, and the engines of war, and gunfire at night was an inspiration to him, and thus also acted as an aphrodisiac. As soon as he arrived in position on 10 April he wrote a long letter-poem to Lou

---

[1] *Poèmes à Lou, Oeuvres poétiques,* 1956, p. 436.
  "O my mystic love o Lou life
    Will give us
  The unassuaged delectation
    We shall know
  A love which will be the unique love
    Farewell my heart"

which began with the lines which he later isolated in the poem of *Calligrammes*, "La Nuit d'Avril 1915." The rest is merely a letter in rhyme, but this *envoi* is a perfect example of how the combination of the beauty and the danger of war could exacerbate his senses until his already intense love of life becomes almost excruciating, and forces itself through densely packed and powerful imagery:

> Nous vous aimons ô vie et nous vous agaçons
> Les obus miaulaient un amour à mourir
> Un amour qui se meurt est plus doux que les autres
> Ton souffle nage au fleuve où le sang va tarir
> Les obus miaulaient
>   Entends chanter les nôtres
> Pourpre amour salué par ceux qui vont périr
> Le printemps tout mouillé la veilleuse l'attaque
> Il pleut mon âme il pleut mais il pleut des yeux morts
> Ulysse que de jours pour rentrer dans Ithaque
> Couche-toi sur la paille et songe un beau remords
> Qui pur effet de l'art soit aphrodisiaque
> Mais
>   orgues
>   aux fétus de la paille où tu dors
> L'hymne de l'avenir est paradisiaque[2]

Apollinaire has been criticised for his apparent celebration of war. He is undoubtedly one of the most considerable of the poets of the First World War, and he is also unique in being able, and daring to write, "Ah Dieu que la guerre est jolie,"

---

[2] *Op. cit.*, p. 434.
"We love you o life and we provoke you
  The shells mewed out a love fit to die
  A love which is dying is sweeter than the others
  Your breath swims along the river where blood finally dries
  The shells mewed
    Listen to our men singing
  Purple love saluted by those who are about to die
  The torrents of spring the night light the assault
  It is raining my soul but it is raining dead eyes
  Ulysses how many days to return to Ithaca
  Lie down on the straw and think up a fine remorse
  Which pure effect of art is aphrodisiac
  But
    organs
      In the pieces of straw where you sleep
  The hymn of the future is heavenly"

or "Que c'est beau ces fusées qui illuminent la nuit." In fact it is not war that he celebrates, but life in the midst of death: "Nous vous aimons ô vie et nous vous agaçons," life that had now become so precious. Old people are sometimes heard to say that their capacities for enjoying the moment have become particularly refined now that each day may be the last. Such was the basis of Apollinaire's plenitude of sensation during the War, and his real inspiration. In the whole body of his poetry, the War forms one of his major themes. It is as if he welcomed it as a poet and made it his own, realising that it could provide him, as few other events in his life, except love, had done, with subjects and settings and images. His imagery, which has always been limited, is immediately enriched: a burnt-out shell is his heart, the love exploded and gone, the gun-flares are women dancing, the snakes in the trenches a woman's sinuous arms, canons and the trenches are obviously sex images, soldiers are like pearls on a necklace, or bottles of champagne, their blood fermenting. Moreover, in the early days the spring was idyllic and the forest a great camping-ground. He was not yet in the front-line and saw little of the actual horror. He was delighted to go about his boy scout duties as *agent de liaison* and feel that he was braving danger and behaving in a most exemplary fashion, while yet having long hours of leisure in which he could write letters and poems and polish those rings that the soldiers used to make out of shrapnel.

He was absolutely delighted that he, the professional poet, was proving that he could be equally successful as a man of action. He did his duties well and above all he was not afraid. "Now one's real character will be revealed." This was the greatest challenge of his life, the testing point for him and for all the others, and he was determined to prove that he, Guillaume Apollinaire, poet and Polish gentleman, could also be a hero.

For the moment there were no great feats to be accomplished: so the heroism consisted in keeping up his spirits and those of the men around him, and living every day to the full. And to do this it was not enough to build and equip his little hut in the forest, and start a newspaper called *Le Tranchman Echo*, the first number of which unfortunately dropped in a cauldron of stew, and to produce a cyclostyled volume of his poems, *Case d'armons* later to be included in *Calligrammes*, and to fire his guns, and encourage the young poets of the battalion: but he had also to keep up every aspect of his old life. All the talk that had gone on in the cafés in Paris, all the gossip and stories and fantasy-weaving now had to be relegated to letters. In June he began again his "Anecdotiques" for the *Mercure de France*. His letters home were innumerable, and the size of his own mail was a legend. It is because of these letters and poems that this whole period of his life is illumined as if by searchlight. One can follow him day by day, know if he slept well, what dreams he had, when he managed to wash. Now one can actually see, not merely divine, just how multifarious and complex his behaviour was, how many moods and modes of being existed in him simultaneously, just as one has seen in his poetry so many different tones juxtaposed. For instance, amongst all the tenderness and reverence and abandon of his passion for Lou he had been capable of describing his affair with her in crude detail in letters to Mollet. Now on 13 April he writes to her, calling her "O Lou mon vice":

> Soldat te souviens-tu du soir Tu étais au theâtre
>> Dans la loge d'un ambassadeur
> Et cette jeune femme pâle et glorieuse
>> Te branla pendant le spectacle[3]

And on the very next day, the sensual delectation has now changed into a great thirst for chastity:

> O Lou, ma très chérie
> Faisons donc la féerie
> De vivre en nous aimant
> Etrangement
> Et chastement[4]

---

[3] "Soldier do you remember that evening You were at the theatre
In the box of an ambassador
And this pale and splendid young woman
Tossed you off during the performance"

[4] "O Lou my darling
Let us live out the fairy-tale
Of living and loving
Strangely
And chastely"

The following day he is still craving for Lou to be a mystic love, his "unique love," and the day after this, still obsessed by his desire for love in whatever shape or form, he remembers the dark-eyed girl whom he had met in January on the train from Nice and who had seemed to be so impressed by him; and far from being satisfied with Lou his unique, mystical love, he now sends another bottle into the sea, in the form of a brief, courteous note apologising for not having sent her the promised copy of *Alcools*. She replies almost immediately, and on the same day that he receives this warm letter from her, there is another from Lou, cold and disdainful. From now on it is obvious what is going to happen. As Lou's star wanes, the young schoolmistress from Oran, Madeleine Pagès, shines more and more brightly in Apollinaire's firmament.

Now he embarks on that most delicate of enterprises, an epistolary courtship and seduction, while at the same time flagellating his old desire for Lou: "Je voudrais éprouver une ardeur infinie." To read the letters sent to Lou and those to Madeleine of the same dates is to surprise him in all his range and subtlety and apparent duplicity. In great erotic bursts he still in imagination perversely possesses Lou, while at the same time in the most circumspect way he makes his approaches to the virgin Madeleine. Intuitively he adapts himself to the two different women. With Lou there is gossip and triviality and almost vulgar *sous-entendus*. With Madeleine, a charming and intelligent girl with a trained mind but still immature emotions and inexperienced senses, he is apparently frank and direct. He shares his daily life with her, analyses his reactions, talks simply of books and his own poetry, flatters her whimsically and with gallantry. She is his "petite fée charmante," he is "her poet." She is a girl whose mind he esteems infinitely and so he sends her exactly the same poem as he sends to Lou his "vice"![5] Then comes the cunning little spear-head of an advance. He writes her another poem, for herself this time, ethereal enough certainly but ending on a characteristic *jeu de mots*: the knot of serpents in his hut trace the name Madeleine, "dont chaque lettre se love en belle anglaise,"[6] a twisted

[5] "Un seul bouleau crépusculaire."
[6] *Tendre comme le souvenir*, 1952, p. 32.

declaration if there ever was one. And then follow the demands for photographs and on receipt of them compliments, insistence, a doubtful story which offends her, and she is on her guard immediately, resisting him, rapping him over the knuckles in an embarrassed sort of way. But however much he may insinuate he is determined to make no declarations this time. The memory of the little traveller, he is aware, is "quelque chose de si ténu de si lointain que d'y penser on arrive à le trop matérialiser."[7] Not merely has he been caught once in his own trap with Lou, and does not want to be so hurt again, but he has well sized up the character of a girl like Madeleine. It is she who must come to him of her own accord. He writes on 22 June:

> My little fairy,
> There you are writing and saying nothing so that I shall speak my thoughts the first. I assure you this is not the moment to play the coquette. You are attractive to me mentally as well as physically. That is why my feelings are more at the mercy of yours than yours at the mercy of mine. So it is a simple matter for you to decide and it will be the only time that I shall obey you, although I am your "servant." Despite this, you are always mistress of our two hearts as much as if you were married you would be mistress in your own home while your husband would be master outside and in the conjugal bedroom. . . . If you feel nothing, it doesn't really matter, a man's heart can bear many a blow.

The wiles and the cunning traps set for the girl are fascinating: and yet at the same time there is this naïve yearning for total love and loyalty. "It is my dream that the most faithful of women should be the most audacious but also the most sincere —just like myself since I am both ingenuous and wary." It is Balzac's dream in *La Cousine Bette* of the ideal wife knowing how to be all women at once, the courtesan being driven out of business by a State "école de gymnastique pour les femmes vertueuses." And all these insinuations are interspersed with comments on *Paradise Lost* and Cervantes and Gervaise de La Touche and Charles-Louis Philippe. Throughout June she still manages to preserve her defences, is still not sure of herself

---

[7] *Tendre comme le souvenir*, 1952, p. 32.

and of him, still refuses even to call him Guillaume. He
redoubles his charm: "I shall teach you anything you wish,
even if I have to invent it." One can well believe this. During
the same period he is still busy "inventing" his great sensual
passion for Lou and still writing poems to her about "ton
derrière merveilleux."

Then came a sudden move north, and after the prestigious
forest which he had so much enjoyed, the site this time was
sinister and full of legions of bluebottles. Harrassed and
depressed he became clamorous. "Come Madeleine, strip
yourself naked, soul, body and heart. Afterwards you will be
so happy to have been truthful." And finally Madeleine does
so, and confesses that ever since she met him she has been in
love with him.

After this the flood-gates are open. Here is the real sister-
soul for whom he has been searching all his life. "I have
always looked for a woman who was my equal but absolutely
mine, more mine than a woman who was inferior to me."
With her he can talk of poetry and ideas, she will make him
work regularly, possibly he will even write plays if she is there to
discipline him. She is calm and steadfast and will counter his
excitability. They exchange their views on religion and on
bringing up a family, for right from the beginning there has
been talk of marriage. He sends her his works, makes his confessions about the loves that have inspired the poems of *Alcools*,
and also rather shamefacedly about the affair of the statuettes.
He finds that she does not like *L'Hérésiarque et Cie*. Although
she will not say why, it is obviously the strain of sadism and
violence which upsets her. But it has now become a challenge
to Apollinaire to impose this whole side of his nature on her.
Almost as soon as he has received her declaration he is preparing the ground:

> I am as you know authoritarian and I want everything that
> you receive from me to be voluptuous. I want you to be mine
> completely for I am your master my darling and your master
> in everything. So I want you to obey me in everything, to
> forget everything for me, to put my wishes before any question
> of good upbringing or indeed before anything at all, and to be
> my little docile slave. In return I shall give you all the joys

that I am capable of and you will have to accept them from me even if they are painful. So our love will be marvellous.

Naturally Madeleine is a little sceptical about this whole idea of voluptuous pain, and time and time again he has to come back to it and explain that this is only a part of love, an aspect of his tenderness. At the same time he is also behaving as he imagines do the most practical of *fiancés*, discussing his money prospects, and on 10 Aug. writing to her mother to beg for her hand.

But his real business with her now, what he needed from her both as soldier and as poet, was complete physical possession even if it had to be only by the pen. His letters to her in the summer and autumn are quite extraordinary. Through them he manages by some magnetism to get the bashful girl really to "strip herself naked, soul, body and heart." Through them he manages to experience "des spasmes de volupté"; through them to transform Madeleine the lily into Madeleine the rose.

It is a considerable feat of the imagination. He has made this one girl into a symbol of all women. She is everything, a St Theresa, mystic, intellectual, his virginal lily, his bacchante and cunning panther, "abandonnée comme Léda, savante comme Hélène." In short she is "l'aspect femelle de l'Univers c'est dire que tu es toute la grâce toute la beauté du monde." His exacerbated and frustrated sensuality gushes forth in great jets of mysticism so that he seems to be worshipping her as a sort of goddess of the life force. In one of the poems in *Tendre comme le souvenir* celebrating her unseen nakedness, he even exclaims, "O toison triangle isocèle tu es la divinité même à trois côtés touffu innombrable comme elle,"[8] which is surely the most pagan of all poetic images. It was in fact a great and prolonged state of auto-intoxication into which he had to whip himself in order to make bearable the life at the Front which was becoming more and more rigorous as the cold set in, in order to face death cheerfully, and also in order to keep on writing poetry.

The letters are extravagant and frenzied: not insincere but desperately charged with wishful thinking. In the poems of *Calligrammes*, however, Madeleine is assigned to her rightful

[8] *Tendre comme le souvenir*, 1952, p. 194.

place, a name for a dream, "O phare-fleur, ô souvenir, à
peine un souffle, un souvenir." "Dans l'abri-caverne" explains his need precisely.   His soul is empty, gone are his
powers of creation, only faceless, nameless half-created beings
exist in him (this always seems to be the way in which
sterility presents itself to him: when he is creative he feels that
he manages to put himself inside every other human being):

Dans ce grand vide de mon âme il manque un soleil il manque
   ce qui éclaire
C'est aujourd'hui c'est ce soir et non toujours
Heureusement que ce n'est que ce soir
Les autres jours je me rattache à toi
Les autres jours je me console de la solitude et de toutes les horreurs
En imaginant ta beauté
Pour l'élever au-dessus de l'univers extasié
Puis je pense que je l'imagine en vain
Je ne la connais par aucun sens
Ni même par les mots
Et mon goût de la beauté est-il donc aussi vain
Existes-tu mon amour
Ou n'es-tu qu'une entité que j'ai créée sans le vouloir
Pour peupler la solitude
Es-tu de ces déesses comme celles que les Grecs
   avaient douées pour moins s'ennuyer
Je t'adore ô ma déesse exquise même si tu n'es que
   dans mon imagination [9]

---

[9] "In this great emptiness of my soul I lack a sun
    I lack illumination
  It is to-day this evening and not always
  Fortunately it is only this evening
  The other days I attach myself to you
  The other days I seek refuge from solitude and all the horrors
  Imagining your beauty
  In order to lift it above the ecstatic universe
  Then I think that I imagine it in vain
  I do not know it by any of my senses
  Nor even by words
  And so is my taste for beauty just as vain
  Do you exist my love
  Or are you only an entity that I have created unwittingly
  In order to people my solitude
  Are you like one of those goddesses that the Greeks invented so as to
    pass the time
  I adore you o my exquisite goddess even if you exist only in my imagination"

The most perfect of his love poems to Madeleine is undoubtedly "Chevaux de frise." It is no accident that he evokes le Paraclet, nor that he makes mention of lilies and "cantiques." Perhaps even unconsciously, now that he is in a state of almost religious fervour and supplication, he falls into the style of the psalms, a style which in fact now becomes one of his favourite forms, in particular for love poetry. Like "Le pont Mirabeau," "Chevaux de Frise" shows him at his most lyrical. Under the apparent ease it is a triumph of suave versification uniting a variety of metre in its rich music. Repetitions, "rimes riches," assonances, parallelism, he uses all the traditional tricks, and a few of his own like the characteristic play on words: "Chevaux muets / Non chevaux barbes mais barbelés." In fact this absolute ease and liberty of movement within the bounds of poetry is the main characteristic of the whole War period of great creativity. By the side of the psalm-like "verset" he is still writing ideograms, still, as for instance in "Du Coton dans les oreilles," trying to produce the simultaneous impressions of the battlefield, explosions and exclamations, and the sound of rain-drops and a military band. In "Océan de terre," dedicated to Chirico, he produces suitably Surrealist images. In September on the request of Marie Laurencin he had also written a series of quatrains, which are like well-water, limpid but deep with the accumulations of the past:

> Mensonge de l'Annonciade
> La Noël fut la Passion
> Et qu'elle était charmante et sade
> Cette renonciation
>
> Si la colombe poignardée
> Saigne encore de ses refus
> J'en plume les ailes l'idée
> Et le poème que tu fus[10]

---

[10] "Refus de la Colombe," *Oeuvres poétiques*, p. 249.
> "Falsehood of the Annunciation
> Christmas was the Passion
> And how charming and sweet
> Was this renunciation
>
> If the stabbed dove
> Still bleeds from its refusals
> I pluck its wings the idea
> And the poem that you were"

He was now at the height of his powers, at the point where as a poet he seemed to be able to do just as he liked, even make a poem out of an accumulation of sentences each beginning with "Il y a." Gone the seeking after novelty. As he wrote to yet another woman, Jeanne Yves-Blanc to whom he had been introduced by a friend in Nîmes and who managed to nip in the bud the advances that despite Madeleine and Lou and Marie, he felt compelled to make: "The fact that one uses traditional forms shows one's liberty."[11] It was indeed the period of his greatest confidence as a poet. Sure of himself and the rightness of his behaviour, sure of having something important to say, and of his means of saying it, sure of Madeleine, and removed now from the febrile competitive spirit of Paris, he pours out his poems fluently and authoritatively. He celebrates Italy's entry into the War, he marks the night of an attack, "nuit des hommes seulement," he describes the beauty of the dug-out which is his "little palace," he identifies himself not only with the young, infinitely touching soldiers, who die in agony on the barbed wire, but with the vast horizon itself and the white trenches. Even the terrible gleam of the gunfire has become his "ardent muse." Because of his real and active role in this significant moment, he feels that he has more than ever earned the right to assert his old claim that he participates in all the life of all the universe at all times:

Je lègue à l'avenir l'histoire de Guillaume Apollinaire
Qui fut à la guerre et sut être partout
Dans les villes heureuses de l'arrière
Dans tout le reste de l'univers
Dans ceux qui meurent en piétinant dans le barbelé
Dans les femmes dans les canons dans les chevaux
Au zénith au nadir aux 4 points cardinaux
Et dans l'unique ardeur de cette veillée d'armes[12]

---

[11] *Lettres à sa marraine*, 1948, p. 18.
[12] "Merveille de la guerre," *Oeuvres poétiques*, 1956, p. 272.
   "I bequeath to the future the story of Guillaume Apollinaire
   Who was at the war and knew how to be everywhere
   In the fortunate towns behind the lines
   In all the rest of the universe
   In those who die entangled in the barbed wire
   In women in cannons in horses
   At the zenith at the nadir at the 4 cardinal points
   And in the unique ardour of this armed vigil"

But once again Apollinaire seemed to have to obey the inevitable pattern of the Greek hero who is struck down at the height of his powers because of his own overweening confidence. Now at this apogee of inspiration, he himself asked to be transferred to the infantry because commissions were easier to obtain there, and he had always been set on becoming an officer. This proved to be a foolhardy move. After his comparatively easy life in the artillery he was suddenly thrown into the extremes of hardship. The front-line trenches were a desolation of mud and ice; there was not enough food, no water, no beds ; the men were kept constantly on the go with everlasting manœuvres when they were not actually preparing for attacks. This now was the real face of war. Apollinaire was horrified. But the horror of this lunar landscape was so complete that it even gave him an æsthetic satisfaction. "The boredom is so intense that it becomes an art, a pleasure," he wrote to Max Jacob.[13] In the same way the prolonged and enforced chastity became a sort of spiritual trial and he tended to see himself clad in the white, shining garments of a Parsifal. This may again seem like histrionics, but even if it was a part that he was playing, at least it had the desired effect of buoying him up through the horror. As an officer he was extremely conscientious. He felt that he had a paternal duty to his men and shared with them any privileges that his rank offered, bed, food, or fire. He never grumbled. It was all a job which had to be done, a moment of history in which he was sharing. And the real qualities of the man now emerged. As he had predicted, this was the crucial testing-ground for character. His shone out brilliantly. He was brave, generous, and dogged, and completely justified in claiming that a poet can behave like a hero.

In January 1916 there was a brief respite. He went on leave to Oran to see Madeleine. What happened there is a matter for conjecture; for the letters and poems naturally stop. According to Madeleine herself[14] everything went perfectly. He was charming and endeared himself to all the family. He acted like the true *fiancé*, respectful and tender:

[13] Adéma, p. 213.
[14] In conversation with the author.

together he and Madeleine explored the town, talking incessantly of the future, and watched ecstatically the phosphorescence on the night sea. But there is no denying that after his return the tone of the letters is different. There are none of the old effusive bouts of mystical eroticism, no harping now on the subject of voluptuous pain: but only cursory formulæ. He excuses himself for the obvious lack by insisting on his fatigue and the extreme demands made on him by his duties. Manœuvres, always manœuvres: he can think of nothing, he is deadened by the incessant toil and severe conditions. He feels very remote from his former life: and for the first time he seems to be complaining. The fact is that he was no longer inspired by her. The poems that he sends to her are not of her charms but of the battlefield: "Du Coton dans les oreilles," "Le Vigneron champenois."

It is obvious that no one woman, however intelligent and attractive and charming—and Madeleine was all of these—could ever reach in stature the whole edifice of his cloudy imaginings. He had been corresponding with a dream. The real woman was like a complete stranger: and her conventional, *bourgeois*, family setting must have been fundamentally alien to him however well he reacted at the time. The whole tone of their exchanges in Oran was at a different level from the fevered demands of the letters. It was true that he had other things to think of, but that had never before prevented him from the effusions of love.

On 14 March a big attack was being prepared. He wrote a brief note to Madeleine announcing that he was going into the front-line, that he bequeathed her everything he possessed, and that she needed to be strong now and always. His premonition was accurate but premature. It was not until after the attack, three days later, while he was sitting peacefully in the trenches reading the *Mercure de France* that there was suddenly a great explosion, and his blood began to stream down over the pages. A fragment of shell had pierced his helmet and wounded him on the right temple.

XIV

L'Esprit Nouveau

ALTHOUGH the wound did not at first seem to be serious he was evacuated to a hospital at Château Thierry and then to the Val de Grâce in Paris. The splinters were taken out and from the Val de Grâce he wrote to Madeleine "My wound is progressing well. Already it's hardly noticeable. Head wounds heal quickly."[1] At the Val de Grâce he asked to be transferred to the Italian Hospital where Serge Férat was working as a male nurse. There he was spoiled and cossetted. His friends flocked to see him and he held court in his bed, with his pierced helmet hanging behind him and the blood-stained copy of the *Mercure de France* on the table, proud of the wound that he had won in the service of his country. It seemed that he was recovering well and he was even allowed to go for walks: but at that point he began to feel dizzy and even fainted once or twice. More menacing still, there was also a hint of paralysis in his left arm. When it became obvious that this was spreading, the doctors were very concerned— head wounds being notoriously treacherous—and eventually decided that he would have to be trepanned, a difficult and risky operation. Apollinaire was quite aware of the seriousness of the situation, but to everybody around him he still appeared to be his usual gay self. The evening before the operation, André Billy went to see him. He was wearing purple pyjamas, a colour that immediately struck Billy as a bad omen, and he laughed and joked in his old carefree way until Billy felt that he could not bear it a minute longer. It was the same on the morning of the operation: Henri Duvernois who nursed him then has described[2] his own feeling of anguish before Guillaume's optimism, and it was Guillaume who appeared to be

---

[1] *Tendre comme le souvenir*, 1952, p. 346.
[2] André Billy, *Guillaume Apollinaire: Poètes d'aujourd'hui*, 1947 (henceforth cited as Billy), p. 33.

consoling his anxious friend for what he himself must suffer.
They talked together as on any other morning, and Guillaume
described his plans for the future, the things that he was writing,
the sketches that he had just scribbled down. The door opened,
"Ah, good! They're coming for me," he said with a smile,
and as they prepared him for the anæsthetic he went on with
his conversation. Everyone marvelled at his courage and
sang-froid.

But the trepanning was successful; the paralysed hands
began to move feebly on the operating table, and Apollinaire
was saved.

Saved, but with long weary months of convalescence ahead.
For some time he stayed at the Villa Molière in Auteuil,
naturally enough a favourite with the nurses. André Rouveyre
remembers paying several visits to him there and meeting the
red-haired Jacqueline Kolb who was later to become his wife.
The dream of Madeleine was swiftly evaporating. He was
now too weak and ill to keep on creating love as a work of art,
but only too glad to accept what reality tangibly offered.
Nor did he feel inclined to launch into any explanations, but
simply kept quiet. Madeleine, in a flurry of anxiety, then
announced that she was going to come to Paris to him, and at
this prospect he reacted quite neurotically:

My dear Madeleine,
　　Above all don't come, that would cause me too much
emotion.
　　And also don't write sad letters, they terrify me.
　　I am going to write to you every week. Write to me like
this as well because the arrival of every letter frightens me.
　　I can't see anybody I know. I haven't written either to
my brother or to my mother and I haven't seen mother
since 15 April. She is upset about it, but I just can't. I
have become very emotional and it will only calm down
slowly.
　　Send my artillery record-book and notes because I shall
probably have to join up again in the artillery, also my gold
signet ring that I can wear again now and the ring with the
round stone.
　　I am going to organise my time and give the poems, if I can
revise them or if not as they stand, to the Mercure for a volume.

I am disgusted with Paris, nobody bothers about the war.
I am in despair about it. It will last another three years at
least, as I see it, it's very very, worrying.[3]

Courage in a specific circumstance, in open combat with
known odds, is one thing, but having to face up to the prolonged siege of fundamental ill health is another, especially
to such a bursting example of robustness as Apollinaire had
always been.

Even though by the autumn he began to go out and about
again and attempted to take up his old life where he left it at
the outbreak of War—to the extent of planning to resuscitate
Les Soirées de Paris—the thought of the coming winter oppressed
him. His one dream seems to have been a quiet retirement
in the south of France, with the freedom to write just what
pleased him. The prospect of earning a living by the old hard
grind of journalism was overwhelming. And what if he were
considered fit enough to be sent back to the army? His whole
experience of the War had only been tolerable because of what
he himself, stimulated and at the peak of mental and physical
strength, had put into it. Now even the idea of it was a nightmare to him. He had always been one for closing chapters
and launching into new ones. To go backwards spelt his kind
of failure. Moreover, as his letter to Madeleine shows, he was
going through one of his bouts of feeling persecuted. His
naturalisation had come through in March just before he was
wounded, but there were still sly digs from unspecified sources,
which are always more frightening than an outright attack, about
his being a foreigner. Unfortunately, too, Cubism just before
the War had been associated with Germany—"Kubismus" it
was called in derision—and Apollinaire's trip to Berlin had not
gone unnoticed. For example an anonymous letter was now
sent to the Inspecteur de la Sûreté Militaire complaining that a
foreigner such as Guillaume de Kostrowitzky should be sent to
the front lines as liaison officer. For somebody who had always
felt and behaved as the most loyal of patriots, this was a most
unfair insinuation and he was quite justified in feeling disgusted
with Paris where the people who were now installed in the

---

[3] *Tendre comme le souvenir*, 195‑. p. 350.

T

comfortable jobs were precisely the ones who had played no
part in the War.   It is hardly surprising that with these
anxieties added to his poor state of health he should write
a melancholy quatrain to Jeanne Yves Blanc in November
presaging his own death.[4]   Nor that that autumn he should
quietly slide away from Madeleine for ever, in a remote and
indifferent letter asking her merely to return copies of books
that he had given her.

One of the books was *Le Poète assassiné* which had been
completed before the War but to which he had added a brief
battlefield finale, "Cas du brigadier masqué," which ends with
his own wound:

> The corporal with the blind mask was smiling lovingly towards
> the future when a large calibre shell hit him on the head,
> and from it like pure blood sprang a triumphant Minerva.
> On your feet everybody to give a courteous salute to victory.

But the most grievous concern of all at this time was the
secret fear that his powers as a poet had been undermined by
this "bloody star" of a wound.   This surely can be the only
implication of "Tristesse d'une etoile":

> C'est pourqoi de mes maux ce n'était pas le pire
> Ce trou presque mortel et qui s'est étoilé
> Mais le secret malheur qui nourrit mon délire
> Est bien plus grand qu'aucune âme ait jamais celé[5]

This suffering, greater than any that has ever before been
experienced by man, must spring from his conviction that he is
some superior form of being and that he has been struck down
just when he is reaching the pinnacle of achievement.   The
Enchanter has been stripped of his magic. And indeed although
he most manfully tries to prove his own fears wrong, the real
moments of inspiration now become rare.   The skill is still
there, but that exuberant creative zest which had so often
carried him away on its tide is seldom now at his bidding—

[4] *Lettres à sa marraine*, 1948, p. 51.

[5] "That is why the worst of my misfortunes
   Was not this nearly mortal wound which has turned into a star
   But the secret suffering that feeds my delirium
   Is much greater than any soul has ever concealed"

perhaps only in full spate in that final poem of *Calligrammes*, "La Jolie Rousse."

His friends too were soon to discover when he began to frequent the Flore and other old haunts, that he himself had seriously deteriorated. André Billy has described the new Apollinaire who replaced the joyous companion of the days before the War:

> An irascible and abstracted Apollinaire with dull eyes and a heavy forehead; a mouth that was pinched with suffering instead of gaily smiling, a head which, under the bandage he still had to wear, seemed to have been flattened, a neck that had thickened along with his whole body.[6]

Sometimes his eyes which were generally so alive and bright, seemed to cloud over; his memory, that marvellous instrument which used to amaze all those who met him, and which, most of all, was responsible for his reputation of erudition, would now sometimes fail him. He would suddenly fly into a temper over nothing at all, and although the next minute he was laughing, this tetchiness alarmed his friends. Moreover he who formerly had been able to work all day and talk all night, who had never known what it was to be tired or seemed to need any sleep, whose energy had been limitless, now complained continually of feeling weary. His friends would talk together about him and share their worries, but what could they do? In the end somebody would always dismiss their fears with: "Never mind, with a constitition like his, he'll get over it."

But if his older friends were worried about him, the younger generation were in no doubt. It was Apollinaire to whom they flocked as their master and figurehead. What Moréas had been to his generation, Apollinaire now was to the generation of Dermée, Reverdy, Soupault, Cocteau, Breton, Tzara. In the spring of 1916 a review had been founded by a then unknown writer, Pierre Albert-Birot, with the expressed aim of: "To love life and to tell you so; to live it and to invite you to do the same." Under the title *Sic* it was to become one of the best known reviews of the post-war period. In October Birot published an interview that he had had with Apollinaire

[6] Billy, p. 33.

while he was still in hospital.   Apollinaire as always, rides his hobby-horse about the necessity for the arts to match the progress of science and constantly to explore new media.   He aims at harmonising the dichotomy that he has always felt between "reason born from the knowledge of the past, and the boldness and foresight that arise from the vision of the future." He also extols a simplicity of outward expression to embody the complex inner riches of the poet—an accomplishment of his own that had been hardly won.   And when asked if he feels that he himself is impelled in a new direction he replies revealingly.   "But the spirit blows where it listeth."

It is in this same number that René Berthier, who had served under Apollinaire in the army gives voice on behalf of the younger writers to the hopes which they all placed in him:

> He does not appear with a style, with new rules and an insolent compass. . . .   But he has simply a chest large enough to breathe in the great depths of noon, and sunlight, and to taste the whole of life.

And this description well sums up the particular kind of influence that Apollinaire exercised and which he could have gone on exercising with increasing effect.   He was a big man with a big personality who would have made his mark and attracted people like a magnet in any walk of life.   The fact that his gifts made him into a poet meant that he could stand as a symbol for the vitality and even the necessity of poetry in the modern world.   It is in this sense that he towers unquestionably above any other French poet of the century, and deserves Aragon's accolade of the "last of the poets."

Nord-Sud, another young, new review, run by Paul Dermée and Pierre Reverdy, reiterated this disciples' cry:

> Not so very long ago, the young poets went in search of Verlaine to pull him out of his obscurity.   Is it astonishing then that we have judged that the moment has come to group ourselves round Guillaume Apollinaire?   More than anybody else to-day, he has traced out new paths, opened up new horizons.   He is entitled to all our fervour, all our admiration.[7]

---

[7] *Nord-Sud*, No. 1, 15 Mar. 1917.

By his example and by the stance that he had taken as a poet it was he who was the real animator of the literature that was emerging from the War.

To give tangible proof of this fervour and admiration, his friends and disciples organised a great banquet in his honour at the end of December to celebrate both his return to normal life—he had just been discharged from the Italian Hospital—and the appearance of *Le Poète assassiné*. The committee was a distinguished one and included, along with old faithfuls like Salmon and Billy and Picasso and Max Jacob, most of the well-known writers of the day, Gide and Régnier, Paul Fort and Jules Romains being only a sample. They hired the enormous ballroom of the palais d'Orléans, but even there there was scarcely room to move, and the crowd became so excited that they refused to listen to any of the pompous speeches in honour of Apollinaire "le poète nouveau," and simply bombarded the speakers with bunches of flowers. Even Apollinaire himself, trying in a light boyish voice to dominate the din as a leader should, was soon shouted down by a laughing crowd dancing and singing students' choruses around him. André Billy says that he can still remember Blaise Cendrars, who had recently been wounded and had lost an arm, doing terrible cart-wheels. It looked in fact like a return to the good old days of Montmartre and the banquet for the Douanier, the true apotheosis of "the resuscitated poet" and Apollinaire left feeling very happy and as if he really had been reborn into an even bigger life. As André Billy says sadly, "This was one of the last good moments for Apollinaire."[8]

It was now his great task to live up to his long coveted role of *chef d'école*. Indeed, he and his disciples were beginning to see him as something more, as the Messiah of a whole new way of thinking about life as well as about art. No longer was it a question of methods, of Cubism or Simultanism, or ideograms, but of a whole "new spirit." Early in 1917 he published in the Bibliothèque des Curieux series an edition of Baudelaire, to which he wrote a very characteristic Preface. Baudelaire, he says, is the first person to have incarnated the

[8] Billy, p. 34.

modern spirit, although he did not manage to analyse clearly
this new spirit with which he himself unconsciously was
imbued. Then comes the considered opinion of Guillaume
Apollinaire, who since he has given his blood for his country
has come to see himself as moralist in chief for the French
nation:

> His influence is coming to an end now, and this is all to the
> good. We have put aside the moral aspect of this work which
> did us a disservice in forcing us to envisage life and things
> with a certain pessimistic dilettantism of which we are no longer
> the dupes. Baudelaire looked at life with a disgusted passion
> which aimed at transforming trees, flowers, women, the whole
> universe and even art into something pernicious. It was a
> bee that he had in his bonnet, and not healthy reality.

Then after the proselytiser, the prophet has his say:

> The use of literary liberty in society will become more and more
> rare and precious. The great democracies of the future will not
> be very liberal to writers: it is good to hoist on high the
> standard of poets like Baudelaire. From time to time they
> can be waved, in order to stir up the small number of slaves
> who still can respond. [9]

Was a tendency to persecution mania as an individual enough
to explain this constant *motif* of poets being persecuted by
society, or was this another example of Apollinaire's penetration
into the future? At any rate it confirmed him in his belief
in the importance of "le poète-drapeau," the poet who milit-
antly assumes his role as one of the saviours of mankind.
Health and strength and robust optimism must now be the
keynotes of the new humanism of "l'esprit nouveau": and not
too much iconoclasm. The thirty-seven-year-old poet saw himself now as the sober, mature, wise man of experience:

> Me voici devant tous un homme plein de sens
> Connaissant de la vie et de la mort ce qu'un vivant peut
>   connaître[10]

---

[9] *L'Oeuvre poétique de Charles Baudelaire*, 1924, p. 4.
[10] "La Jolie Rousse," *Oeuvres poétiques*, 1956, p. 313.
"Here I am in front of you all a man full of sense
Knowing all that a living creature can about life and about death"

He was middle-aged and had lived through the extravagances of youth. Privately he admitted that the next citadel that he wanted to storm was the Académie française. He was chary of associating with such extremist movements of the newest *avant-garde* as Dada, although personally he remained on good terms with Tzara. Putting aside his own past outbursts of destruction and of distributing "merda" right and left amongst the ranks of established reputations, he is now become, so he thinks, the apostle of order and good sense. It is true that what Apollinaire regarded as good sense might sometimes appear to other people as nonsense, but at least he had no professed desire to indulge in nonsense for nonsense sake.

As was his habit, even now in his diminished physical condition, and being forced once more to apply himself to a daily job—this time, ironically enough for such a writer, at the Censorship Office—he let no opportunity slip by for hammering home his beliefs.

In May he writes the programme notes of the famous ballet *Parade* where for the second time he uses the word "sur-réalisme" and declares that this is the

> point of departure for a series of manifestations of the New Spirit . . . which will undoubtedly seduce the élite and which promises to imbue both art and social habits from top to bottom with universal joyousness, for common sense demands that they should at least reach the same level as scientific and industrial progress.

In June as an earnest of his own efforts to imbue both art and social habits with universal joyousness he produces for the world the Jarryesque play left over from 1903: *Les Mamelles de Tirésias*. For some long time the editors of *Sic* had been nagging him to give a play and he had found this in his jealously guarded store of manuscripts and read it to them. They agreed to put it on; Apollinaire added one scene, a Prologue, and a Preface, and it was produced with Serge Férat's *décor* amidst great scandal on 24 Jun. 1917. It is difficult to know why after Ubu and Marinetti, Apollinaire's piece created such a hubbub. Many of the older Cubist painters dissociated themselves from him because of it, claiming that he had made them look ridiculous. Once again it was an occasion for the Establishment to inveigh against the young and the rebels, and Apollinaire who had just, with great difficulty and use of influence, installed himself at the Censorship Office was afraid that he would lose his job because of it. The trouble was probably due to Apollinaire's habitual lack of regard for chronology. To produce a lark from one's student days when one is established as a leading man of letters, then to announce that it is basically a serious work because it treats that most urgent of all problems facing the country—the need to increase the birthrate—and to have the Prologue admonish the audience in all good faith: "Ecoutez ô Français la leçon de la guerre Et faites des enfants vous qui n'en faisiez guère," is to ask for trouble. Thérèse who decides to change sex and throws her breasts into the audience as balloons, and her husband who then takes on himself the task of producing children at the rate of a hundred a day, are very funny, even hilarious, but are they worthy precursors of the new humanism? In his Preface Apollinaire did his persuasive best to present them as such. "The Theatre," he says, almost in excuse, "is no more a slice of life than a wheel is a leg." He has chosen

> on a serious, touching subject to give free course to that fantasy which is my way of interpreting nature, and which manifests itself according to the day with more or less melancholy, satire and lyricism.

The stumbling-block here is his own complexity. He was so easily capable of being serious and flippant, naïve and sophisticated at the same time. He was not joking when he declared:

> The fault is graver, the vice more profound for the truth is this: we do not make enough babies in France because we do not make love enough. Everything hangs on that.

Since the War, he, the patriot and hero, had in his own mind assumed moral responsibility for the whole nation. But his audience, witnessing the gay brain-child of his youth swaddled in this new pomposity could not believe in his sincerity and saw only the *blague*. He must be poking fun at them. Nobody

quite gave him credit for the range and diversity of his temperament, nor for the fact that the outrageous joker of Bohemian
days might be changing into a *bourgeois* family man, nor even
for what he himself described as "a benevolent irony" which
allows one to laugh even at adversity, and "a deep-seated
optimism which consoles and leaves room for hope to wax and
grow."[11]   Once again he was misunderstood, and made to
feel a lone voice crying in the wilderness.

However he was not daunted for long and in November
1917 he returned with a frontal attack, the famous lecture in
which he came down to defining "L'Esprit nouveau." Of all
Apollinaire's pronouncements this is the most important, and
vital for an understanding of his attitude to his art and to
life generally. It is really a credo summing up all that he has
been trying to formulate and embody throughout his life, and
a most manifest example of his real single-mindedness of
purpose. "Les jours s'en vont je demeure."

It is interesting to note that Apollinaire's "new spirit,"
which if he had lived he would probably have had the influence
to impose as the major movement in post-war literature, lies
at the opposite extreme in every way from the wave of Exist-
entialism that dominated French ways of thinking after the
Second World War. Undoubtedly the reasons for this lie not
in literary or philosophical influences but in Apollinaire's
own personality. Energy, optimism, irony, laughter, fantasy,
common-sense, and a transcendent idealism, these are all his
personal attributes. And he is harnessing them here in an
attempt to re-create a new role for poetry in a changing world.
The new spirit is in fact no purely literary phenomenon, but a
clarification of what in 1912 he was calling Orphism, a "magnificent exuberance of life":

> that divine idea which lies within us so vital and so true,
> that perpetual renewal of ourselves, that eternal creation,
> that ceaselessly resurgent poetry by which we live.

And in many ways he fears that poets have been left behind
in the attempts to express the real creative spirit of man. The
old goad is still pricking him on in the race between the two

[11] Preface to *Les Mamelles de Tirésias, Oeuvres poétiques*, 1956, p. 869.

cultures. "Mathematicians have the right to say that their dreams, their preoccupations often far surpass the crawling imaginations of poets." Possessed by his old nostalgia for shouting out the battlecry, he attempts to lead poets on into the new fields that they must conquer if poetry is still to exist. They must be ready to explore every possibility of new methods and techniques even if these lead to a dead end or to disaster. They must never be satisfied with confining themselves to narrow schools of thought. Progress consists not in a Messianic march forward, but in the discovery of ever new natural combinations. That is how science proceeds: poetry must do the same. The old adage of "there is nothing new under the sun" may be true for the sun, he says, but not for men. Through the miracles of science, he has seen the inside of his own head. To rival that achievement poetry must be prepared to make use of new discoveries both in the infinitely great universes within ourselves—that is, the analysis of the subconscious and of dreams—or in the infinitely great universes around us in space. It can borrow from the techniques of the cinema and the gramophone, or from the visual arts. It can hoist itself on to the shoulders of prophecy, or stoop to pick up a mere handkerchief. It can present itself in a great guffaw of laughter, and most of all in the devastating, eye-opening shock of surprise:

> Poetry and creation are one and the same thing: the name "poet" should be given only to the inventor, the creator, at least he who creates to the extent that man can ever create. The poet is the discoverer of new joys even if they are painful to bear. One can be a poet in every domain: it is sufficient that one should be adventurous, and go forward in exploration.

So this is the point which, after all these years as a practising poet, he has at last reached. Lyricism is not enough, but "only one of the domains of the poetry of to-day." It would seem to be a measure of the largeness of his vision and of his courage, and also of the irony that invests him like an aura that he should here relegate what is his own strongest gift to a minor role in the whole task of nourishing humanity.

And characteristic too that he should use an outwelling of particularly lyrical prose in this visionary attempt to transcend lyricism.

> As the richest and least known domain, the one of infinite extent, is the imagination, it is not astonishing that we have reserved the name of poet for those who are searching for the new joys which stake out its enormous spaces.
>
> The least event is for the poet, the postulate, the point of departure for an unknown immensity where all the bonfires of multiple meanings are ablaze.

He had begun his lecture on a sober note cataloguing the national and traditional characteristics that form the base for his rocketing new spirit. As he follows its soaring trajectory he is transported by vibrant enthusiasm and the lecture takes on the tone of an inspired sermon. He actually ends his declaration of faith in the tones of a prophet:

> Poetry is still only at the stage of *incunablia*. But wait, the prodigies will speak with their own voices and the new spirit which makes the universe swell with life will manifest itself formidably in letters, in the arts and in every known thing.

And here this inspired but sick man shows that he too like Baudelaire, is the real "poète-drapeau," still, so long after his death, capable "of stirring up the small number of slaves who can still respond."

The poet must practice what he has preached and Apollinaire's remaining year of life is one desperate and prolonged effort to do just this. There is one poem which of all his others best seems to exemplify "the new spirit"; and this is "Les Collines" of *Calligrammes*. Until recently it has generally been considered of 1913 vintage because of its position in the volume, which unlike *Alcools* does seem to follow a chronological pattern. But consistency in this matter was never one of his habits and this argument can bear no weight. Recently the American critic, Scott Bates, has convincingly argued[12] the case for it being written in 1917 or early 1918 as a concrete example of L'Esprit nouveau; and without being able to be

---

[12] Scott Bates, "Guillaume Apollinaire," *La Revue des lettres modernes*, 1962, p. 25.

categoric about it, because so far the evidence is entirely
internal, I incline to his opinion. In particular the references
to "suffering" and "the time for goodness" seem to situate
it as belonging to this period when he has explored and himself exemplified, both qualities, and when he makes a point of
underlining them in other poems. If it was not written to
embody the new spirit, then the new spirit must have been
formulated in order to embody the programme of "Les Collines,"
so nearly do the two correspond. There is the announcement
of the art of prophecy:

> Sache que je parle aujourd'hui
> Pour annoncer au monde entier
> Qu'enfin est né l'art de prédire[13]

of the explorations of dream, of the depths of consciousness:

> Profondeurs de la conscience
> On vous explorera demain
> Et qui sait quels êtres vivants
> Seront tirés de ces abîmes
> Avec des univers entiers[14]

and even of man's capacity for suffering:

> L'âge en vient on étudiera
> Tout ce que c'est que de souffrir
> Ce ne sera pas du courage
> Ni même du renoncement
> Ni tout ce que nous pouvons faire[15]

The time has come when the magic of man's imagination must
create prodigies:

> Voici le temps de la magie
> Il s'en revient attendez-vous

---

[13] "Know that I speak to-day
  To announce to the whole world
  That at last is born the art of prophecy"

[14] "Depths of consciousness
  You will be explored tomorrow
  And who knows what living beings
  Will be dragged from these abysses
  Along with entire universes"

[15] "The time is coming we will study
  All that it means to suffer
  It will not be courage
  Nor even renunciation
  Nor all that we can do"

A des milliards de prodiges
Qui n'ont fait naître aucune fable
Nul ne les ayant imaginés[16]

the same conception on which he had terminated his lecture, and which takes him right back to his adolescent play with the whole idea of Merlin the Enchanter. There is the same basic life energy which he has consecrated as the mainspring of "L'Esprit nouveau": "La grande force est le désir," and finally, as he reveals the little secrets that have been divulged to him when he soared into the empyrean of the ideal, there comes the shock of surprise, the use of trivial details in "ever new natural combinations," the lever which lifts up the universe and reveals the blaze of "multiple meanings":

Un chapeau haut de forme est sur
Une table chargée de fruits
Les gants sont morts près d'une
   pomme
Une dame se tord le cou
Auprès d'un monsieur qui s'avale

Le bal tournoie au fond du temps
J'ai tué le beau chef d'orchestre
Et je pèle pour mes amis
L'orange dont la saveur est
Un merveilleux feu d'artifice[17]

---

[16] "This is the time for magic
   It is coming back expect
   A myriad prodigies
   That no fable has yet brought forth
   Because nobody has imagined them"
[17] "A top-hat is on
   A table weighed down with fruit
   The gloves are dead next to an apple
   A lady wrings her own neck
   Next to a gentleman who is swallowing
      himself

   The dance whirls round in the depths
      of time
   I have killed the handsome band leader
   And I peel for my friends
   The orange whose savour is
   A marvellous firework

Tous sont morts le maître d'hôtel
Leur verse un champagne irréel
Qui mousse comme un escargot
Ou comme un cerveau de poète
Tandis que chantait une rose[17a]

Inevitably the poem is more personal. Apollinaire gathers together again his chosen images to present his own tensions. He launches the poem with the combat of two large aeroplanes fighting in the Parisian sky to represent the warring poles of his nature: youth and the past against maturity and the future, all the possible conflicting extremes of his richly endowed but precariously balanced nature. There are the flower and the star of his youth, the flame of his martyrising ambition, the ship of constant rebirth and the lift of ceaseless exploration, the dead corpse of past loves, the sea and the wind waving away time, even the harlequin miming phantoms, and the crossroads of one of his earliest poems, "Merlin et la vieille femme." It is as if in announcing that he is a prophet seeing into the future, instead he turns backwards and sums up all his past. He includes the pæan of his megalomania:

Je dis ce qu'est au vrai la vie
Seul je pouvais chanter ainsi
Mes chants tombent comme des graines
Taisez-vous tous vous qui chantez
Ne mêlez pas l'ivraie au blé[18]

along with his sense of human inadequacy and failure:

Mais pleure pleure et repleurons
Et soit que la lune soit pleine
Ou soit qu'elle n'ait qu'un croissant

[17a] They are all dead the *maître d'hôtel*
Pours out an unreal champagne for them
Which froths like a snail
Or like a poet's brain
Whilst a rose was singing"

[18] "I tell what life is really like
Only I could sing thus
My songs fall like seeds
Be quiet all of you who sing
Do not mingle the chaff with the wheat"

> Ah! pleure pleure et repleurons
> Nous avons tant ri au soleil[19]

In the last verse he condenses in his most masterly manner his whole exquisitely sensual perception of the mysterious alchemy of life:

> Des bras d'or supportent la vie
> Pénétrez le secret doré
> Tout n'est qu'une flamme rapide
> Que fleurit la rose adorable
> Et d'où monte un parfum exquis[20]

Even if "Les Collines" was written earlier it still remains the best single summary of what he thought poetry must be. It is the final and most harmoniously orchestrated answer to the questions that he had so tortuously formulated in his adolescent efforts.

Unfortunately the new spirit, like any other as he himself had admitted, blows where it listeth. Ill and weary, oppressed by his daily work—he was eventually transferred to the Colonial Ministry where he sat disconsolately under a map of Madagascar wondering what to do—and the usual inconsequential spate of journalism, he managed to produce several works; only a few of which proved to have been worth his pains.

La Femme assise is notably the most bungled piece of pot-boiling. He even acknowledges that here prose is what best suits his haste. It is a hotch-potch of articles about Montparnasse strung together on the thread of the most tenuous story, along with what remained of his great work on the Mormons. He wrote Prefaces to many exhibitions including a perspicacious introduction to Paul Guillaume's exhibition of "art négre," and he gave a lecture at the same gallery announcing the arrival of "l'art tactile." He wrote the libretto of a comic-opera, *Casanova,* and a short story "La Promenade de l'ombre" which was published in *L'Excelsior.* He was also

---

[19] "But weep weep and let us weep again
And whether the moon is full
Or whether it is only a crescent
Ah! weep weep and let us weep again
We have laughed so much in the sun"

[20] "Arms of gold support life
Penetrate the golden secret
All is but a rapid flame
Crowned by the adorable rose
Whence rises an exquisite perfume"

planning a film-script with André Billy, *La Bréhatine*. The event of greatest moment, however, was the publication of *Calligrammes*, of which only the three last poems, "Tristesse d'une étoile," "La Victoire," and "La Jolie Rousse" are known to have been written after he had returned from the War. And it is only these, and the little collection of limpid verses in *Vitam impendere amori* that present anything like the quality that he had achieved apparently without effort and often daily in the trenches.

"La Victoire," like "La Jolie Rousse" and "Les Collines," is a poem about poetry. The victory is that which he described in "L'Esprit nouveau" of the poet perpetually renewing both himself and poetry:

> La victoire avant tout sera
> De bien voir au loin
> De tout voir
> De près
> Et que tout ait un nom nouveau[21]

But now he seems to be overwhelmed by the odyssey that it entails. If "La Victoire" is a disquieting poem with its staccato interpolations, its incessant switching from one set of images to another, and the hysterical pitch of its advice to: "Imitez le son de la toupie / Laissez pétiller un son nasal et continu," it is because it follows the fluctuations and imperfections of the man's temperament which is struggling to keep pace with the poet's ideal, always, for him, the greatest battle of all:

> Ma voix fidèle comme l'ombre
> Veut être enfin l'ombre de la vie
> Veut être ô mer vivante infidèle comme toi[22]

To do this he has recourse again to the same limited group of images that he has been using since 1904, the poor sailors,

[21] "The victory will be above all
To see clearly things far away
To see everything
From close to
And that everything should have a new name"

[22] "My voice faithful as the shadow
Craves finally to be the shadow of life
Craves o sea to be quick and faithless as you"

men like bunches of grapes, the pure emerald of his Mediterranean childhood, the white splendour of the poetic ideal ("Jardins de la lumière où j'ai cueilli des bouquets") which may also be linked with the incandescent southern sky of his early days, and then all the symbols of the bad dream, which is his failure to achieve both his ideal and love—the port, taverns, the sea, an oasis of arms waving. His aspiration now takes the form of a search for a new language, and it seems that he becomes almost desperate when he imagines such a task. Indeed he has reason to do so. As he is beginning to formulate it, it is the negation of poetry itself and most certainly of the kind of poetry that he excels in writing. After the intensity of his experience of the War and the remarkably natural way in which he manages to transform it into poetry, he is back again in the cleft stick of exaggerated cerebration and theorising. And ironically he knows it. If he advocates the noise of hawking and spitting as a new consonant he must merit "l'ardente moquerie" of the public: but he is "plus têtu que non l'hydre de Lerne," and so he will go on, buffeted to and fro between the air pockets when his inspiration lets him fall like a stone (the road which he is exploring with his hands simply disappears), and the upsurges of the divine spirit.

In *Vitam impendere amori* and "La Jolie Rousse," the spirit manifests itself for the last time. Although the little collection of verses which makes up *Vitam impendere amori* was published in November 1917 with illustrations by André Rouveyre, and "La Jolie Rousse" first appeared in the review *L'Eventail* in March 1918, the unpublished manuscripts[23] of *Vitam impendere amori* show that the two are more closely linked than has previously been suspected: notably the page which contains the first draft of "Tu n'as pas surpris mon secret" is headed by the scored-out lines:

> Tes cheveux sont d'un or discret
> Mais vif
> Tes cheveux sont d'—[24]

---

[23] Photostat copies of these were given to the author by André Rouveyre.

[24] "Your hair is of a discreet gold
  But bright
  Your hair is"

which, of course, is a tentative first sketch of the famous lines
of "La Jolie Rousse":

> Ses cheveux sont d'or on dirait
> Un bel éclair qui durerait . . .[25]

Vitam impendere amori is a review of his past loves, the procession of women which has advanced and then retreated into
shadows and memories, the phœnix that has been reborn from
its own ashes, the spring that has vanished only to return with
greater tenderness. At first sight these limpid verses seem
merely to deal in generalities, with their conventional images
—rose, fountain, water, chains of memory, set against a formal
Symbolist *décor* of twilight gardens. The comparison with
Moréas must impose itself. Nevertheless they have also a
density and an incisiveness which is not at all Symbolist. The
convention has been deliberately chosen for a definite effect.
The evocation of the different women is in fact based on actual
precise memories, masked purposely because of his present
involvement with "la jolie rousse," and his desire to see the
past fade. Their reduction here to a sort of stylised essence is
the poet's way of exorcising them. The manuscript version of
the third poem, reproduced as Plate 6, underlines this process:

> Tu ne m'as pas dit ton secret
> Vois ce cortège qui s'avance
> M'en resterait-il un regret
> Si nous étions de connivence
>
> Les masques ont passé par bandes
> La rose flotte au fil de l'eau
> Et ce secret que tu demandes
> Il tremble en moi comme un grelot[26]

---

[25] "Her hair is gold like
A beautiful burst of lightning that lasts for ever"

[26] "You have not told me your secret
Look at this procession that draws nearer
Should I have any regret for it
If we were of one mind

The masqued revellers have passed by in groups
The rose floats on the surface of the water
And this secret that you ask of me
Trembles within me like a bell"

In this form the poem has an obvious enough meaning. It is addressed to Jacqueline who has not yet "told him her secret, nor he his to her. They are obviously "trembling" on the threshold of love. If they were "de connivence," he would have no nostalgia for the cortege of his past loves. In the final, published version, the secret is transferred to him, and the connexion between it and the regret is no longer made so obvious:

> Tu n'as pas surpris mon secret
> Déjà le cortège s'avance
> Mais il nous reste le regret
> De n'être pas de connivence[27]

Other of these little poems can be similarly traced to a particular woman. The first in which love is identified with spring and rebirth, having died "entre les bras," would seem to refer to Annie ("je l'aimais charnellement")—the first big love of his life which reached the idyllic pitch in the spring of the year. In the second, the memory which lies in chains is "le dernier des Phénix noire perfection," which is an appropriate image for the dark-haired Madeleine, last of his loves. who herself was enchained in her memories of him. "Ton souvenir gît enchaîné." In the fourth, however, "Le soir tombe et dans le jardin / Elles racontent des histoires," several dark-haired women—Mia, Mareye, Marie, Madeleine?—are invoked together in the collective, erotic symbol of the rose: "Rose toi qui te défends Perds tes odeurs inégalées." The fifth represents an Ophelia-like figure floating on the "onde nocturne," a generalised enough image, but the glancing reference to a soldier passing leads straight back to Lou, and it seems feasible to suppose that the idea of suicide could have been Apollinaire's own at that time, and that he has thus finally rid himself of it by transferring it to the loved one.

The last poem was metamorphosed out of all recognition between the first and the final drafts. André Rouveyre has

---

[27] "You have not surprised my secret
Already the procession comes nearer
But we still regret
That we are not of one mind"

claimed that it was because of his sharp criticism that Apollinaire scrapped the original poem. If so, he was in fact well justified. The manuscript shows that it was one of those banal pieces of scribbling into which Apollinaire's facility could sometimes lead him.

> Sera-ce un nimbe ou l'auréole
> De nos transfigurations
> Une lumière ou le symbole
> Des passions[28]

runs the second stanza for instance. Fortunately Apollinair e was provoked by Rouveyre's protests into producing a poem which is now the best of the sequence.

Again it can be linked with "La Jolie Rousse" in its nostalgic farewell to his castaway youth. When he reviews his present, uneasy position on the verge of maturity, he is invaded once more by a sense of loneliness and veers into a nostalgia for love. Here the images go right back into the Marie Laurencin period: "Le paysage est fait de toiles." "Un clown est l'unique passant." The portrait smiling in the shadow re-emerges from "Zone," the revolver-shot reiterates the persecution complex of that time and the eternal *mal-aimé* theme. The past is exploded, "la vitre du cadre est brisée," but there is nevertheless a hint of a new beginning. "Un air qu'on ne peut définir"; enough for him at least to contemplate burying his regrets.

In the interval between *Vitam impendere amori* and "La Jolie Rousse," this tentative, new love affair has blossomed out and his own confidence with it. The new season has become the time not of regrets but of "la raison ardente." And yet, although the avowed intention is that it should serve as prelude to a new departure, with its initial statement of his own *curriculum vitae* and his qualifications not merely as leader of the New Spirit but as arbiter in the age-old quarrel between tradition and invention, ironically too there are very conscious

---

[28] "Will it be a halo or the aureole
Of our transfigurations
A light or the symbol
Of passion"

echoes of Villon's *Testament*. There always seems to be a tendency in Apollinaire for opposites to be also alternatives[29] (for example, the substitution in the manuscript of the third poem of *Vitam impendere amori* of "s'avance" for "s'éloigne"). It cannot be only the reminiscence of Villon which thrusts him out of his august judge's seat into the suppliant position of the guilty prisoner. "Pitié pour nos erreurs pitié pour nos péchés." What is this guilt, what the sins? He has just stated the aims of the new adventurous spirits in one of his most inspired passages:

Nous ne sommes pas vos ennemis
Nous voulons vous donner de vastes et d'étranges domaines
Où le mystère en fleurs s'offre à qui veut le cueillir
Il y a là des feux nouveaux des couleurs jamais vues
Mille phantasmes impondérables
Auxquels il faut donner de la réalité
Nous voulons explorer la bonté contrée énorme où tout se tait
Il y a aussi le temps qu'on peut chasser ou faire revenir
Pitié pour nous qui combattons toujours aux frontières
De l'illimité et de l'avenir
Pitié pour nos erreurs pitié pour nos péchés[30]

Is the guilt a sense of his own inadequacy, the plea for pity a sigh because he is unable to embody as fully as he would wish those grandiose mirages which since earliest days have hovered tantalisingly on the horizon of his vision?

Characteristically, in this inevitable impasse, he seeks to escape again into human affection, the new consolation offered by the "adorable rousse." But the words which in the manuscript of *Vitam impendere amori* had refused to take shape, now,

[29] Cp. Margaret Davils, "L'Ironie de Guillaume Apollinaire," unpublished thesis for Doctorat de l'Universite de Paris, 1948.

[30] "We are not your enemies
We want to give you vast and strange domains
Where the floating mystery offers itself to those who want to pluck it
There are new fires there colours never seen
A thousand imponderable phantasms
To which we must give reality
We want to explore goodness that huge land where all is silent
There is also time which one can drive away or recall
Pity for those of us who always fight on the frontiers
Of the limitless and the future
Pity for our errors pity for our sins"

presumably, because the secret has been shared, flow forth in a rush of lyricism:

> Ses cheveux sont d'or on dirait
> Un bel éclair qui durerait
> Ou ces flammes qui se pavanent
> Dans les roses-thé qui se fanent[31]

But of course the consolation is not complete. Nothing is, nor ever could be for Apollinaire. Even this, alternatively the great manifesto of his maturity or his last will and testament, ends only with one mood indecisively shifting into another like bands of mist on a sunny morning. Back he steps into an abject cloud of self-pity, "Mais riez, riez de moi," and yet even then this self-abasement is shot through with the rays of the life-long Enchanter complex: "Car il y a tant de choses que je n'ose vous dire / Tant de choses que vous ne me laisseriez pas dire": these things—the "flowering mystery," the "lays for queens," the consuming fire, the whole elusive subject matter of poetry which must constantly be created anew. What lends particular poignancy to this beautiful poem is the implication that there are also "tant de choses que je ne sais vous dire."

So it had to remain, for Apollinaire now had to use his best energies merely for the task of keeping himself alive. In January 1918 he had a severe attack of bronchitis and went back to hospital for three months. In May he married Jacqueline, and now, craving for a proper home and children, he worked harder than ever at his journalistic odd jobs. Even when he was on holiday with his wife in Brittany he did not permit himself to take a rest from writing. He was planning to embark on a whole new series of *Les Maîtres de l'amour* on "les grandes amoureuses,"—Cleopatra, Ninon de Lenclos, Messalina. He was also contemplating once again a collected volume of his poems on painters, this time to be called *Le Marchand d'oiseaux*. But his deepest concern at that time was

[31] "Her hair is gold like
A beautiful burst of lightning that lasts for ever
Or those flames which parade
In tea-roses that fade"

for the play *Couleur du temps* which was to be put on in the autumn. All his life he had been attracted by the theatre: for so many writers it seems to present the greatest challenge of all and they insist on breaking their heads against the iron curtain of its disciplines. Apollinaire was no dramatist, and *Couleur du temps* makes sad reading. It contains some splendid lines of poetry firmly stamped by his seal, and it has a passage about the birds of the air assembling, which is reminiscent of "Zone" though without any of its *élan*. But it is no play. The characters of the poet, the scientist and the rich man are abstract symbols; the plot of their search for an ideal contains not an ounce of drama. But what really chills one's heart is the whole glacial, dead atmosphere. *Couleur du temps* stands at the opposite pole from the swarming, crowded life of *L'En-chanteur pourrissant*. Then his imagination was so crammed that it could barely be contained by language. Now words are merely words and represent only the nothingness of death. The frozen wastes of the final scenes, the death of all the characters for an ideal which itself is death, the last sigh "Adieu Adieu il faut que tout meure" symbolise the inevitable and final defeat. His life has almost ebbed away. Gone the hopes of a violent summer season; he is plumb in the middle of the winter of impotence, sterility, cold, and silence. One can only admire the way in which he faces up to his last task as a writer, pointless but for such a man who has made poetry his life, necessary, of mirroring this process of extinction.

In November while he was working on the final revision of the play, harassed, overworked, weary, and still unable outwardly to admit the defeat that his work, for poetry can never lie, proclaims, he fell an easy prey to the epidemic of Spanish influenza which was raging like the plague through Paris. His last struggle, now just for the breath of life, was as hectic as any of his others. He begged the doctor to save him. "I want to live, I want to live" he kept repeating. "I have still so many things to say." But the odds were against him. Both his lungs were affected and he lasted only five days. Jacqueline who herself had had the illness was so overwhelmed that she had no time to warn his friends or even his mother. His death was a total shock. Coming when it did right at the end of the War, it came to symbolise for his friends the end of youth, gaiety, a way of life, a whole epoch. "A light was extinguished," "the sunshine had gone out of our lives": this is how they express their sense of deprivation. "Truthfully," wrote Max Jacob, "neither the success of my friends nor those of our victorious country can bring to life again what his death has withered in me for ever. I did not know that he was 'my life' to this extent. For me something has broken somewhere. If I were a little more sensitive I should feel that I myself had died." It was inconceivable that he who in his life and his work had more than any of them embodied "the magnificent exuberance of life" should have been so mown down. In his death they had a foretaste of their own. Uncannily, for the rest of the Kostrowitzky family the symbol became fact, and both his mother and Albert were to die within a few months.

And as he lay stretched out on his death-bed with, as he would have wished, his helmet beside him, the fermenting crowds in the streets celebrated the Armistice and cried out their anti-Kaiser slogans, "A bas Guillaume," a final irony that the poor assassinated poet would well have savoured.

Bibliography

The following lists are highly selective. The most complete bibliographies are in the Pléïade edition of *Oeuvres poétiques* and Marcel Adéma: *Apollinaire le mal-aimé*. Mme Durry: *Alcools* and Michel Décaudin: *Le Dossier d'Alcools* give lists of works likely to prove useful to students. Editions cited in footnotes are marked *.

I. APOLLINAIRE

1. *The main volumes of works published in Apollinaire's lifetime*

For the appearance of individual poems, articles and stories see *Oeuvres poétiques*, and *Apollinaire le mal-aimé*. For Introductions, Prefaces, catalogues, works done in collaboration, and pornographic works see *Apollinaire le mal-aimé*.

L'Enchanteur pourrissant, woodcuts by André Derain. *Paris (Kahnweiler) 1909.
L'Hérésiarque et cie. Paris (Stock) 1910, *1936.
Le Bestiaire ou cortège d'Orphée, woodcuts by Raoul Dufy. Paris (Deplanche) 1911.
Les Peintres cubistes (Méditations esthétiques). Paris (Figuière) 1913.
Alcools. Paris (Mercure de France) 1913.
Le Poète assassiné. Paris (Bibliothèque des Curieux) 1916. *Ed. Michel Décaudin, Paris (Club du meilleur livre) 1959.
Vitam impendere amori. Paris (Mercure de France) 1917.
Les Mamelles de Tirésias. Paris (Edition Sic) 1918.
Calligrammes. Paris (Mercure de France) 1918.
Le Flâneur des deux rives. Paris (Editions de la Sirène) 1918.

2. *The main posthumous editions*

Anecdotiques. Paris (Stock) 1926.
Contemporains pittoresques. Paris (Editions de la Belle Page) 1929.
L'esprit nouveau et les poètes. Paris (Jacques Haumont) 1946.
Ombre de mon amour. Geneva (Cailler) 1947.
La Femme assise. Paris (N.R.F.) 1948.
Lettres à sa marraine. Paris (Pour les fils du roi) 1948.
Il y a. Paris (Messein) 1949.
Couleur du temps. Paris (Editions du Bélier) 1949.
Tendre comme le souvenir. *Paris (Gallimard) 1952.

Casanova. Paris (Gallimard) 1952.
Le Guetteur mélancolique. Paris (Gallimard) 1952.
Oeuvres poétiques. *Paris (Bibliothèque de la Pléiade, N.R.F.) 1956.
Chroniques d'art. *Paris (Gallimard) 1960.

II. OTHERS

ADÉMA, MARCEL: *Apollinaire le mal-aimé* [= Adéma]. Paris (Plon) 1952.
ÆGERTER, EMMANUEL and LABRACHERIE: *Guillaume Apollinaire.* Paris (Julliard) 1943.
BILLY, ANDRÉ: *Apollinaire vivant.* Paris (La Sirène) 1923.
——: *Poètes d'aujourd'hui: Guillaume Apollinaire* [= Billy]. Paris (P. Seghers) 1947.
BRETON, ANDRÉ: *Les Pas perdus.* Paris (N.R.F.) 1924.
CADOU, RENÉ-GUY: *Testament d'Apollinaire.* Paris (Debresse) 1945.
CARMODY, FRANCIS J.: *The Evolution of Apollinaire's Poetics 1901-1914.* Berkeley and Los Angeles (University of California Press) 1963.
CENDRARS, BLAISE: *Blaise Cendrars vous parle.* Paris (Denoël) 1952.
DÉCAUDIN, Michel: *Le Dossier d'Alcools* [= Décaudin]. Geneva (Droz) 1960.
DELAUNAY, ROBERT: *Du cubisme à l'art abstrait.* Paris (S.E.V.P.E.N.) 1957.
DURRY, MARIE-JEANNE: *Guillaume Apollinaire, Alcools,* VOL. I [= Durry]. Paris (Sedes) 1956.
FABUREAU, HUBERT: *Guillaume Apollinaire, son œuvre.* Paris. (Nouvelle revue critique) 1952.
FAURE-FAVIER, LOUISE: *Souvenirs sur Apollinaire* [= Faure-Favier]. Paris (Grasset) 1945.
FETTWEISS, CHRISTIAN: *Apollinaire en Ardenne.* Brussels (Henriques) 1934.
FLEURET, FERNAND: *De Gilles de Rais à Guillaume Apollinaire.* Paris (Mercure de France) 1933.
GIEDION-WELCKER, C.: *Die neue realität bei Guillaume Apollinaire.* (Benlibern-Bümpliz) 1945
GOFFIN, ROBERT: *Entrer en poésie.* [= Goffin]. Brussels (A l'enseigne du chat qui pêche) 1948.
JACOB, MAX: *Correspondance,* VOL. I. Paris (Editions de Paris) 1958.
JANNINI, P. A.: *La Fortuna di Apollinaire in Italia* [= Janinni]. Milan (Cisalpino) 1959.
LÉAUTAUD, PAUL: *Entretiens avec Robert Mallet.* Paris (Gallimard) 1951.
——: *Journal littéraire,* VOLS. II and III. Paris (Mercure de France) 1955-6.
LUCA, TOUSSAINT-: *Guillaume Apollinaire, Souvenirs d'un ami* [= Toussaint-Luca). Monaco (Editions du Rocher) 1954.
MONTFORT, EUGÈNE: *Apollinaire travesti.* Paris (P. Seghers) 1948.
MOULIN, JEANINE: *Manuel poétique d'Apollinaire.* Paris (Les Cahiers du Journal des Poètes) 1939.
——: *Guillaume Apollinaire, Textes inédits* [= Moulin]. Geneva (Droz) 1952.

OLIVIER, FERNANDE: *Picasso et ses amis* [= Olivier]. Paris (Stock) 1933.

ORECCHIONI, PIERRE: "Le Thème du Rhin dans l'inspiration de Guillaume Apollinaire," in *Lettres modernes* 1956.

PIA, PASCAL: *Apollinaire par lui-même.* Paris (Editions du Seuil) 1954.

ROQUES, MARIO: *Etudes de littérature française.* Geneva (Droz) 1949.

ROUVEYRE, ANDRÉ : *Souvenirs de mon commerce.* Paris (Crès) 1921.

——: *Apollinaire,* Paris (N.R.F.) 1945.

——: *Apollinaire.* Paris (Editions Raison d'être) 1952.

——: *Amour et poésie d'Apollinaire* [= Rouveyre]. Paris (Editions du Seuil) 1955.

SALMON, ANDRÉ: *Souvenirs sans fin,* VOLS. I, II and III. Paris (Gallimard) 1955-6, 1961.

SHATTUCK, ROGER: *The Banquet Years.* London (Faber) 1960.

SOFFICI, ARDENGO: *Rete Mediterranea.* Florence (Vallecchi) 1920.

——: *Ricordi di vita artistica e litteraria.* Florence (Vallecchi) 1930.

SOUPAULT, PHILIPPE: *Guillaume Apollinaire ou les reflets de l'incendie.* Marseille (Cahiers du sud) 1927.

STEIN, GERTRUDE: *Picasso.* Paris (Librairie Floury) 1938.

——: *Autobiography of Alice B. Toklas.* Paris (Gallimard) 1934.

TAUPIN, R. and ZUKOFSKI, L.: *Le Style Apollinaire.* Paris (Les Presses modernes) 1934.

VLAMINCK, MAURICE DE: *Portraits avant décès.* Paris (Flammarion) 1943.

WOLF, E. M.: *Guillaume Apollinaire und das Rheinland.* Dortmund (Husen) 1937.

III. PERIODICALS DEVOTED TO APOLLINAIRE

For individual review articles see *Oeuvres poétiques.*

Sic, Nos. 37-9, Jan.-Feb. 1919.

Vient de paraître, No. 24, 15 Nov. 1923.

L'Esprit nouveau, No. 26, Oct. 1924.

Images de Paris, Nos, 49-50, Jan.-Feb. 1924 and Nos. 56-7, Sep.-Oct. 1924.

Présence d'Apollinaire. Paris (Galerie Breton) Dec. 1943, Jan. 1944.

Rimes et raisons. Paris (Editions de la tête noire) 1946.

La Table ronde, No. 57, Sep. 1952.

Le Flâneur des deux rives, Bulletin d'études apollinairiennes, No. 1, Mar. 1954; Nos. 7-8, Sep. and Dec. 1955.

La Revue des sciences humaines, No. 83, Oct.-Dec. 1956.

La Revue des lettres modèrnes, Sep. 1962.

General Index

Index of Apollinaire's Works Quoted or Referred to in the Text